The Female Body

Gordon Gagliano, *Introspective Nude*, 1989.

# The Female Body

## Figures, Styles, Speculations

Laurence Goldstein, Editor

*Ann Arbor*

THE UNIVERSITY OF MICHIGAN PRESS

Copyright © by the University of Michigan 1991
Published in the United States of America by
The University of Michigan Press
Manufactured in the United States of America

1994   1993   1992          4 3

A CIP catalogue record for this book is available from
the British Library

Cover illustration: Virginia Maksymowicz, *History of Art*, ongoing series.
Cast paper and acrylic. Life size. Photo: Blaise Tobia.

**Library of Congress Cataloging-in-Publication Data**

The Female body : figures, styles, speculations / Laurence Goldstein,
    editor.
        p.   cm.
    Includes bibliographical references.
    ISBN 0-472-09477-7 (alk. paper). — ISBN 0-472-06477-0 (pbk. :
alk. paper)
    1. Body, Human—Social aspects.   2. Women Physiology.   3. Women
in art.   4. Women in literature.   I. Goldstein, Laurence, 1943–
GT495.F46   1991
391'.6—dc20                                            91-31453
                                                           C I P

# CONTENTS

# INTRODUCTION

The contents of this book have been selected from two oversize issues of *Michigan Quarterly Review*, Fall 1990 and Winter 1991. As I began to assemble the issues, sending out calls for manuscripts and writing letters of solicitation, I became aware of two very different responses to my announcement of the special topic. My fellow academics praised it as a timely and judicious choice. The female body is, as Margaret Atwood writes, "a hot topic" being scrutinized in a number of recent books, in college courses and conferences, and with increasing sophistication in feminist publications in every professional field. Social issues like abortion, pornography, rape, and new technologies of reproduction have guaranteed a continuing, perhaps eternal, controversy about the rights and violations of the female body, not to mention the no less political matter of medical treatments related to anorexia, cancers affecting women, PMS, mortal illness, and other conditions. Scholars have produced an extraordinary amount of research in the last two decades in order to situate the female body in a diversity of historical and theoretical contexts. Like textuality, or technology, or the discourse on race—and these are all pertinent to the female body—this topic has emerged as a central one in contemporary academic scholarship.

At the same time, I made a point of mentioning the forthcoming issues to people remote from the university. Here the response was entirely different. Women usually greeted my announcement with a thin smile of resignation and a remark like, "You'll certainly sell a lot of copies of that issue." Men were more likely to respond with a conspiratorial nudge and ask if I planned to include a centerfold.

These different reactions are related, of course. It is because the female body has for so long been identified as an erotic object, canonized in the nudes of high art and the sex symbols of popular culture, that efforts to locate and describe alternative images became a paramount goal of the feminist movement and (therefore) of the culture at large. This is not to say that such alternatives exclude the erotic; far from it. Most women would not protest John Updike's remark that "a naked woman is, for most men, the most beautiful thing they will ever see." It is not desire per se that has caused suspicion but the masculine appropriation of desire in a society that renders such desire as power, often overwhelming power. Women who see themselves as essentially objects of male desire can make a place for themselves in a patriarchal society that grants them certain privileges, but they can also suffer from the harrowing fear anatomized by Andrea Dworkin in her fiction, "In October 1973." Her narrator, looking through the lewd eyes of male passers-by, imagines herself as nothing but "bait," a "fucking invisible ghost" whose desperate resistance takes the form of writing her endangered selves into being.

Resistance begins with the recognition that the body is, in Carol Gilligan's phrase, "a repository of experience and desire" unique to the individual, an ever-nourishing source for self-realization. Gilligan shows how women have usefully imagined themselves as *subjects* of desire, whether it is Anne Frank constructing in her diary a moral vision from the intuitions of her adolescent sexuality, or the student in her term paper who rebuffs the strategies of sexual possession enacted in Andrew Marvell's poem of seduction, "To His Coy Mistress." Such resistance has changed the female body, in the public imagination, from a playground to a battleground as actors of different gender contest the nature of erotic and social experience in a struggle of vital interests.

Ironically, as Susan Bordo suggests, a counterresistance may well characterize the second generation of the feminist era, as a postmodern sensibility rejects the "totalizing" rhetoric that confidently speaks of female gender as a universal category (when gender is defined as the social organization of sexual difference). Using examples from the media, Bordo shows how white women and women of color alike have reacted negatively to the moralism (as they see it) of an older feminism that stigmatizes the traditional arts of "feminine beauty" and body enhancement. Bordo cautions against the trivializing of hard-won freedom. Freedom has no significant meaning, she argues, if it causes women to abandon commendable personal and social goals in favor of media-driven distractions (fun and fashion) until they are maneuvered back into the gravitational orbit of an unjust and prejudiced society.

There is nothing trivial about the issue of abortion, and Carl Cohen rightly addresses himself to the question of how *not* to argue about this most arguable of topics. We are not free to argue the subject in ignorance of biology, he reasonably assumes, and proceeds to test the hypotheses of pro- and anti-abortion advocates by measuring them against the scientific facts as we have them and the inescapable philosophical implications of such facts. In other medical venues, too, as Ruth Behar points out, the choices women face can leave scars both real and metaphorical. Is it free choice or necessity that compels women to "acquiesce to the master narrative of medical science" when driven by the body's imperatives into irreversible operations? The hospital or clinic can be imagined as a life-giving mission, but also as the haunted castle in some Gothic melodrama of the female body's journey through life. Negotiations with the medical community, as with society at large, rely on such tropes as aids to understanding. Indeed, metaphors, myths, and texts of the historical past recur in contemporary discourse at every turn. Homunculism informs the abortion debate just as the figures of Venus, Ophelia, Lysistrata, and Leda govern the imagery of female embodiment.

Because the female body is not just an anatomical object but a cultural construction, authors have focused pervasively on "body language"—the language of posture, gesture, movement, dress, and cosmetic alteration. I confess to being surprised at what a large proportion of the material submitted for the issues focused on matters of apparel and bodily display; but the obsession makes perfect sense at a time when gender identity is a topic of energetic contention. All the fiction in this book, and a major portion of the poetry, as well as essays by Kim Edwards, Anne Herrmann, and Sally Peters, comment on the opportunities for self-expression and self-transformation in the complex role-playing fostered by a tolerant culture. Some artifacts of self-design are ephemeral, but others, like dress or dances, or even tattoos, belong to traditions that unite or differentiate women across borders and generations.

Media representations of the body are important because they model the options available to women, options of resistance as well as options of submission. The naked patient being operated on by Dr. Agnew in Thomas Eakins's famous painting is an obvious model of submission, but as Judith Fryer shows in her analysis of this painting, the nurse positioned by the table mediates between the patient and the assemblage of male spectators, including the artist figure. As we look at contemporary artworks, gazing at the variety of images collected by Darcy Grimaldo Grigsby, our attitudes toward the female body are

likely to change in keeping with the artists' own self-conscious awareness of their hands-on status as makers. Contemporary artists are likely
to use humor or anger to signify resistance to voyeurism, turning the
erotic into a challenging joke. How does a male relate to the hyperbolic
sexuality of Marilyn Monroe, and to the transvestism of her admirers
Tony Curtis and Jack Lemmon, in *Some Like It Hot*? How does a
woman relate to them, or to the stages of pop singer Madonna's self-
creation? What about the female muse in that other lyric form, poetry?
Jefferson Humphries offers some surprising ideas about how male and
female poets body forth their inspiration. And Stephanie Kiceluk
studies some of the ways modern fiction has revised our attitudes by
remolding and reimagining the female body in a series of radical
experiments.

Will our attitudes toward the male body change as they change
toward the female? Many works in this collection weigh the options
available to men as the female person increasingly authorizes her self,
mind and body alike, by strategies of resistance modeled for her in life
and art. ("Art is man's nature," wrote Edmund Burke, meaning women
as well.) A too exclusive concentration on the female body, it has been
argued, perpetuates the concept of the female as "other" or "exotic," an
object of scrutiny in a society tainted by voyeurism and fantasies of
control. But the purpose of this book is precisely to move beyond the
defensive anxiety engendered by the older, more abrasive politics of
gender—move beyond it with maturity and wisdom, and good humor.

The perspectives on the female body collected here are provisional
and contemporary. They do not render earlier readings obsolete or
foreclose future discoveries. There is considerable contention among
the authors represented here, with no possibility, and no need, for
harmonious resolution. This is as it should be in a cultural milieu where
the intellect has full freedom to discourse about anything, including the
bodies upon which our society inscribes its variety of desires. Each
writer has been affected by the mandate to speak the truth as he or she
sees it, and many chose, with my encouragement, to speak personally
of how the "I" is involved in the rites and tribulations of the female
body. The ongoing conversation of males and females on this subject
will, I hope, be enhanced in this last decade of the century by the
writings that lie before you.

MARGARET ATWOOD

# THE FEMALE BODY

". . . entirely devoted to the subject of 'The Female Body.' Knowing how well you have written on this topic . . . this capacious topic . . ."

—letter from *Michigan Quarterly Review*.

1.
I agree, it's a hot topic. But only one? Look around, there's a wide range. Take my own, for instance.

I get up in the morning. My topic feels like hell. I sprinkle it with water, brush parts of it, rub it with towels, powder it, add lubricant. I dump in the fuel and away goes my topic, my topical topic, my controversial topic, my capacious topic, my limping topic, my nearsighted topic, my topic with back problems, my badly-behaved topic, my vulgar topic, my outrageous topic, my aging topic, my topic that is out of the question and anyway still can't spell, in its oversized coat and worn winter boots, scuttling along the sidewalk as if it were flesh and blood, hunting for what's out there, an avocado, an alderman, an adjective, hungry as ever.

2.
The basic Female Body comes with the following accessories: garter belt, panti-girdle, crinoline, camisole, bustle, brassiere, stomacher, chemise, virgin zone, spike heels, nose ring, veil, kid gloves, fish-net stockings, fichu, bandeau, Merry Widow, weepers, chokers, barrettes, bangles, beads, lorgnette, feather boa, basic black, compact, Lycra stretch one-piece with modesty panel, designer peignoir, flannel nightie, lace teddy, bed, head.

3.

The Female Body is made of transparent plastic and lights up when you plug it in. You press a button to illuminate the different systems. The Circulatory System is red, for the heart and arteries, purple for the veins; the Respiratory System is blue; the Lymphatic System is yellow; the Digestive System is green, with liver and kidneys in aqua. The nerves are done in orange and the brain is pink. The skeleton, as you might expect, is white.

The Reproductive System is optional, and can be removed. It comes with or without a miniature embryo. Parental judgement can thereby be exercised. We do not wish to frighten or offend.

4.

He said, I won't have one of those things in the house. It gives a young girl a false notion of beauty, not to mention anatomy. If a real woman was built like that she'd fall on her face.

She said, If we don't let her have one like all the other girls she'll feel singled out. It'll become an issue. She'll long for one and she'll long to turn into one. Repression breeds sublimation. You know that.

He said, It's not just the pointy plastic tits, it's the wardrobes. The wardrobes and that stupid male doll, what's his name, the one with the underwear glued on.

She said, Better to get it over with when she's young. He said, All right but don't let me see it.

She came whizzing down the stairs, thrown like a dart. She was stark naked. Her hair had been chopped off, her head was turned back to front, she was missing some toes and she'd been tattooed all over her body with purple ink, in a scrollwork design. She hit the potted azalea, trembled there for a moment like a botched angel, and fell.

He said, I guess we're safe.

5.

The Female Body has many uses. It's been used as a door-knocker, a bottle-opener, as a clock with a ticking belly, as something to hold up lampshades, as a nutcracker, just squeeze the brass legs together and out comes your nut. It bears torches, lifts victorious wreaths, grows copper wings and raises aloft a ring of neon stars; whole buildings rest on its marble heads.

It sells cars, beer, shaving lotion, cigarettes, hard liquor; it sells diet plans and diamonds, and desire in tiny crystal bottles. Is this the face that launched a thousand products? You bet it is, but don't get any funny big ideas, honey, that smile is a dime a dozen.

It does not merely sell, it is sold. Money flows into this country or that country, flies in, practically crawls in, suitful after suitful, lured by all those hairless pre-teen legs. Listen, you want to reduce the national debt, don't you? Aren't you patriotic? That's the spirit. That's my girl.

She's a natural resource, a renewable one luckily, because those things wear out so quickly. They don't make 'em like they used to. Shoddy goods.

6.
One and one equals another one. Pleasure in the female is not a requirement. Pair-bonding is stronger in geese. We're not talking about love, we're talking about biology. That's how we all got here, daughter.

Snails do it differently. They're hermaphrodites, and work in threes.

7.
Each female body contains a female brain. Handy. Makes things work. Stick pins in it and you get amazing results. Old popular songs. Short circuits. Bad dreams.

Anyway: each of these brains has two halves. They're joined together by a thick cord; neural pathways flow from one to the other, sparkles of electric information washing to and fro. Like light on waves. Like a conversation. How does a woman know? She listens. She listens in.

The male brain, now, that's a different matter. Only a thin connection. Space over here, time over there, music and arithmetic in their own sealed compartments. The right brain doesn't know what the left brain is doing. Good for aiming though, for hitting the target when you pull the trigger. What's the target? Who's the target? Who cares? What matters is hitting it. That's the male brain for you. Objective.

This is why men are so sad, why they feel so cut off, why they think of themselves as orphans cast adrift, footloose and stringless in the deep void. What void? she asks. What are you talking about? The void of the Universe, he says, and she says Oh and looks out the window and tries to get a handle on it, but it's no use, there's too much going on, too many rustlings in the leaves, too many voices, so she says, Would you like a cheese sandwich, a piece of cake, a cup of tea? And he grinds his teeth because she doesn't understand, and wanders off, not just alone but Alone, lost in the dark, lost in the skull, searching for the other half, the twin who could complete him.

Then it comes to him: he's lost the Female Body! Look, it shines in the gloom, far ahead, a vision of wholeness, ripeness, like a giant melon, like an apple, like a metaphor for *breast* in a bad sex novel; it shines like a balloon, like a foggy noon, a watery moon, shimmering in its egg of light.

Catch it. Put it in a pumpkin, in a high tower, in a compound, in a chamber, in a house, in a room. Quick, stick a leash on it, a lock, a chain, some pain, settle it down, so it can never get away from you again.

JOHN UPDIKE

# VENUS AND OTHERS

"Thy navel is like a round goblet, which wanteth not liquor," says
the male voice in The Song of Solomon, "thy belly is like a heap of
wheat set about with lilies. Thy two breasts are like two young roes
that are twins." Robert Graves, in *Watch the Northwind Rise*,
quotes a vernacular rendering of these verses which goes, "Your
belly's like a heap of wheat, / Your breasts like two young roes. / O
come to bed with me, my sweet, / And take off all your clo'es!" A
naked woman is, for most men, the most beautiful thing they will
ever see; on this planet, the female body is the prime aesthetic
object, recreated not only in statuary and painting but (as Ms.
Atwood points out) in the form of doorknockers, nutcrackers, lamp-
stands, and caryatids. For the Victorians, it was everywhere, naked
in brass, while their real women were swaddled and padded and
reinforced like furniture; in this century, the female body haunts
merchandising from top to bottom, from the silky epidermal feel of
a soft cigarette pack to the rumpy curves of a Porsche 911. The
female body is a masterpiece of market design, persuading the race
to procreate generation after generation, extracting semen from
mesmerized men with the ease of a pickpocket at a girlie show.

This captivating mechanism pays a price for its own complexity:
cancer attacks breasts and ovaries, menstrual cramps and hysteria
impair performance. Its season of bloom, of potential fertility, is
shorter than that of the male body, though more piquant and powerful. Kafka, in a male-bonding letter to Max Brod, unchivalrously
remarked of women, "Not until summer does one really see their
curious kind of flesh in quantities. It is soft flesh, retentive of a great
deal of water, slightly puffy, and keeps its freshness only a few
days." He goes on, with his scrupulous fairness: "Actually, of course,
it stands up pretty well, but that is only proof of the brevity of
human life." Just so, the actuarial longer-lastingness of the female
body demonstrates the relative biological disposability of the male,

5

hormonally inclined toward reckless exertion and indulgence, and the salubrious effects of lifelong exercise in the form of housework.

If the main social fact about the female body is its attractiveness, the main political fact is, its weakness compared with the male body. There may be some feminists ardent enough to dispute this, but the truth is elemental. As Elizabeth Hardwick, reviewing Simone de Beauvoir's *The Second Sex*, put it with admirable firmness, "Women are certainly physically inferior to men and if this were not the case the whole history of the world would be different . . . . Any woman who ever had her wrist twisted by a man recognizes a fact of nature as humbling as a cyclone to a frail tree branch." This fact lies behind many facts of feminine circumstance, such as the use of women as domestic drudges and beasts of burden in the world's fundamental economy, or the superior attentiveness and subtlety of women in the private maneuvers of advanced societies. Watching a movie, women as well as men, scientific research has disclosed, will watch the face of the woman on the screen. In a female face, the things that can open, the eyes and the mouth, open wider. Women talk, Women see. "The fastidiousness of women," Stendhal wrote in *On Love*, "is the result of that perilous situation in which they find themselves placed so early, and of the necessity they are under of spending their lives among cruel and charming enemies."

This physical weakness and the cruelties that result are the truth but not all the truth, and from the standpoint of the species not even the main truth. An interesting thought-experiment, for an adult male, is to try to look at a prepubescent girl, one of ten or eleven, say, with the eyes again of a boy the same age. The relative weakness, the arresting curves, the female fastidiousness are not yet in place, but the magic is. The siren song, the strange simultaneous call to be kind and to conquer, the swooning wish to place one's life *beside* this other. To be sure, cultural inducements to heterosexuality bombard us from infancy; but they fall, generally, upon terrifically receptive ground.

The female body is, in its ability to conceive and carry a fetus and to nurse an infant, our life's vehicle — it is the engine and the tracks. Male sexuality, then, returning to this primal source, drinks at the spring of being and enters the murky region, where up is down and death is life, of mythology. The paradoxical contradictoriness of male attitudes toward the female and her body — the impulses to exalt and debase, to serve and enslave, to injure and comfort, to reverence and mock — goes back to some point of origin where emotions are not yet differentiated and energy has no distinct direction. The sex act itself, from the male point of view, is a paradox, a transformation of his thrusts into pleasure, a poke in the gut that is gratefully received. Sadism and masochism naturally flirt on the edges of our, as Katherine Mansfield said, "profound and terrible . . . desire to establish contact."

And naturally modern women feel a natural impatience with being mythologized — being envisioned (talk about hysteria!) as madonnas and whores, earth-mothers and vampires, helpless little girls and implacable dominatrices — and with male inability to see sex simply for what it is. What is it? A biological function and procedure, presumably, on a plane with eating and defecation, just as woman are, properly regarded, equally entitled human beings and political entities with minds of their own. Well, men have been known, inadvertently, in lapses of distraction or satiety, to see the female body as just a body, very like their own, built for locomotion as well as procreation, an upright watery stalk temporarily withstanding, with its miraculous molecular chain reactions, the forces of gravity and entropy. It is a lucid but dispirited moment, seeing a nude woman as a kind of man, only smaller, lighter-framed, without a beard, but matching us tuft for tuft otherwise, and with bumps, soft swellings, unmale emphases stiffened with fat, swayed by gravity . . . a heap of wheat set about with lilies . . . those catenary curves, that curious considerate absence . . . the moment of clear vision passes.

We can only appeal, in asking forgiveness of women for our mythologizing of their bodies, for being *unreal* about them, to their own sexuality, which is different but not radically different, perhaps, from our own. For women too there seems to be that tangle of supplication and possessiveness, that descent toward infantile undifferentiation, that omnipotent helplessness, that merger with the cosmic mother-warmth, that flushed pulse-quickened leap into overestimation, projection, general mix-up. The Song of Solomon has two voices; there is a female extoller as well, who claims, "My beloved is white and ruddy, the chiefest among ten thousand. His head is as the most fine gold; his locks are bushy, and black as a raven . . . his belly is as bright ivory overlaid with sapphires," etc. The male body, can it be? — its defenseless boneless belly above the one-eyed priapic oddity — may also loom as a glorious message from the deep, with an Apollonian (to be exact, a Martial) beauty beyond the bodily. In Ms. Atwood's last novel, *Cat's Eye*, the heroine, in one of the many remarkable passages about growing up female and human, reflects upon the teen-aged boys she talks to on the telephone: "The serious part is their bodies. I sit in the hall with the cradled telephone, and what I hear is their bodies. I don't listen much to the words but to the silences, and in the silences these bodies re-create themselves, are created by me, take form." Some of this is sexual, she reflects, and some is not. Some is purely visual: "The faces of the boys change so much, they soften, open up, they ache. The body is pure energy, solidified light." For male and female alike, the bodies of others are messages indicating what we must do — they are the glowing signifiers of our own existence.

ZONA TETI

# FROM NESTOR TO HELEN NOW OF TROY

To the rocks the sea leaves foam
from the wreckage of dead waves:
death-foam like fairy hair,
flimsier than the froth of a beard
or the foam-haired pudenda
making gods in the clash of love.

The Love-goddess rises from the foam
like a mist pushed out to curves by wind.
This pale air suggests only the finer points
of sex, as clean as a nursery stork.

From sea-foam she came, say scholars who cite
Greek *Aphro*dite from *aphros*, "foam," as though
of all meanings one alone aims home.

Consequence of foam indeed
is double-formed Love,
but not the foam the bubble breath of sea.
The fact behind the froth is the thin
white milk, the scuds of love, the manly cream.

Lust is sufficient ocean to raise a god
for any excusing emotion. Like winds
we clothe the form in mist
and puff our cheeks, and call it love.
Dear form until new breasts take the eye.
Then we kill the god blocking our way.

# THE DREAM

I would always wake up in a cold sweat, checking the space between my legs to be sure it was still empty.

And when the therapist asked, "Were there disturbing dreams when you were young, the kind that occurred again and again?" I lied, said nothing, claimed that my memory was as clean as unlined paper. I thought they knew by the sweat soaking my blouse, how

as a child I would dream I was discovered behind the green flow-ered couch at one of my parents' cocktail parties, where I liked to hide and listen to what Mom and Dad would say about us children, how Lisa was the smartest in her class and Janet, the athlete, was among the best junior riders in the state. I was cross-eyed, though they all hoped to fix me.

So far, three operations had failed, and you know how important appearance is for a woman. I had been their last hope for a boy, and seemed like one after all, Dad always said. All at once I would be discovered,

naked, hidden, and one guest would say, "Why, congratulations, it's a boy!" I would look down and see there, resting between my white and freckled thighs, a little boy's penis, and all those well dressed guests smelling of perfume and shaving creams, would be touching me with their cold, wet hands, the women's polished fingernails descending like a rare kind of African bird. Men and women would gush and admire the little penis. With all the attention the penis would grow

becoming child size, all on its own, one-legged, needing to hop, and able to say only one word, "Oh." And you know how penises are, rather friendly fellows, this one being no exception, hopping about in search of good company, personal attention, growing larger by the minute, becoming quite a towering young fellow, the kind with a future.

My mother who never liked to hold me, would remark in her crisp New England voice, "How perfectly grotesque."

The penis would wilt all at once until it felt ashamed of itself and hid under the green couch, and I would be scolded for hiding behind the couch. Dad would pick me up with his huge, hairy hands, and spank me in front of all those men and women, insisting loudly, "I have to be strict with my girls, to raise them into proper ladies in these permissive times."

The guests would withdraw into outer darkness, denying that the penis ever existed. But the penis would rise again, night after night.

I wouldn't tell this to anyone for fear of what it might mean.

CAROL GILLIGAN

# JOINING THE RESISTANCE: PSYCHOLOGY, POLITICS, GIRLS AND WOMEN

## 1.  In the Museum:

It is Tuesday. It is raining. And the writing, outing and theater club
is going to the museum. Eight eleven-year-old girls, members of the
sixth grade at the Atrium School in Watertown, Massachusetts, and
two women, psychologists interested in girls' development, climb
into the school van and begin to make their way through the rain-
washed streets into the city. It is June. School is over for the year.
The sixth grade has graduated, and the girls from the class have
returned for a week of outings, writing, and theater work, designed
to strengthen healthy resistance and courage. They gather in the
coatroom of the Fine Arts Museum, shedding backpacks and rain-
coats, retrieving notebooks; they are ready. Today, I explain, they
are to be investigative reporters; their assignment is to find out how
girls and women appear in this museum.

"Naked," Emma says, without hesitation. A current of recognition passes swiftly, silently, through the group. Like Dora, Freud's
patient who remembers standing in the Dresden art gallery for two-
and-a-half hours in front of the Sistine Madonna, Emma will be
transfixed by the images of women, by their nakedness in this cool,
marble building. Later, when asked to write a conversation with
one of the women, Emma chooses a headless, armless Greek statue,
weaving into the conventions of polite childhood conversation her
two burning questions: are you cold? and would you like some
clothes?[1]

But why am I telling you this story? I am interested in the relationship between political resistance and psychological resistance—

An earlier version of this essay was presented as the Tanner Lecture in
Human Values at The University of Michigan, on March 16, 1990.

both highly-charged subjects in the twentieth century. And I have observed a moment of resistance which occurs in girls' lives at the edge of adolescence. Emma's playfully innocent, slightly irreverent conversation with the statue in the museum bespeaks her interest in the scenes which lie behind the paintings and sculpture which she is seeing—an inquiry into relationships between artists and models: what each is doing and feeling and thinking; a curiosity about the psychological dimensions of this connection between men and women. The statue's response—"I have no money"—to the question about whether she wants some clothes, reveals how readily this inquiry becomes political and sets up the dynamic I wish to follow: the tendency in girls' lives at adolescence for a resistance which is essentially political—an insistence on knowing what one knows and a willingness to be outspoken—to turn into a psychological resistance: a reluctance to know what one knows and a fear that such knowledge, if spoken, will endanger relationships and threaten survival.

Freud located this intersection between psychology and politics— between the child's desire for relationships and for knowledge and cultural prohibitions on knowing and seeing—as a turning point in boys' early childhood and named it "the Oedipus complex," after Sophocles' tragedy about knowledge and blindness.[2] In studying girls' development, my colleagues and I have observed a comparable turning point in girls' lives at the time of adolescence.[3] This is the time when girls' desire for relationships and for knowledge comes up against the wall of Western culture and a resistance breaks out which is, I will claim, potentially of great human value.

Let me return for a moment to the museum and record the doubling of voice and vision which characterizes girls' perception and conversation. Mame's eye for the disparity between outside and inside, between calm surface and explosive laughter, is evident as she describes the painting of "Reverend John Atwood and his family." His two oldest daughters, she writes, sustaining the possessive, "have no expression. They're just staring straight ahead, but one of them looks like she is going to burst out laughing." His wife, she concludes on a more somber note, "looks very worn and tired." By paying close attention to the human world around them and following the changing weather of relationships and the undercurrents of thoughts and feelings, girls come to discern patterns, to notice repeating sequences and to hear familiar rhythms, and thus find under the surface of the apparent disorder of everyday living an order which is the psychological equivalent of the Mandelbrot equations of the new chaos physics.

Yet girls' "unpaid-for-education" — Virginia Woolf's name for "that understanding of human beings and their motives which . . . might be called psychology"[4] — leaves girls with knowledge that may well run counter to what they are told by those in authority. So that they are often left, in effect, with two truths, two versions of a story, two voices revealing two points of view. Malka, perhaps reflecting this experience, writes not one but two conversations between herself and the Queen of Babylon. The first is the official version. Speaking in the voice of a reporter, Malka addresses the Queen in a manner befitting her station. "Hello Madam," she says to the woman in the painting who is brushing her hair while receiving news of the revolt, "What is it like ruling so great a land?" "Glorious," the Queen replies, "It is great fun, although," she adds with a yawn, "it does tax time and strength sometimes." In the second conversation, Malka speaks in her own voice to this bored, haughty Queen, asking her simply: "Whatchya doing?" The Queen, in a sudden reversal of priorities, replies: "Brushing my hair. I was interrupted this morning by a revolt."

Whose agenda, what is important, what can be spoken and what is tacitly to be ignored — looked at but not seen, heard but not listened to? The play of girls' conversation, the questions and comments that dart in and out like minnows, followed by looks, scanning faces, and listening to what happens, seeing what follows, taking the pulse, the temperature of the human climate — is anyone upset? what is permitted, admitted (in both senses of the word)? Conflict erupts among girls like lightning — something has happened, someone has stepped over a line. Rejection — the thin dark line of rejection: not you; we — whoever "we" are — do not want to be with you.

Girls' questions about who wants to be with whom are to them among the most important questions, and they take sharp notice throughout the day of the answers given to these questions, as revealed through nuance and gesture, voices and glances, seating arrangements, choices of partners, the responses of adult women and men, the attitudes of authorities in the world. Emma's voice in saying that the nudes are naked, Mame's voice in speaking about the irreverence of the daughter and the tiredness of the mother in Reverend John Atwood's family, Malka's voice in revealing by reversing the relationship between hair-brushing and quelling revolts, are the same three voices which are suppressed in the first published version of Anne Frank's diary — the excised passages which reveal that Anne has looked at and seen her own naked body, that she has recorded disturbing thoughts and feelings about her mother, and that she knows from her reading whose activities people record and imbue with value and is disturbed by the disparate attention given to the courage and suffering of women and men. On June 15, 1944, in one of the deleted passages, she writes:

> A question that has been raised more than once and that gives me no inner peace is why did so many nations in the past, and often still now, treat women as inferior to men? Everyone can agree how unjust this is, but that is not enough for me, I would also like to know the cause of the great injustice . . . . It is stupid enough of women to have borne it all in silence for such a long time, since the more centuries this arrangement lasts, the more deeply rooted it becomes . . . . Many people, particularly women, but also men, now realize for how long this state of affairs has been wrong, and modern women demand the right of complete independence! But that's not all, respect for woman, that's going to have to come as well! . . . Soldiers and war heroes are honored and celebrated, explorers acquire immortal fame, martyrs are revered, but how many will look upon woman as they would upon a soldier? . . . Women are much braver, much more courageous soldiers, struggling and enduring pain for the continuance of humankind, than all the freedom-fighting heroes with their big mouths![5]

That girls' knowledge — of the body, of relationships, and of the world and its values — and girls' irreverence provide the grounds for resistance has been known since the time of *Lysistrata*.

## 2.    If only women . . . .

In 411, B.C.E., in the midst of the disastrous war between Athens and Sparta, Aristophanes plays out a plan for ending the war in a bawdy comedy, *Lysistrata*. If only women, he thinks, who are able to see the absurdity of men's fighting, who are wise, moreover, in the ways of human bodies and psyches, and who can have an effect on men, would take the salvation of Greece into their hands, they could, he imagines, stop the violence. At the opening of the play, Lysistrata calls the women of Athens and Sparta together, preparing to explain her plan, and the voice and expressions of this classical rendition of a peace-making woman resonate strongly with the voices and gestures of eleven-year-old girls in the twentieth century.

"I am angry . . . I am very angry and upset," Sarah says, protesting with her whole face and body. Somberness gathers across her eyebrows, joining them together as she says directly: "I was treated by Ted like trash." Tension is in the air. Sarah and Emma walk back and forth across the room, heads down, arms around each other's shoulders. The social texture has suddenly become dark, opaque, like sudden shadows, hurt feelings easily moving to tears, then out, talking, contact, an opening, light and shadow, the play of relationships, the somberness which gathered across Sarah's face moves off, dissipates . . . the girls line up chairs, dragging them into a row, two chairs apiece, bottoms on one, feet on another. They open their journals and begin writing.

"What's bothering you Lysistrata?" Calonice says at the beginning of Act One, in Alan Somerstein's 1973 Penguin Classics translation. "Don't screw up your face like that. It really doesn't suit you, you know, knitting your eyebrows up like a bow." "Sorry, Calonice, but I'm furious. I'm disappointed in womankind." Lysistrata is upset because the women of Athens and Sparta have not shown up for her meeting — and she knows they would do so at once for Bacchus. Calonice, taking on the task of speaking to someone who is too angry to listen, reminds Lysistrata that "it is not so easy for a wife to get out of the house."[6]

The women come, and Lysistrata explains that if women will vow to give up sex until men vow to give up fighting, they should succeed in bringing about peace — in essence by substituting the mutual pleasures of sex for men's single-minded pursuit of violence.

The strategy is as follows: the women will do everything in their power to arouse the desire of their husbands and lovers, and then they will run out of their houses and lock themselves up in the Acropolis. The plan succeeds brilliantly in the theater. The Peloponnesian War, however, continues.

More than two millennia later in Puritan New England, where the only war described is the unremitting war in the heart of the Puritans, Hawthorne puts forward a similar vision: that a woman must bring the new truth that will establish relations between women and men "on a surer ground of mutual happiness." And then, in a stunning exegesis, with the brilliant economy of a single letter, demonstrates why this vision is bound to eventuate in failure. The very knowledge and passion which enable a woman to escape from "the iron framework of reasoning" also disable her, by causing her to be labeled an impure woman: a woman who has been adulterated.[7]

This double vision which at once enables and imprisons women is explicated in the chapter entitled "Another View of Hester," after seven-year-old Pearl, in "The Minister's Vigil," trenchantly gives another view of the Reverend Arthur Dimmesdale ("Thou wast not bold! . . . thou wast not true! . . . Thou wouldst not promise to take my hand, and mother's hand tomorrow noontide!").[8] The scarlet letter, the narrator explains, revealing Hester's passion and also her knowledge of relationships which the Puritan eye cannot discern, gives her "so much power to do and power to sympathize . . . with her fellow creatures" that many people said that the A meant Able rather than Adultery, "so strong was Hester Prynne with a woman's strength."[9]

Living at once inside and outside the framework, Hester is able to see the frame. The "lawless passion" which broke the bonds of convention and released her from the chain of the good, enabled her mind to run free — leading to silent speculation which, the narrator surmises, the Puritan forefathers "would have held to be a deadlier crime than that stigmatized by the scarlet letter," a crime which threatened not simply her own position but the very foundation of the Puritan order.[10]

Like the hysterical women of the late nineteenth century — the women whose features Freud lists in describing his early patient, Fraülein Elisabeth von R., noting as characteristic "her giftedness, her ambition, her moral sensibility, her excessive demand for love which, to begin with, found satisfaction in her family, and the independence of her nature which went beyond the feminine ideal and found expression in a considerable amount of obstinacy, pugnacity and reserve,"[11] Hester Prynne has the character of a resister: "a mind of native courage and ability," a woman whom fate and fortune had set free.

> The scarlet letter was her passport into regions where other women dared not tread. Shame, Despair, Solitude! These had been her teachers, — stern and wild ones, — and they had made her strong, but taught her much amiss.[12]

In the end, then, she must be corrected — and unlike Dora, Freud's later patient who flees from what had become the iron framework of his treatment, leaving her analysis in mid-stream, Hester, in the dark conclusion to Hawthorne's brooding novel, takes on the Puritan mantle. Assuring the women who come to her for counsel and comfort that a new truth will reveal a new order of living and that "the angel and apostle of the coming revelation must be a woman," she explains that this woman—whom she once thought might be herself—must in contrast be "lofty [and] pure" as well as beautiful, and "wise not through dusky grief, but the ethereal medium of joy . . . and sacred love."[13] Thus the very woman who is able to envision a new order of human relations is, by the same token, unable since the experience which enables her also adulterates her in the eyes of the community. Released from goodness, she is imprisoned in badness, within the iron framework of a puritanical order.

This imprisonment of women becomes the subject of Claudia Koonz's scathing jeremiad—her 1987 study of women in Nazi Germany which she entitles *Mothers in the Fatherland*. Koonz asks on a political level the question which currently rivets psychotherapists: how could women, how could mothers especially, have stayed with and supported such fathers? Interviewing Gertrud Scholtz-Klink, the "Lady Führer über Alles," chief of the Women's Bureau—the oxymoronic Nazi social service agency—and author of *Woman in the Third Reich*, Koonz is spellbound by her protestations of goodness, by a moral piety and smugness which seemingly admit no pity. "Crimefeel" is the term she coins for this unrepentant woman's insistence on describing herself as both a good mother and a good Nazi— the emotional analogue to the murderous "crimethink" which Orwell describes in *Nineteen Eighty-Four*. That women did not resist Hitler in any more significant numbers than did doctors, clergy, professors and others is surprising only in that the main form which resistance could take under the relentless eye of the Nazi terror was, it would seem, characteristically female, falling into "what we think of as 'women's work' " — grounded less in the rhetoric of heroism than in a realistic sense of vulnerability, involving "manipulat[ion] [of] the situation, intelligence and the ability to assess the enemy's personality."[14] Yet women as a group did not do this work but instead actively supported and voted into power the openly sexist and avowedly misogynistic Nazi Party, with an idealization of mothers which provided only the thinnest of veils over the underlying rage and contempt. Soldiers and mothers—the imagery of Hitler's Germany; what were they doing in one another's company?

The relationship between soldiers and mothers surfaces in the very different context of Diana Russell's 1989 study, *Lives of Courage: Women for a New South Africa*, creating a paradox which Russell highlights for her reader. Interviewing politically courageous women, Russell heard repeatedly about the importance of women in the resistance movement and the extraordinary strength and resilience of women not only in the face of daily adversity but also under the extreme conditions of political detention and torture. Many women in one way or another echoed Albertina Sisulu's conviction that "women are the people who are going to relieve us from this oppression and depression."[15] Yet when asked why there are relatively few women leaders, these same women referred to "women's internalized sense of inferiority, their poor education, their lack of assertiveness, and the strong beliefs in traditional gender roles that still prevail in African cultures." I find it difficult, Russell tells her reader,

> to reconcile these two perspectives. The fact that only 5 percent to 12 percent of the political detainees are women suggests that women are underrepresented not only in leadership positions but also in the rank-and-file of the movement.[16]

Her discussion then turns to the crucial role women play in enabling men to be politically active and also to the fact that women are mothers and often faced with raising children singlehandedly and providing for them on severely inadequate wages. Like Anne Frank, Russell laments the inattention given to mothers' courage and bravery. And yet, this leaves unanswered the question which Virginia Woolf raises in *Three Guineas*: is there a way in which women can help men prevent rather than wage what has historically been the male act of war — the violence which, whatever its causes, leaves in its wake a litter of dead bodies and ruined houses?

In her darkly cautious and brilliantly far-reaching address to this question, Woolf gently shifts the focus of attention away from mothers and to the "daughters of educated men," for whom she lays out a three-step passage out of the private house of their fathers and into the public world where they will form a "Society of Outsiders." The steps which Woolf sees as essential are university education and admission to the professions so that women can gain what is to be their only weapon: the power of independent opinion supported by independent income. Because women's experiences in living and women's relation to the tradition differ from men's, women may succeed in "finding new words and creating new methods,"[17] and thus may help men to break what otherwise is a vicious cycle.

The dangers inherent in this process are what Woolf calls "adultery of the brain" and "brain-selling" or writing "what you do not want to write for the sake of money." And the danger in these sins arises in part from the fact that these practices create and let loose upon the world "anaemic, vicious and diseased progeny," which infect and corrupt other people. So that women become complicit in perpetuating what women do not want by saying what women do not want to say.[18]

The deeply-knotted dilemma, then, which lies at the center of women's development is how can girls both enter and stay outside of, be educated in and then change, what has been for centuries a man's world? And yet, if "the public and the private worlds are inseparably connected, . . . [if] the tyrannies and servilities of the one are the tyrannies and servilities of the other," if we live in one world and cannot dissociate ourselves from one another, and if the psychology of fathers which has ruled the private house is writ large in legal codes and moral orders and supported by the ever-present threat of what is considered to be a legitimate use of force or violence, how can daughters be anywhere other than inside and outside of these structures?[19]

Perhaps girls' doubling of voice and vision offers an answer to this question, especially if girls resist the temptation to solve this doubling by simply correcting for male perspective. This is the central lesson girls learn in the move from primary to secondary education — how to make this seemingly simple algebraic or geometric correction which aligns girls' vision with the Western tradition, so that girls can enter without changing what has been called "the human conversation." Once this correction is made, the framework becomes invisible, and then, in the words of one wise twelve-year-old girl, "you don't have to think."

In an extraordinary film about South Africa, which has the slow-motion quality of recovering memory, Shawn Slovo returns to the year when she was thirteen — the year her mother was taken away to prison — to consider, in the context of this difficult relationship between mother and daughter, "how to merge the politics with the personal without detracting from the importance of either."[20] Slovo is the daughter of Ruth First, the journalist who was one of the few whites centrally involved with the African National Congress, a woman whose militant opposition to Apartheid led her to be arrested and detained twice by the South African government in 1963, the year of the film's action, and then, in 1982, to be killed by a parcel bomb while working with the resistance in Mozambique.

Set at that edge of girls' development, between childhood and adolescence, the film catches an angle of perception which is at odds with conventional ways of speaking about mothers and daughters, especially with conventional images of what constitutes good and bad mothering. And this shift in perspective is, inadvertently, a discovery of the film. Slovo, as she records in her introduction to the diary she kept in the course of her writing, set out to write in what are essentially conventional terms about

> the relationship between a white woman, politically committed to the fight against Apartheid, and her thirteen-year-old daughter who must contend against politics for the love, care and time of her mother. Set against the backdrop of increasingly violent repression, [the film] chronicles the effects of the break-up of the family.[21]

And yet Slovo has written a very different film. Showing the break-up of the family, she chronicles the connection between mother and adolescent daughter, a connection instigated by the daughter's insistence on entering the emotional center of her mother's life. Thirteen-year-old Molly, in the critical scene, literally breaks her mother's silence by opening her secret drawer and reading her diary. What she discovers is what she most feared. That her mother had "tried to leave us," that she had tried to kill herself in prison. "You don't care about us. You shouldn't have had us," the dialogue runs.[22]

Slovo discovers in writing out this accusation of bad mothering — the accusation readily made by Pauline Kael and other critics — that she hears her mother's voice as well as her own. The scene which she had resisted writing, "the conversation, the confrontation, my mother and I had never had" and which "in life . . . was what kept us apart," turns out to have been "there all the time, just waiting for the last moment."[23]

The scene as written has the quality of remembering and also the ring of familiarity, resonating with other moments when daughters fight for relationship with their mothers and mothers let them in. Then the desire for human connection overrides the restraints on relationships between mothers and daughters imposed by cultural images of good and bad women, and leads, in the case of Shawn

Slovo, to a reformulation of the basic question at a much deeper level: What does it mean to be a good mother to an adolescent daughter, coming of age in a violent and racist society? and, What can women teach girls about resistance and courage and love in the face of indifference, cruelty and violence?

The illusion, still blinding the critics but seen through in the film, is that mothers and daughters *can* live in a world apart. Slovo steadily directs the viewer's eye to the enclosure—the imprisonment of conventionally good South African white mothers in elaborately fenced-in private houses. Her conclusion is that mothers cannot stay with their daughters without joining the resistance, at least once their daughters are able to see beyond their enclosure, *and* that daughters and mothers need to find ways to be with one another in this struggle.

## 3.   Resistance

Five psychological truths:

1. What is unvoiced or unspoken, because it is out of relationship, tends to get out of perspective and to dominate psychic life.

2. The hallmarks of loss are idealization and rage, and under the rage, immense sadness. ("To want and want and not to have.")

3. What is dissociated or repressed—known and then not known—tends to return, and return, and return.

4. The logic of the psyche is an associative logic—the free-falling logic of dreams, poetry, and memory—as well as a formal logic of classification and control.

5. One learns the answers to one's own questions.

Anna at twelve, tall, thin, her dark hair cut short, her green eyes looking steadily out of a quiet and somewhat wary face, raises the question: how can you tell if what people are saying is true, "if what they are saying about you, if they really mean it, or if they are just doing it to be mean, and it's hard to tell, I mean, with a lot of people you can't tell how they are." What she is trying to understand is the difference between the surface banter of teasing, making fun, putting people down which went on among her friends (although she does not know if they were really her friends) at the public school she went to, and being mean, "really mean," or cruel. At her new school—a girls' school—Anna notices that everyone is "nice," and she feels good about herself when she is "nice to people or . . . not being mean," and bad about herself when she is mean or hurts people but "sometimes you just can't help it." Anna feels that people can tell how she feels, even when "inside I'm really sad about something but outside I'm trying to be happy," because "if you're feeling sad, you just can't make yourself happy."[24]

Malka writes about the disparity between inside and outside after the outing club's trip to Plum Island — a beach and bird sanctuary on Boston's north shore:

> A sand castle, life on a small scale. Kingdoms rise and fall, water ebbs in and out. Water rises, in and out. Channels, pools, castles, forests. The outside view. But on the inside — are babies being born? Are children playing? Are crafts being learned? Are people being married? Are battles being fought? Are people dying? Love, fun, smiling, and crying. Life. A sand castle.

At the edge of adolescence, girls draw attention to the disparity between an insider's view of life which they are privy to in childhood and an outside view, intimating that the insider's knowledge is in danger of being washed out or giving way. The connection between inside and outside becomes explicitly a focus of attention when girls reach adolescence and become subjected to a kind of voice and ear training, designed to make it clear what voices people like to listen to in girls and what girls can say without being called, in today's vernacular, "stupid," or "rude." On a daily basis, girls receive lessons on what they can let out and what they must keep in, if they do not want to be spoken about by others as mad or bad or simply told they are wrong. Anna, dealing with this problem of containment, says that she would like to be "just a better person or have better ways of thinking" and explains:

> Sometimes I will get really mad, and I can outburst or something, and I can't be like that . . . . I have to learn how to work with people, *because sometimes I just get really mad at people who can't understand what I am saying*, and I get so exasperated. It is like, "Why can't you just . . .? What's wrong with you? Why can't you see this my way?" And I have to really go for what I want though. I can't let this stuff take over me. And I have to, you kind of have to fight to get what you want. [emphasis added]

In essence, Anna states the problem of resistance as a problem of relationship. She feels pressure to hold herself in, "not to be like that . . . [not to] get really mad," or, even worse, "outburst." At the same time, she realizes she must not let go of what she wants, that "I can't let this stuff take over me." One resistance is psychological and will lead Anna to take herself out of relationship, not to fight for the understanding she wants but to become "nice" and as she now views it "successful." The other resistance is political, and, by staying in relationship Anna will come into conflict with others.

Anna struggles between these two forms of resistance at the age of twelve. With her mother, she experiences the central dilemma of relationship: how to speak honestly and also stay in connection with others. When they go shopping for clothes, Anna explains,

> She will pull something out and she'll say, "Well, what do you think of it?" And then if I say I don't like it, then she'll get really mad, and she'll put it back . . . . And then, she'll forget about what happens when I really give her my opinion, and then she'll say, "Tell me what you really think about it." And then she gets mad when I tell her . . . . And I'll say, "Well, you don't really want it because you already screamed at me when I gave it."

Eleven-year-old Tessie articulates the importance of voicing conflicts in relationships, explaining why it is necessary to "tell someone about it" so that you are "telling it from both sides" and can *"hear* the [other] person's point of view."

> When you are having an argument . . . and you just keep it inside you and don't tell anyone, you never hear the person's point of view. And if you are telling someone about it, you are telling it from both sides and so you hear what my mother said, or what my brother said. And the other person can say, well, you might be mad, but your mom was right, and you say, yeah, I know. So when you say it out loud, you have to listen.

Tessie also observes that fighting—by which she means verbal conflict or voicing disagreement—is good for relationships: "fighting is what makes relationships go on," in the face of trouble, and "the more fights you get in and the more it goes on . . . the stronger it gets because the more you can talk with that person." The subtlety of Tessie's understanding of how people come to know one another and what kind of knowledge is necessary if friends are not to hurt one another's feelings is evident as she explains that it is through fighting, rather than "just saying 'I'm sorry' to them," that you learn "how that person feels," and then you know how "not to hurt their feelings." Yet fights also carry with them the danger of not speaking and "then you seem to grow apart."[25]

I emphasize this detailed, specific psychological knowledge based on careful listening and sustained observation and characterized by finely-wrought distinctions — a naturalist's rendering of the human world — because girls' knowledge when brought into the public world is often dismissed as trivial or seen as transgressive, with the result that girls are told repeatedly not to speak, not to say anything, or at least not to talk in public about what they know.

Asked at twelve whether she has changed as a learner, Anna explains that she has come to think about things which she never thought about before, meaning the origins of things which formerly she just took for granted because "you just kind of trusted the teacher," like 2 + 2 = 4, or the letters of the alphabet. "You don't sit there and say, 'A — what a dumb letter.' You don't think about it."

Now, thinking about thinking and about different ways people "look at something," Anna says you might think someone is "crazy" but, struggling with the problem of difference — the problem of relationship and of relativism — "that is their opinion . . . as long as it's not going to hurt anybody." As a scholarship student in a private school, she is acutely aware of difference and wonders about how she fits into this world where "it's just friendly and everything is nice. It is really nice, I think," and where to her delight she is encouraged to speak — for Anna, an irresistible invitation. "Most of the time," Anna concludes at twelve, "I'm in a pretty good mood, and sometimes I'm not. Sometimes I am mad at the world."

When Anna is interviewed at age thirteen, as an eighth grader, her interview is peppered with "I don't know" (spoken now over twice as many times as the previous year, increasing from 21 times at age twelve to 67 at age thirteen, with no corresponding increase in the length of the interview transcript). Anna is struggling explicitly with a reluctance to know what she knows and an inclination to suppress her knowledge and go along with the group. Asked about whether she has work that she loves, this child who loves learning and loves school says "reading and singing . . . and I can just sort of get lost in them and not have to think about things." Talking about herself as a knower, she observes that "you can interpret things differently" and describes the way thoughts and feelings cascade differently from different beginnings, so that depending on where you start from — for example, in reading a poem — you arrive at different endpoints.

But now conformity has a hold on Anna as she begins to feel like a member of her new school, not only a top student but also a part of her class. She watches others to see which way to go and does not, she says, "massively disagree on anything." With friends, if she disagreed, she would be "kind of mad at myself, have kind of a messed up feeling." With adults, "they would overpower me most of the time." Anna is learning to bring herself into line with the world around her, to bring herself into agreement with others so as not to mess up relationships with friends or experience the helplessness of being overpowered by adults. Paradoxically, for the sake of relationship and also for protection, she is disconnecting her self from others.

At fourteen, in ninth grade, Anna bursts out, becoming outspoken and drawing the interviewer's attention to the change she hears in her voice: "I used to be really quiet and shy and everything, and now I am really loud." Again, the phrase "I don't know" has doubled (from 67 to 135), but now it alternates with the phrase "you know"[26] and punctuates a tale of resistance which is clearly political: an insistence on knowing what she knows and writing the paper she wants to write, even though she knows it will make her English teacher angry. "I see things from a lot of points of view," Anna explains, and calling her ability to see from different viewpoints "creative" now rather than "crazy," she tells the following story.

The class was asked to write a hero legend, and Anna did not see the hero in the same way as her teacher: "There was a ladeedah hero who went and saved all humankind." Anna explains,

> if you see this hero from a different viewpoint, from a different standpoint, everyone could be a hero. So I wanted to write it from a Nazi standpoint, like Hitler as hero, and she really did not go for that at all. And I started to write, and she got really mad, and she was, like, I am afraid you are going to come out sounding like a little Nazi . . .

Anna's solution was to write two papers, two versions of the hero legend: "a ladeedah legend and the one I wanted to write." She turned both papers into her teacher along with a letter explaining her reasons. "She gave me an A on the normal one. I gave her the other one because I just had to write it. It sort of made me mad."

Anna wrote about Hitler "from the point of view of a little boy who was joining one of those groups that they had, and he was so proud to have a uniform and he went to try to salute . . . . It did not come out about Hitler as much as about the reasons for Hitler,"— which interested Anna who was part German and whose father had been unemployed. In addition, Anna has seen, by watching her father and her brother easily resort to what she calls "brute force" in the face of frustration, how the need to appear strong or heroic can cover over vulnerability and lead to violence. To Anna, the hero legend is an understandable but dangerous legend.

In choosing to disagree openly with her teacher and, in Woolf's terms, not to sell her writing or commit adultery of the brain, Anna said she was "just really mad" and that her teacher "was just narrow-minded" in her insistence that Hitler was an "anti-hero" rather than a hero.

"It was an urge," Anna says. "I had to write that paper because I was so mad . . . . I had to write it to explain it to her, you know; I just had to . . . . I just had to make her understand."

This urgent need to "make her understand," the overwhelming desire for human connection — to bring one's own inner world of thoughts and feelings into relationship with the thoughts and feelings of others — feels very pressing to girls who fight for authentic relationships and who resist being shut up, put down, turned away, ignored. Anna's friend went to talk with the teacher on Anna's behalf, and her mother encouraged her to write the paper but to do so in a way that would not antagonize the teacher. In the end, Anna concludes that her teacher "probably saw it as more annoying than anything else." What she learned from this experience, she said, "was not to antagonize people," her mother's caution. In fact, she was able both to speak and not antagonize people — in part, she suspects because she had not been heard, because her teacher did not understand, but also because her teacher, however annoyed, was willing to listen and read both papers.

Anna at fourteen sees the framework of the worlds she lives in. Painfully, she has become aware of the inconsistencies in the school's position on economic differences — where money is available and where it isn't, the limits of the meritocracy which is espoused. And seeing inconsistencies, she becomes riveted by the disparity between the names of things and the realities and plays with the provocation of being literal in an effort to call things by their right names.

At fifteen, Anna begins to ask some literal questions about the order which is taken to be unquestionable in the world she lives in — questions about religion and violence. And she discovers that her questions are not welcomed by many of her classmates and her opinions are often met with silence; in the midst of an intensely controversial classroom conversation, she notices who is not speaking: "there were a bunch of people who just sat there like stones and listened."

Anne Frank in one of the suppressed diary entries, comments on the silences which surround the subject of sex. On March 18, 1944, at the age of fourteen, she writes:

> Parents and people in general are very strange when it comes to [sexual matters]. Instead of telling their daughters as well as their sons everything when they are 12 years old, they send the children out of the room during such conversations and leave them to find things out for themselves. If the parents notice later on that the children have learned things anyway, then they assume that the children know either more or less than they actually do . . . . Grownups do come up against an important obstacle, although I'm sure the obstacle is no more than a very small barrier, they believe that children will stop looking on marriage as something sacred and pure when it dawns on them that in most cases the purity is nothing more than eyewash.[27]

What puzzles Anna is the reluctance of people to speak about cruelty and violence. Like Anne Frank, she notes the readiness of adults to cover over what they do not want children to look at — so that children, especially as they reach adolescence, are encouraged, tacitly, not to know what they see or not to listen to what they hear, or to see everything as "nice." And yet Anna is also bothered by her mother's refusal to wash over the realities of her life and confused by what she is taking in — in part because of the disparity between what women are saying in the two worlds that she lives in.

The acuity of Anna's perception is striking, and her description of life in her family is almost identical to Glen Elder and Avshalom Caspi's depiction of families living under economic hardship, where fathers are unemployed and emotionally volatile and where mothers and daughters bond. Anna's family constellation (herself and younger brothers) matches the picture for maximal psychological risk in children, given the consistent finding that when families are under stress, the children who are most psychologically in danger are boys in early childhood and girls at adolescence.[28] Anna's relationship with her mother thus seems critical to Anna's resilience. Her closeness with her mother and the openness of their conversation is sometimes painful. Anna feels her mother's feelings "gnawing at" her. And it is sometimes confusing for Anna to know how her mother thinks and feels. She realizes that her mother's is "only one viewpoint" and she does not "know how much of it is dramatized." And yet, she "can see that a lot of what my Mom says is true."

"You can't see someone like my Dad," she says, as an eleventh grader in the fifth year of the study, returning to a question she introduced at the start, "without realizing how easily people are taken in." At school, she has "gotten a glimpse" behind the scenes and seen women whom she thought of as nice and compassionate "give away their color," after which, she astutely observes, "all you can see is that part." "It is awful," she says, despairing at the capacity of people to cover over reality, the chameleon-like way her father changes his voice when,

> in the midst of screaming and yelling and ranting and raving at everyone in our house, the phone rings: "Hello" — like that. And it is really awful. Everyone thinks he is the strongest person, and when you see the other side you just get so annoyed when people do that.

I could, Anna muses, "probably give *the* best senior speech in the world in terms of shocking people, but people just don't, you know, it is so different, because there is just no one," she says with adolescent fervor, "no one who has to deal with anywhere near the same thing [as I do]." The violent outbursts of her father toward her brothers have brought social service agencies to the house; her brother's violence toward her mother has brought the police. Because of the social class difference, Anna may think that hers is the only family (in her school) where violence happens. And yet, she concludes, "Pollyanna" — that epitome of the nice girl — "would have problems . . . . Thinking that life is peaches and cream is not realistic. It's not real . . . . It really grates on you when you have someone around you who is like Pollyanna . . . that is really scary, you know; you can't deal with someone like that." The niceness which governs and sustains the school which she goes to cannot admit the world which she knows from experience . . . and Anna knows it. They are, she says, "totally different outlooks on life."

The real world, Anna begins: "I have a bunch of friends that I talk to and, you know, they understand and everything, but it is not very many people. This school," she concludes, "is not the real world." Anna, who loves school, who wants to take everything that there is to take, to know everything she can know about the world — to know Chinese and Latin as well as French and English, does not know how to imagine her future: whether she will enter the world which the people in her school think of as "normal" — the world which is reflected in the norms — or whether she will join Woolf's Outsiders' Society and armed with an independent income to support her independent opinions, will be one of those people who go through college and get a Ph.D. and I'll live at the bottom of a mountain in Montana. Just one of those weird people. Have a chicken farm. I don't know. Then I will just write books or something,

remaining, as Woolf envisioned, "outside (and) experiment[ing] not with public means in public but with private means in private."[29]

## 4.   Psychology and Politics: Perfect Girls and Dissidents

"The anxious bird," Jorie Graham writes in her poem, "The Age of Reason,"

> . . . . . . . . . . . . in the wild
> spring green
> is *anting*, which means,
> in my orchard
> he has opened his wings
> over a furious
>
> anthill and will take up
> into the delicate
> ridges of quince-yellow
> feathers
> a number of tiny, angry
> creatures
>
> that will inhabit him, bewildered
> no doubt,
> travelling deep
> into the air
> on this feathery planet
> new life . . .
>
> We don't know why
> they do it.
> At times they'll take on
> almost anything
> that burns, spreading
> their wings
>
> over coals, over cigarette
> butts,

even, mistakenly, on bits
of broken glass.
Meanwhile the light keeps
stroking them
as if it were love.

The poem is an inquiry about love. Love means opening; it means taking in. And Graham asks the question: what, in the name of love, is taken in? The world of nature, with its ever-present reminder of death — "The garden / continues its work / all round them, the gradual / openings that stand / for death." And the world humans cultivate, the stories that grow in the hothouse of culture: "Under the plastic / groundcover the human / garden grows: help-sticks / and knots, row / after row. Who wouldn't want / to take / into the self / something that burns / or cuts, or wanders / lost / over the body?"

Who would, or wouldn't, in the name of love, take in films like Werner Herzog's *Woyzek*, where

the hero whom
we love
who is mad has
murdered

the world, the young
woman
who is his wife,
and loved her,
and covered himself
with blood,

he grows frightened
by how quickly
she softens and takes on the shape
of the soil.

The emphasized lines, the short lines of this poem, in their staccato insistence telling, flashing, a warning to women, like Emilia in the brothel scene of *Othello* desperately trying to tell Desdemona before it is too late what she needs to know about what Othello is thinking, and feeling, Graham's words capturing the essence of that warning, like nautical flags flying or newspaper headlines: "*murdered /*

*woman / and loved her / with blood.*" How often, how far do we take this truth in? How do philosophers reason about this, what are reasonable answers to the poet's questions: "How far is true / enough? / How far into the earth / can vision go and / still be / love?"[30]

When eleven-year-old Tessie is asked, at the end of November, what stays with her in looking back over the past year, she says, "the summer, things that we do in the summer . . . like the sailing that we do and all the fun that I had going swimming and doing different things." Asked how she would describe herself to herself, Tessie says simply, "I like myself." Pleasure runs through Tessie's life like water flowing, swirling around her friends in the summer, her fights with her brother, swimming, reading, writing stories, her closeness with her mother, her special relationship with her father who "always wanted a daughter," her confidence and pleasure — in taking care of children, in throwing sawdust on a classmate who has made her angry, in deciding it was worth it to get into trouble, in helping people with difficult things or problems, in meeting new people, "that's fun, you get to know more people as you go on."

But Tessie also has taken in, in the name of love, an image of perfection, exemplified by her grandmother, the person whom she admires:

> She is *always* smiling and *always* laughing. She's *always* doing something helpful. I don't know. She goes to a nursing home, and she writes letters for people who can't write letters . . . . She *always* has things made and *always* has little things for little kids . . . . She makes big terrariums and everything that she sells at the Church fair, and she enjoys what she is doing, she loves her grandchildren and her children. And she seems to be an *always* happy person and *always* willing to help you and everything. (emphasis added)

The repeated word, "always," catches the stillness at the center of this frozen image; Tessie's free-flowing world has suddenly stopped.

Ellen, at eleven, asked whether there is someone whom she admires, describes a variant of this image — a perfect girl who seems an offshoot of the always good woman, and the repeated word "really" in her description suggests that Ellen may question whether what she is seeing is real.

There is this girl in our class who is perfect . . . . She's *really* tall, not *really* tall, she's tall, and is pretty and she's good at everything. You could say something, and she could do it perfectly. And she's smart, and she is good at any sport, and she's good at art, and she's good at everything. She's like a person I know, like my mother's friend in college. She's good at everything. There is not one thing she cannot do. She's *really* nice and . . . she's *always* being herself.

Claudia, the astute nine-year-old narrator of Toni Morrison's novel *The Bluest Eye*, sums up "this disrupter of seasons," the girl who enters the late elementary school classroom and "enchanted the entire school."[31]

The familiarity of this girl, her regular appearance at the edge of adolescence in girls' lives and in women's novels, signals a shift in the cultural framework which is key to the psychology and politics of girls' adolescence. Suddenly girls feel the presence of a standard which does not come out of their experience and an image which, because embodied, calls into question the reality which they have lived in — the moving, changing world of thoughts and feelings, relationships and people. Feeling the mesmerizing presence of the perfect girl, girls have entered the world of the hero legend, and experience the imposition of a framework which seemingly comes out of nowhere — a world view superimposed on girls but grounded in the psychology of men. With the arrival of the perfect girl, who exemplifies the incredible, girls are in danger of losing their world. But they are also in danger, in the world of the hero legend, if they continue to know what they know and especially if they say it in public. What once seemed ordinary to girls — speaking, difference, anger, conflict, fighting, bad as well as good thoughts and feelings, now seems treacherous: laced with danger, a sign of imperfection, a harbinger of being left out, not chosen.

Like the hero or the superheros of boys' early childhood, the perfect girl of girls' early adolescence is an emblem of loss — signifying an idealization which replaces relationship, covering over a rage which is unspeakable and a sadness which seems endless, and thus marking an inner division or psychic chasm: a taking of the self out of relationship in the name of love. This is the move enacted by the hand which censored Anne Frank's diary, removing her slightly from the reader (especially the puritanical American reader), imposing a kind of innocence or psychological virginity, so that she — who knew so much — would appear more perfect or more acceptable or more protected in the eyes of the world by seeming to know less than she knew. The evidence covered over reveals the extent of Anne's connection with her body, with desire, with her mother, and with the world which she lived in — a world which contained both the story of Woyzeck and the Nazis. Living in the midst of real terror, she had not lost her world.

If girls' knowledge of reality is politically dangerous, it is both psychologically and politically dangerous for girls not to know what is going on — or to render themselves innocent by disconnecting themselves from their bodies, that repository of experience and desire, and thus, in essence, disassociating themselves from themselves, from relationships and from what they know about the world. Because girls are encouraged to make this disconnection at the time of their adolescence, girls' dissent at this time becomes psychologically essential, and potentially healing for boys as well. And yet at adolescence, girls' knowledge and girls' passion are bound to make trouble in the world girls are entering.

When Rosie is interviewed at age fourteen, her vitality is infectious. She speaks openly in the privacy of the interview setting about desire as sexual — in somewhat the same tentative yet resolute manner that Anne Frank describes in preparing to speak about her body ("When the subject [of what a naked girl looks like] comes up again," she says to herself in her diary, "how in heaven's name will you be able to explain what things are like [down there] without using examples? Shall I try it out here in the meantime? Well then get on with it!").[32] Rosie's pleasure in her body and her exuberance at age fourteen are unmistakable. At the same time, she is in trouble at school for her outspokenness, her irreverence, and her refusal, despite her evident brightness, to be the perfect student.

At fifteen, Rosie and her boyfriend are caught in the park by a ranger who calls her mother to come and take Rosie home. Rosie was embarrassed and scared about what was going to happen to her, and also worried about disillusioning her mother who "had this image of me . . . as close to the perfect child." Asked to describe this perfect child, she says, without hesitation: "She gets straight As and has a social life, but still gets home exactly on the dot, on time, and does everything her parents say, and keeps her room neat." I ask Rosie, "Are there girls like this?" She says, "Perhaps; saints." "Do saints have sex?" I wonder, thinking of Rosie. "I don't know," she begins, and then fills in her solution: "If they want, as long as they don't get caught; as long as nobody knows."

Once her mother knew, Rosie "hunted her down and . . . made

her talk to me. And it wasn't like a battle or anything . . . . I just
wanted to talk to her and see what she had to say." Like Anna who
wants to connect her own with her teacher's view of the hero, by
"making her understand," Rosie wants to discover what connections
are possible between herself and her mother, what her mother is
willing to say.

Rosie's clarity, her playfulness, her irreverence in refusing to dis-
embody saints, and her courage in staying in her own body coexist
with confusion about the world she lives in. Despite her efforts, she
cannot find the emotional center — the place where desire or passion
or pleasure live in her mother's busy life. From her mother, she takes
in the caution that she must be more careful about her body, more
attentive to the warning signals and the flags of danger. Perhaps the
seemingly disembodied perfect girl who her mother and teachers
envision she could be really exists and is admirable, exemplifying the
way Rosie should live in order to take care of herself in a world
where imperfection often means rejection and where, more darkly,
sex can be fatal, love can mean murder, and fighting can mean
violence.

At the end of *Oedipus Rex*, that psychological telling of the hero
legend, after the truth about family relations has been uncovered
(that Oedipus has unwittingly murdered his father and married his
mother, and that it was his mother who — cannily, uncannily? —
gave him away to the herdsman), Oedipus blinds himself, Jocasta
strangles herself, their sons run off to become kings and war against
one another, and their daughters are summoned to accompany their
father in his blindness. A quick scanning of Sophocles' *tableau
vivant* of life in the patriarchal family suggests that the wounds
which fathers suffer in early childhood infect their daughters in
adolescence. Yet in a play which is filled with riddles and
questions — where the chorus asks about Jocasta's silence ("How
could the Queen whom Laïus won, / Be silent when that deed was
done?"),[33] no one asks on behalf of the daughters: why did Oedipus
blind himself?

## 5.  Women Teaching Girls

It is September, and the sky over New England is Fra Angelico
blue. We, two women, psychologists at Harvard University, are
flying to Cleveland, to talk with the Laurel School teachers about
our research with the girls they are teaching. It is the beginning of

the second year of the project, and the library fills as we enter, the faculty sitting in short rows crossing the room with a long aisle running down the center. School—the microcosm in children's lives of the public world, the public space which Hannah Arendt sees as the crucible of democracy, the place where the natality and plurality, the ever new and always different nature of the human condition can flourish.

The school is governed by an honor code, which is working well according to the school's recent evaluation, maintaining an order of living where people can bring themselves and leave their things in safety. In the privacy of the research interview, girls spoke about the honor code from a different angle, describing dilemmas of relationship which arose in the wake of honor code violations; how, they wondered, could they stay in connection with themselves and also be in connection with others? Since there seemed no way to speak about these problems of relationship in the public arena, many girls had publicly agreed to an honor code which they did not believe in.[34] And, taking matters of public governance into their own hands, girls took them into a private world of relationships and settled them in private places, drawing on that psychological knowledge—that intricate physics of relationship which girls learned by keeping an eye on the human weather and following the constant play of relationships, thoughts, feelings and actions as it moves across the sky of the day.

This girls' school, like a perfectly run household, was being governed as if effortlessly. In fact, it was being run by an underground society of girls whose knowledge and activities on behalf of the school were going for the most part unseen and unnamed. To encourage girls' involvement in political matters, to educate girls who hopefully as women will participate fully as citizens in a democratic state, it seemed necessary to bring girls' questions about public governance into the public arena—to name girls' activities and their knowledge that were contributing to the public welfare and also to encourage girls to deal publicly with their differences and their disagreement.

To my right, in front, a woman—small bones, white hair, intense face concentrating energy as her thoughts and feelings connect with sound and come out into the air of the room on her voice—said: "How can we help girls learn to deal with disagreement in public, when we"—she looked across the rows, quickly scanning the faces of her colleagues, women and men—"when we," meaning now women, "cannot deal with disagreement in public ourselves?"

Silence washed the room. The research was uncovering the underground. Girls' voices, recorded in private and amplified in the public space of the school, were resonating with women teachers, encouraging women to ask: what were they teaching girls about relationships, about speaking, about conflict, about difference, about political and psychological resistance?.

Two questions about relationships clarified a woman's position: Where am I in relation to the tradition which I am practicing and teaching? and Where am I in relation to girls, the next generation of women? Are women vessels through which the culture passes? Are women oracles of the disciplines, conveying, like the oracle of Apollo — the priestess who voiced the wisdom of the Delphic oracle — the wisdom of male gods? Provocative questions, but it was the relationship between girls and women which proved to be transformative, and most specifically, the relationship of women to girls at the edge of adolescence.

Education is the time-honored, non-violent means of social change, the alternative to revolution. And education at present in this country is largely in the hands of women, who, as mothers, teachers, and therapists, are directly in contact with people's desires for relationships and for knowledge, and also in touch with the resistance. Perhaps women are currently in a position to constitute an Outsiders' Society.

The old question stirs: what if women . . . irrepressible question! half the population in every generation. Could women, as Madeline Grumet envisions, turn the practice of teaching — a relational practice — from "women's work" into "the work of women," so that instead of leading what Grumet calls "the great escape" from the daily rhythms of the maternal order to the clock time of the paternal state,[35] women would institute a new order (using private means in private as Woolf would have it) by teaching a different knowledge and creating a different practice of human relationships?

At the beginning of the second act of *Lysistrata*, Lysistrata despairs; the women are leaving the Acropolis and rushing home to their husbands. "I know you miss your husbands," she says, "but don't you realize that they miss you as well? . . . Be strong sisters," she enjoins the women: "There is an oracle that we will triumph if only we don't fall out among ourselves."[36]

Sara Ruddick heals what is perhaps the major division within and among women — the division between mother and resister — by defining a women's politics of resistance which is relationally rather than heroically conceived. This practice of resistance is rooted in the body (its vulnerability, its promise, its power); it is a practice of "preservative love." Taking her cue from the Madres of Argentina and the women of Chile, Ruddick describes a strategy which draws its imperative from the singularity of human being and the irreplaceability of human relationships, rather than from visions of immortality or superhuman strength. If only women would make a shift within their existing practice as mothers, separating out those elements which support militarism (the worshipping of martyrs and heroes) from those which subvert it (women's irreverent language of loyalty, love and outrage), women could move readily, Ruddick suspects, "from denial to truthfulness, from parochialism to solidarity, from inauthenticity to active responsibility."[37] In short, women could move from psychological to political resistance.

Central to this journey is a recovery of anger as the political emotion par excellence — the bellweather of oppression, injustice, bad treatment; the clue that something is wrong in the relational surround (a fin on the horizon, a sudden darkening, a bad shadow). Teresa Bernardez, writing about women and anger from the two-culture vantage point of an Argentinean born, North American psychotherapist, reminds her reader that cultural injunctions against anger in women turn into psychological inhibitions which "prevent rebellious acts," with the result that women come to feel complicit in their own misery. The process of psychotherapy then involves a kind of reverse alchemy whereby anger which has soured into bitterness and hatred becomes once again simply anger — "the conscious response to an awareness of injustices suffered or losses and grievances sustained . . . [the anger] which involves self-love and awareness of the responsibility of making choices."[38] Like eleven-year-old Sarah's anger which lives in the daylight of her relationships, or Tessie's anger which sits comfortably side-by-side with self-love. Bernardez notes that when people are living under conditions of political oppression or terror, they often come not to know what they know and "have forgotten what they have forgotten." She also observes that anger silenced "contributes to the making of depression." And depression in women tends to begin in adolescence.

Perhaps women have forgotten girls. And not remembered this disconnection at adolescence. So that relationships between adolescent girls and women hold a key to the psychology and the politics of women's resistance.

When Anjli brought her paper on "To His Coy Mistress" to her English teacher, Mrs. Franklin, Nancy Franklin realized that she was hearing the poem in a way she had never heard it before — very differently from the way she had learned to listen in the course of her graduate training. Anjli had been asked to analyze the poem for tone; she was taking an advanced class taught simultaneously at several schools in the area. Nancy Franklin was one of the women pursuing the question: what does it mean to be a woman teaching girls, and it is to this group of women, in the third year of their meeting, that she speaks about Anjli's paper and her decision to join Anjli's resistance.

Anjli in the midst of writing her analysis — listening to the tone of the poem in her house late at night — suddenly begins writing in the first person as she takes in what she is hearing: the voice of an older man bent on overcoming a young woman's resistance ("Had we but world enough, and time, / This coyness, Lady, were no crime"). And Nancy Franklin, taking in Anjli's voice, feels the power of the poem anew and also the force of what Anjli is hearing. Anjli writes, her teacher recalls, "I am writing this paper and it is late at night, and I am terrified because this is such a morbid poem ("Thy beauty shall no more be found, / Nor, in thy marble vault, shall sound / My echoing song: then worms shall try / That long preserved virginity, / And your quaint honor turn to dust, / And into ashes all my lust."). This is such a frightening poem."

Anjli's paper was submitted to six teachers for cross-grading exercises, designed to insure consistency of standards. One woman, Franklin recalls, "actually wrote on the paper: 'She doesn't understand *carpe diem*. Why doesn't she know this term? This is not a college level paper.'" Another wrote "She misreads Marvell's playfulness." And yet — Nancy Franklin says, caught momentarily by the standards of her colleagues and then resisting their disconnection from Anjli and their dismissal of her reading — "this paper was beautiful, and it made me see the poem in a new way." Sustaining this connection, she draws out its implications for Anjli, for herself, and also for society:

> This is a young girl; this is a seventeen-year-old, very innocent but very bright girl. Reading this, Lord knows, you go back and read that poem, at two o'clock in the morning. And she was terrified — the voice of an older man speaking to a young girl. And the comments she got on this paper. They all said: C-, you know, no good. "Doesn't know stanzaic patterns, missed all this playfulness, and *carpe diem, carpe*

*diem.*" Now there's the educational system at work. What did it tell her? Go underground; to survive, go underground, at least until you get out of this system. Or worse.[39]

Anjli read the graders' comments, discussed them with her teacher, remembered hearing about *carpe diem*, reread the poem, and, Nancy Franklin writes, "found that indeed she could see the poem that way but more importantly, she could see it both ways." She knows that "she could rewrite the paper now that she understands the way she was supposed to react saying what she is supposed to say . . . 'If you were a guy,' she says, smiling, 'It might be really funny.' " But Anjli also still cringes at the poem's morbid images: "I don't think," she concludes, "a class full of girls could really laugh at this."[40] What is puzzling, then, given Anjli's perspective, and also potentially treacherous, is the position of the women graders; Anjli assumes that she will be understood by girls, but she cannot assume such understanding from women.

At the intersection between political resistance and psychological resistance, at the time of adolescence, girls' psychological development becomes indelibly political. If girls know what they know and bring themselves into relationships, they will be in conflict with prevailing authorities. If girls do not know what they know and take themselves out of relationship, they will be in trouble with themselves. The ability of girls to tell it from both sides and to see it both ways is not an illustration of relativism (the abandonment of an absolute truth) but rather a demonstration of girls' understanding of relationship raised to a cultural level and a provisional solution to a difficult problem of relationship: how to stay connected with themselves and with others, how to keep in touch with themselves and with the world. As eleven-year-old Tessie underscores the importance of voicing her argument with her mother, so Anjli voices the disparity between how she reacts and how she is supposed to react, what she says and what she is supposed to say, according to the authorities who correct and grade her. And Tessie's openness, at least in theory, to her friend's hearing her mother's voice differently from the way she does, corresponds to Anjli's generosity toward those who hear the poem differently: the guys and the graders. Women teaching girls, then, are faced with a series of intricate problems of relationship. Girls must learn the traditions which frame and structure the world they are entering and they also must hold on to their own ways of hearing and seeing. How can women stay with girls and also teach cultural traditions? How can girls stay with women and also with themselves? What can women teach girls about living in a world which is still governed by men?

"What happens to girls when they get to that age?" Sharon Miller asks. A teacher of twelve-year-olds and the mother of a twelve-year-old daughter, she returns to what has been the riddle of female development—to Freud's question and the question posed by women therapists across the century: Why is it that girls, who seem "more intelligent and livelier than boys of the same age; [who] go out more to meet the external world and at the same time form stronger [connections with people]," seem to become less intelligent and less lively when they reach adolescence?[41] Freud observes that "the constitution will not adapt itself to its function without a struggle," and then goes on to talk about the function of women. Our research on girls' development has focused on elucidating the struggle, which is readily observed in girls at the time of adolescence.

Like girls in novels and poems written by women,[42] girls interviewed in contemporary school settings speak about taking themselves out of relationships as they approach adolescence: about "building a little shield," about "getting afraid to say when you're mad at somebody," about "losing confidence in myself. I was losing track of myself, really, and losing the kind of person I was."[43] Paradoxically, girls are taking themselves out of relationship for the sake of relationship and self-consciously letting go of themselves. This doubling of the psychological language augments the confusion girls experience at this time—the inability in a way to say what is happening because the very words "self" and "relationship" have doubled in meaning, as if one psychology has been superimposed on another, causing girls to lose track of their own experience as they move into the larger world.[44] Lyn Brown, analyzing girls' narratives of relationships, notes that as girls approach adolescence they tend to withdraw authorization from their own experience and to replace realistic with inauthentic or idealized descriptions of relationships. Perhaps for this reason, girls who are developing well according to standard psychological measures and cultural yardsticks, are also

> engaging in difficult and sometimes painful personal battles around issues of voice and authorization, unsure of the accuracy of their own perceptions, afraid that speaking up will damage relationships or

compromise their image in the eyes of others . . . showing signs of an impasse in their ability to act in the face of conflict.[45]

What happens to girls when they reach this age? "I think," Sharon Miller says, "they have let go of themselves. I think it is the unusual middle school girl who can say . . . if you don't like me the way I am, fine. Most girls can't say that because there is no one there." Why not? I ask her. I am thinking of the girls who are so resolute, so present at eleven. "Well, that's the question, you know; what happens to girls when they get to that age? Well, because that is the age when girls start identifying with adult women." And then, suddenly, seeing the circle closing, she says, hand rising, covering her mouth, "My God," as tears begin flowing, "And there is nothing there."[46]

Like a film running backwards, women teaching girls arrive at the moments of their own resistance and come up against their own solutions to the problems of relationship which girls face. Then women may encounter their own reluctance to know what they know and come to the realization that such knowledge is contained in their body; and may discover that they have succumbed to the temptation to model perfection by trying to be perfect role-models for girls and thus have taken themselves out of relationship with girls—in part to hide their imperfection, but also perhaps to keep girls from feeling their sadness and their anger. Women teaching girls, however, also may discover that they are harboring within themselves a girl who lives in her body, who is insistent on speaking, who intensely desires relationships and knowledge, and who, perhaps at the time of adolescence, went underground or was overwhelmed. It may be that adolescent girls are looking for this girl in women, and feeling her absence or her hidden presence. And it may be that women, in the name of being good women, have been modeling for girls her repudiation—teaching girls the necessity of a loss or renunciation, which girls question.

Perhaps there is a new cycle that, once beginning, will break up an old impasse in women's development and affect men as well. If women and girls can stay with one another at the time when girls reach adolescence, girls' playfulness and irreverence may tap the wellsprings of women's resistance. And women in turn, taking in girls' embodiment, their outspokenness and their courage, may encourage girls' desire for relationship and for knowledge and teach girls that they can say what they know and not be left all alone.

**Coda:**

"Dear Kitty," Anne Frank writes on January 6, 1944, at the age of fourteen, in a passage from her diary which her father edited — in exactly the manner she predicts in the passage:

> I have three things to confess to you today . . . . I *must* tell someone, and you are the best to tell, as I know that come what may you always keep a secret . . . . You know that I've grumbled a lot about Mummy, yet still tried to be nice to her again. Now it is suddenly clear to me what she lacks. Mummy herself has told us that she looked upon us more as her friends than her daughters; now that is all very fine of course, but still a friend can't take a mother's place. *I need my mother as an example which I can follow, I want to be able to respect her and though my mother is an example to me in most things she is precisely the kind of example that I do not want to follow.* I have the feeling that Margot thinks differently about these things and would never be able to understand what I've just told you. And Daddy avoids all arguments about Mummy. [deleted passage is italicized][47]

*"One Conclusion,"* Emma writes, beginning a new page in her journal,

> One of the conclusions I come to is that many/most of the paintings/ statues/artwork of women I have seen are of women naked. A lot of the art of women that I saw was done by men. Maybe because the women posed. None of the girls I saw were naked. Maybe because artists like to have people pose naked, and they think women are better because they have more growth.

One question, Malka writes at the end of her second conversation with the Queen of Babylon, "Did these people, places, painted, sculpted, did they live? Did they live in the heart of the painter, sculptor?"

"Wouldn't there have been," Anna says irreverently — she has just finished writing a paper on the Church and Galileo — "Wouldn't there have been a lot of animal stuff on Noah's ark after forty days?"

"I think I am trying," Rosie says, "to attach value to things. This is important. This is not important. Maybe order things more." What do you order them to, I ask, wondering what key she is tuning to, what standard she has in mind. And Rosie, the embodied saint, the underground woman, suddenly turns philosophical:

I don't know . . . but I guess I know that there should be an order, and I was trying to decide what that order was. Maybe that is part of what I am looking for . . . is an order to my life. This is getting deep, philosophical.

I am listening to girls' questions — following girls' inquiry into relationships as it becomes more philosophical, more critical, and also more psychologically and politically dangerous. Emma's curiosity is edging toward men's feelings about women's bodies; Malka begins to trace the channels connecting men's hearts with cultural icons. If this inquiry continues, girls will find the line which connects the personal and the political, the line between the psychology of men and the cultural framework, and wonder how they fit in.

"I don't know . . ." Rosie says, Socrates plaint. "I guess I know," she follows, in rapid succession. She is observing how her mother spends her life, her time, asking in effect the same question which Malka asks the Queen of Babylon: "What are you doing?" And seeing what her mother has to say — whether her mother might come up with the Queen's funny answer: "Brushing my hair. I was interrupted this morning by news of a revolt," the answer which captures the doubling of women's lives and also speaks to girls' questions about what gives women pleasure and what women value.

Rosie, the sharp-eyed adolescent, notices that her mother's "small study and bedroom are messy." She will have to create her own order of living, find some way to orchestrate her life. "I don't know . . . I know . . . you know . . . do you know? . . ." voices of the underground, speaking under the sign of repression, marking dissociations which are still tenuous, knowledge which is fragile, reaching out for connections which can sustain the promise that a secret underground one day will become a public resistance. Then a healthy resistance which is evident in girls at adolescence, rather than turning inward and becoming psychologically corrosive, can stay in the open air of relationships. And by remaining political, work to bring a new order of living into the world.

## ACKNOWLEDGEMENTS

The research which underlies this paper was encouraged and supported by Joan Lipsitz and the Lilly Endowment, by Steven Minter and the Cleveland Foundation, by Judith Simpson and the Gund Foundation, by Lawrence Cremin, Marion Faldet, Linda Fitzgerald and the Spencer Foundation, by the American Association of University Women, by Benjamin Barber and the Walt Whitman Center at Rutgers

University, and also by Leah Rhys, Principal of the Laurel School in Cleveland, Ohio, Virginia Kahn, founder of the Atrium School in Watertown, Massachusetts, and Patricia Graham, Dean of the Harvard Graduate School of Education. I am deeply grateful to the girls who participated in these projects and to the women who have accompanied me most closely on this journey: Lyn Mikel Brown and Annie Rogers — the two psychologists I refer to in the paper — and also Judy Dorney and Patricia Flanders-Hall, who took the lead in the project on Women Teaching Girls, and all of the teachers who participated in the retreats. Normi Noel added theater to the writing, outing and theater club, Kristin Linklater taught me about the embodiment of voice, and Tina Packer, artistic director of Shakespeare and Company, stimulated my thinking and made the connection between mothers in the fatherland and family violence.

# NOTES

[1]The quotations from the eleven-year-old girls are taken from the girls' journals and also from my journal. The Outing, Writing and Theater Club is part of the project, "Strengthening Healthy Resistance and Courage in Girls," being conducted by Annie Rogers and myself in public and private schools in the Boston area. Among the sixth grade girls at the Atrium School, a private coeducational elementary school, there is some diversity in cultural background and family composition; cultures represented in this group of girls include North American Protestant, Jewish, and Latino. The women involved in the project, including Normi Noel who does the theater work, are also somewhat culturally diverse. The absence of black girls and women in this group is a clear limitation, and not characteristic of the public school Outing, Writing and Theater Club or the larger Harvard Project on the Psychology of Women and the Development of Girls.

[2]Sigmund Freud, *The Interpretation of Dreams*. 1899/1900. Vol. IV and V of *The Standard Edition of the Complete Psychological Works of Sigmund Freud* (London: The Hogarth Press, 1955). See also *The Complete Letters of Sigmund Freud to Wilhelm Fleiss, 1887-1904* (Cambridge, Mass.: Harvard University Press, 1985).

[3]Carol Gilligan, *In a Different Voice: Psychological Theory and Women's Development* (Cambridge, Mass.: Harvard University Press, 1982); "Prologue" and "Teaching Shakespeare's Sister: Notes from the Underground of Female Adolescence," in Gilligan, Lyons and Hanmer [Eds.], *Making Connections* (Cambridge, Mass.: Harvard University Press, 1990); Carol Gilligan, Lyn Mikel Brown, and Annie Rogers, "Psyche Embedded: A Place for Body, Relationships and Culture in Personality Theory" in A. I. Rabin et al. [Eds.], *Studying Persons and Lives* (New York: Springer, 1990).

[4]Virginia Woolf, *Three Guineas* (San Diego: Harcourt Brace Jovanovich, 1938), p. 6.

[5]*The Diary of Anne Frank*, The Critical Edition (New York: Doubleday, 1989), p. 678.

[6]Aristophanes, *Lysistrata/The Acharnians/The Clouds* (London: Penguin Books, 1973), pp. 180–181.

[7]Nathaniel Hawthorne, *The Scarlet Letter* (New York: The Modern Library, 1950 [1850]), pp. 299, 184.

[8]*ibid.*, p. 178.

[9]*ibid.*, p. 184.

[10]*ibid.*, pp. 187–88.

[11]Sigmund Freud, "The Case of Fraulein Elisabeth von R." from Joseph Breuer and Sigmund Freud, *Studies on Hysteria*. 1893–95. Vol. II of *The Standard Edition*, p. 161. See also Elaine Showalter, *The Female Malady* (New York: Penguin Books, 1985).

[12]Hawthorne, *op. cit.*, p. 227.

[13]*ibid.*, p. 299.

[14]Claudia Koonz, *Mothers in the Fatherland* (New York: St. Martin's Press, 1986), pp. 310, 332.

[15]Diana E. H. Russell, *Lives of Courage: Women for a New South Africa* (New York: Basic Books, 1989), p. 24.

[16]*ibid.*, p. 24.

[17]Woolf, *op. cit.*, p. 143.

[18]*ibid.*, p. 143.

[19]*ibid.*, p. 142.

[20]Shawn Slovo, *A World Apart* (London: Faber and Faber, 1988), p. x.

[21]*ibid.*, p. ix.

[22]*ibid.*, p. 107.

[23]*ibid.*, pp. xi, 18.

[24]Anna's quotations are taken from interviews conducted over the course of a five-year study on girls' development at the Laurel School in Cleveland, Ohio. Papers from the project, which involved girls and women who were diverse in racial as well as economic background, were presented at the Harvard-Laurel Conference on "The Psychology of Women and the Education of Girls," held in Cleveland, April 1990, and are being prepared for publication by Harvard University Press.

[25]Tessie was one of ten eleven-year-old girls living in a suburb of Boston and interviewed by Sharry Langdale in 1981 as part of the Project on the Psychology of Women and The Development of Girls conducted at Harvard University.

[26]This analysis was carried out by Lisa Marie Kulpinski, a graduate student in the Human Development and Psychology Program at Harvard University, and reported in her paper, "Adolescence: Hitting a Fork in the Road," 1990.

[27]Frank, *op. cit.*, p. 545.

[28]Glen Elder and Avshalom Caspi, "Studying Lives in a Changing Society: Sociological and Personological Explorations," in A. Rabin *et al.* [Eds.], *Studying Persons and Lives* (New York: Springer, 1990), pp. 226–28. See also Anne Peterson, "Adolescent Development" (*Annual Review of Psychology*, 39, 583–607, 1988).

[29]Woolf, *op. cit.*, p. 113.

[30]Jorie Graham, *Erosion* (Princeton: Princeton University Press, 1983), pp. 16–21.

[31]Toni Morrison, *The Bluest Eye* (New York: Pocket Books, 1970), p. 53.

[32]Frank, *op. cit.*, p. 557.

[33]Sophocles, *Oedipus the King*. In the more literal Loeb Classics translation, this line reads "How could the soil thy father eared so long / Endure to bear in silence such a wrong" (Cambridge, Mass.: Harvard University Press, 1912), p. 113. In the text, for purposes of clarity, I have cited Fitzgerald's freer translation.

[34]Dianne Argyris and Judy Dorney, graduate students in the Human Development and Psychology Program at Harvard University, compiled and analyzed the girls' thoughts and feelings about the Laurel School honor code, and this work was the basis for the presentation to the faculty.

[35]Madeline R. Grumet, *Bitter Milk: Women and Teaching* (Amherst: University of Massachusetts Press, 1988), pp. 58, 25. See also Jane Roland Martin, *Reclaiming a Conversation* (New Haven: Yale University Press, 1985), and Mary Blenky, et al., *Women's Ways of Knowing* (Basic Books, 1986).

[36]Aristophanes: *op. cit.*, p. 212.

[37]Sara Ruddick, *Maternal Thinking: Toward a Politics of Peace* (Boston: Beacon Press, 1989), pp. 227–230.

[38]Teresa Bernardez, "Women and Anger: Cultural Prohibitions and The Feminine Ideal" (Wellesley College: Stone Center Working Paper Series, 31, 1988), p. 5. See also Jean Baker Miller, *Toward a New Psychology of Women* (Boston: Beacon Press, 1976) for a discussion of women and anger and the roots of anger in women's political oppression.

[39]Quotations taken from the taped transcript of the Women Teaching Girls project, Harvard-Laurel retreat, February, 1990. The retreats which brought together psychologists and teachers, and crossed the educational span from nursery to university, were designed and led by Judy Dorney (see note 34).

[40]Nancy S. Franklin, "Teachers' Tales of Empowerment: A Story from an English Teacher." Paper presented at the Harvard-Laurel Conference on The Psychology of Women and The Education of Girls, April 6, 1990, Cleveland, Ohio. Conference papers are being prepared for publication by Harvard University Press.

[41]Freud, "Femininity," Lecture XXXIII, (*New Introductory Lectures on Psycho-Analysis.* (1933 ), Vol. XXII of *The Standard Edition*), p. 117, and also "The Transformations of Puberty" in *Three Essays on the Theory of Sexuality* (1905), Vol. VII. See also Karen Horney, "The Flight from Womanhood" (*International Journal of Psychoanalysis*, 7, pp. 324–339, 1926); Clara M. Thompson, "Adolescence" and other papers in *Interpersonal Psychoanalysis* (New York: Basic Books, 1964), and Jean Baker Miller, "The Development of Women's Sense of Self," (Wellesley College: Stone Center Working Paper Series, 12, 1984).

[42]See for example, Charlotte Bronte, *Jane Eyre*, Toni Morrison, *The Bluest Eye*, Jamaica Kincaid, *Annie John*, Carson McCullers, *The Member of the Wedding*, Margaret Atwood, *Cat's Eye*, and also Michelle Cliff, "Claiming an Identity They Taught Me to Despise," in *The Land of Look Behind*, and Sharon Olds, "Time-Travel," in *Satan Says*.

[43]Lyn Mikel Brown, "A Problem of Vision: The Development of Relational Voice in Girls Ages 7 to 16," Unpublished paper, 1990, Project on the Psychology of Women and the Development of Girls, Harvard University. See also Brown, "Narratives of Relationship." Ed.D. Dissertation: Harvard University, 1989). Lyn Brown who was my companion on the journey to Cleveland was the research director of the Harvard-Laurel project.

[44]For a fuller discussion of this phenomenon, see Gilligan, *In a Different Voice* and "Teaching Shakespeare's Sister," and also Lori Stern, "Disavowing the Self in Female Adolescence: A Case Study Analysis" (Unpublished Ed.D. Dissertation: Harvard University, 1990).

[45]Lyn Mikel Brown and Carol Gilligan, "The Psychology of Women and The Development of Girls." Paper presented at the Harvard/Laurel Conference on The Psychology of Women and The Education of Girls, April 5, 1990, Cleveland, Ohio. Conference papers being prepared for publication by the Harvard University Press.

[46]Quotations taken from the taped transcript of the Women Teaching Girls Project, Harvard-Laurel Retreat, October, 1989.

[47]Frank, *op. cit.*, p. 440.

ELIZABETH SOCOLOW

# OPHELIA

So wet.
In this whole country
there had never been a pond like this,
man-made, dug with the sound of a voice,
the mere reach of an arm
—the water filling in the widening place.

No geese flew there and landed.
No fish swam,
and the frogs did not yet croak,
not in a place empty of flowers
and the crisis of green to hold them dry.
I cannot tell you how quiet it is when this happens.

Women do not swim in such pools of nature;
we bathe ourselves, we drown in a wet vacancy
so large and hidden, no one even knows it is there.
For swimming, the long dive
is necessary. For diving a man, please.

Months, I wanted flowers,
birds whose sharp beaks of need
do not summon fathers with platitudes
from wisdom books. The Apocryphal Ecclesiasticus
walked on the thin legs of my father.
He whispered words from behind all hiding places
as if he knew everything about money

and nothing about water.
*Do not trust water, the new wet at the center of yourself*
*made by a man whose voice you need.*

That was my wisdom. I spoke it in the face of my father's rules
like oil poured on greens before the sour vinegar sauces it
to savory crisps.

I spoke my wisdom to myself and he thought I meant geese
and flowers.
Where is the old book of wisdom
that allows a woman
her own answered need?
Without such wisdom — swimmers answering
water in the heat for the pure refreshment,
the attendant pleasure — do not trust water.

There are no men in this country
who do not feel unmanned
when their desire claims them.
No wonder they are sailing away
to find a new world.
There desire itself could be something else,
a fruit we have never tasted,
a fruit like a map and a journey,
the eating a form of travel.

*The governor has gone from the land,*
Hamlet would say, pressing Ex Caliber
at the lake of me, out the other side
for some Arthur to grab.
My thighs are the beach of a landlocked body,
water he created
and never entered, swimming lateral, littoral,
along the shores. He would reach down my back
with his own good hand to claim his sword
in its emergency,
spurting the white blood of such sporting.

I survived. He killed my father and I could have died
of the silence, the wrong wish answered. But I lived,
still wishing that the pond would find a swimmer
in the full afternoon, a man from a place where water
is for pleasure as well as thirst.

SARAH MESSER

# CHOOSE

The first two weeks I search the sheets for blood,
lift my skirts in secret looking. Rolled apart
to bedside, I pound a desperate fist into my gut
each night, mouthing, *bleed, bleed,* while you

softly speak of choice — the former girlfriend
who had five and was all right. I try to imagine
their aborted lives, maybe nine or ten years
old by now, with scrubbed faces and shining shoes

ready to greet the big wide, and all the why's
to be explained: a mother too young,
who runs finger-in-throat to bathrooms,
a father on cocaine; the one-lunged, armless,

web-toed kids, blinded from a herpes kiss,
born with a tail curled like a pig's; or those slid
out wet and healthy, to slowly starve in a heatless
flat between potato bags and cans of instant milk.

Now we walk to a stirrup-horned place. Not knowing
what to say, you talk incessantly of women's swelling
bodies; skin stretched tight as fruit, swollen ankles,
strange hair growth, and how breasts jiggle,

grow to globes in pregnancy, spilling
milk like tilting bowls. But in the room
of white circle lights, still, it's only me
who lies during the pinch of a long-barreled

needle — legs spread in sheets

like a back-spun beetle — as the curled
nub of my cervix contracts and expands.
It's only me who bites the wings of cotton

that the nurse gives for the pain —
"bite down, look away — "
The lights, white globes jiggling, and the flutter,
"just a flutter" of the 45-second "evacuation — "

a butterfly in a dark jar. Still, it's me
who gets the red-candy pills, yellow ergotrate —
I who cannot unclench my cotton-crammed thighs,
or spread my jaws to speak of sores

left to my sex from birth, and all choices
carried behind me like a tail.

CARL COHEN

# HOW NOT TO ARGUE ABOUT ABORTION

So intense is the moral controversy over abortion that partisans —
both abortion liberals and abortion conservatives — are tempted, for
rhetorical effect, to rely upon ill-considered arguments. But to do so,
whatever one's moral position, is counterproductive; confidence in
intellect and integrity is shaken, even true conclusions may be
undermined. The price of using bad arguments is high.

The terms "liberal" and "conservative" have special meanings in
this realm: conservatives here — those who view the fetus as a person
from conception, condemn the killing of the fetus as profoundly
wrong, and who call themselves "pro-life" — are often quite liberal
in other matters; liberals here — those who hold that whatever one's
view of abortion only the pregnant woman has the moral authority
to decide upon an abortion for herself, and who call themselves
"pro-choice" — are often quite conservative in other matters. Adopting this common usage, my aim is to expose bad arguments on both
sides.

## 1. Liberal Fallacy

I begin on the liberal side. One argument very commonly presented by liberals goes like this:

> We liberals believe it is permissible for a woman to terminate her
> pregnancy because the pregnancy is hers alone, and therefore moral
> decisions pertaining to it are rightly hers to make. Our conservative
> opponents believe abortion not permissible, basing their conclusion
> upon moral beliefs about the fetus that we think mistaken. Neither
> side can prove the other wrong. To restore social harmony all parties
> should agree to forgo coercion — as is done in religious disputes — and
> to respect the rights of others to be guided by their own principles. No
> one need condone what he thinks evil; all are free to express moral
> judgments openly and forcefully, of course. But we must not perse-
> cute those whose practices we think immoral. Liberals must respect

the rights of those who believe that abortion is morally wrong to refrain from terminating pregnancies. Conservatives must likewise respect the rights of those who believe that decisions about pregnancy are only for the pregnant woman to make. Let each party act in accord with its own honest moral convictions, no one forced to abide by the moral code of another. Why is our willingness to be tolerant not matched on the other side?

This argument assumes that if no agreement can be reached upon the moral principles that govern a pregnant woman, the matter must be left to the decision of the woman herself, since it is her conduct alone that is at issue. Thus the religious analogy: About the gods we cannot agree — so you pray in your way, and allow me to pray in mine. Let moral agents mind their own business.

Conservatives can never accept this, of course. For them, the tolerance practiced in religion (or in other spheres) cannot be practiced with respect to abortion because in this sphere, unlike those, it is the well-being of a separate moral being, the unborn child, that is at issue. Say they in effect:

> You may worship false gods and go to Hell, and that is your business. You two may fornicate or join in other sinful practices, and that is, jointly, your private business. But when your conduct threatens the life of another person that conduct ceases to be your business alone; you are not to be permitted, under the flag of private morality, to kill an innocent person.

> Slaveowners, responding to abolitionists, used precisely the argument of the abortion liberals: "Since we cannot agree upon the morality of the conduct at issue, let us agree not to coerce one another. We respect your right to act in accordance with your beliefs; you must respect our right to act in accordance with ours. Let the owning of slaves be practiced only by those who believe it to be morally right. Live and let live."

> Outrageous. But why? Because slavery cannot be justified by the honest convictions of moral monsters. They are free to believe what they choose, but they must not be permitted to *act* upon heinous beliefs when that action injures innocent others. The lives of the human beings whom they would enslave stand independently opposed to them — and in defense of those lives all decent people are obliged to intervene. Owning slaves cannot be allowed on the ground that the slave owner's private moral code must be respected. No more

> can abortion be allowed [the conservative concludes] because the private moral code of some pregnant women must be respected.

The liberal replies:

> Your analogy with slave-holding is grossly unfair; slavery is an abomination, of course—but that is because those enslaved were *persons* of unquestioned humanity, possessing moral rights like all other persons. You seek to forbid my practice of abortion because you believe that the fetus is here analogous to the slave. You think they are both persons, with rights to life—but that is precisely what we deny!

The conservative rejoins:

> We understand that you deny it, and we respect your right to defend that mistake. But your argument is circular and worthless when you urge tolerance of certain acts, on the assumption that that denial is sound. This assumption is the very point at issue between us.

The conservative complaint is just. One begs the question—the classical name of the fallacy is *petitio principii*—when he assumes in the premises of his argument the truth of the conclusion he seeks to establish. Liberals who urge mutual toleration of different moral codes assume in their urging that the act in question, performing an abortion, is of moral concern only to the pregnant woman. That is the claim whose truth the conservative denies. And no argument against the conservative position can have merit if it *assumes* precisely what it aims to *show*.

The liberal position may of course be correct even though this common defense of it is fallacious. Recognizing deficiency in argument may help liberals to see how they must argue to advance their case. The heart of the dispute over abortion, illuminated by this logical quarrel, lies in conflicting beliefs about the moral status of the fetus. The common unwillingness of liberals to be forthright about this matter infuriates their opponents, conveys the impression (sometimes justified) that they are not listening to thoughtful conservative complaints, and thus exacerbates the conflict between the parties.

What *is* the fetus? What *rights* (if any) does a fetus possess? What *obligations* (if any) are owed to it? In determining the morality of abortion, these are questions the liberal, along with all others, cannot avoid.

## 2. Conservative Pseudo-Science

On the conservative side the focus is correct, and the logic impeccable. But the foundation upon which the reasoning is built is often defended badly. Conservatives commonly reason thus:

> The pre-born child, whose life is terminated by an abortion, is a human person. It is morally wrong to kill any person deliberately, except perhaps in circumstances of the most dire necessity. Abortions (save in those rare cases in which the life of the mother is gravely threatened by the pregnancy) are therefore killings without justification and are thoroughly evil.

The reasoning here is good in form; it is not circular, nor is it otherwise fallacious. The truth of its first and major premise (that the fetus is a human person) is critical, of course; it is often asserted on religious grounds, but it remains disputable. So conservatives often present a *defense* of their first premise based upon the genetic history of the fetus; the argument goes essentially like this:

> The mother's egg contains 23 chromosomes; the father's sperm another 23. The 46 chromosomes in the single cell of the newly-fertilized egg constitute the complete genetic makeup of a unique human being. When sperm and egg combine the DNA (desoxyribonucleic acid) of a new human being is formed, uniquely and for life. Hence the human being into which that embryo later develops is already there, *is* the embryo itself. The embryo must be a human being because a human being it becomes, and nothing is added to it — and out of nothing nothing comes.[1]

This argument is seriously defective; it ought to be rejected by thoughtful conservatives, in their own interest. It is bad because it rests upon a *misunderstanding* of scientific report; and it is bad because its *use* of science in moral argument is confused.

First, *misunderstanding*. From the genetic uniqueness of the fertilized egg cell it does not follow, nor is it true, that that cell, the zygote, and the individual later exhibiting its genetic pattern, are *identical*. The genes give and limit potential, but the human being is very much more than a tangle of nucleic acids bearing genetic codes. It is not the case that nothing of vital importance is added to the zygote as it subsequently develops; a very great deal is added after fertilization. From the fertilized egg cell arises a clump of undifferentiated cells; that clump changes fundamentally within the womb. These changes are not determined by the DNA alone. Cells interact fortuitously, apparently responding to their positions within the clump of cells. Individual cells develop differently, literally becoming different types of cells, depending upon their position in the clump.[2] And the development of groups of cells is critically affected by chemical substances in their immediate environment, substances external to the DNA.

Limits upon what the zygote may become are buried in the DNA; human zygotes never yield spaniels. But the conservative genetic account supposes the fertilized egg cell to be a very small ball of extraordinary wisdom, somehow unwinding to produce human brain or muscle in accord with an organic plan already *pre*determined. The tiny zygote is imagined somehow to contain an internal genetic diagram of the person to be, roughly analogous to an electrical wiring plan, or architectural blueprint, a detailed design not yet expressed but nevertheless complete and wholly incorporated within. This is a mistaken account.

In a less enlightened age, before the fertilization of the human egg by human sperm was understood, it was widely believed that the mother's womb was no more than the place of growing, and that the little human was shot into that place — very tiny but already perfectly formed, a minuscule homunculus — from the male penis. All the baby's parts being there in miniature at the outset, the uterus was supposed (in this archaic view) to be simply where the tiny baby grows to be large, like a fetus. Preposterous, of course. And yet, in the thinking of many contemporary conservatives, the same underlying blunder lies buried: a very tiny person (of one cell) will simply grow into a much larger person (of hundreds of billions of cells) but it will remain unchanged in essence. The new homunculism differs from the old in allowing that mother as well as father make a contribution to the tiny being, and the modern will allow that the minute parts are there only in design and not in actual shape. But common to both is the fantasy that once the homunculus is in place, the rest is essentially no more than an unfolding.

This notion — that there is a very little but completely designed human being hidden in that fertilized egg, or zygote — is not supported by genetic science. As the first cell divides and its daughter cells divide, what takes place is largely a development that cannot be wholly explained by the genetic codes in the nucleic acids. Each one of the cells (called blastomeres) in the earliest stage of development possesses the same genetic information, and each one could become an embryo. Yet the simple multiplication of these early cells by cleavage comes to a stop, and a very different process, that of cell differentiation, begins. In this process, cells identical in their DNA endowment diverge in structure and in function. Some genes in some cells are activated, "turned on," in other cells other genes are activated – but the DNA in the liver cell is no different from the DNA in the skin cell. Hence there must be additional information provided – and that additional information essential for this process of differentiation cannot come from within; some critical interaction between the molecules of the zygote, and molecules outside the zygote, must occur.

Some, but not all, of the sources of this externally provided information are known. The formation of the membranes and layers of the embryo are largely derived from the relative positions of cells (as noted above), and therefore from information not provided by the genes. But the full impact of cell position upon development cannot be specified in advance.[3]

As the clump of cells enlarges, development of the embryo involves differentiation (in which the several cells acquire specialized functions) and pattern formation, and morphogenesis (in which the embryo is shaped). Morphogens, molecules of special chemical substances that function as signal-givers to the developing cells, seep past the undifferentiated cells, helping to determine cell migration and development. The amounts and placements of these morphogens – believed now to be bits of retinoic acid – vary for reasons not known, yielding different organs, organs of different shapes, entirely distinct cell specializations. If too much retinoic acid is applied to the limb buds of a chick fetus or a mouse fetus, for example, the animal develops monstrous or defective organs – twin wings facing one another, or twin paws on a single limb. The various cells in every embryo encounter different amounts of the critical morphogens at different times; events like these (and probably others that we know not of) greatly influence what those cells become.[4]

Strong evidence, clinical and experimental, supports the conclusion that a human being, as we normally use that expression, is not present in the embryo. Two human embryos, twins in the uterus, sometimes later combine into a single healthy embryo. This would be utterly impossible if a human being had been pre-figured in those strings of nucleic acids found in the newly fertilized cell. The zygote has distinctively human DNA, to be sure – but that individual zygote, even when perfect, is not a pre-formed human being, and, furthermore, does not even contain all of the information necessary for the development of a human being.

The very uncertain future of the fertilized egg has been demonstrated dramatically in mice, with the following experiment: the fertilized egg of two white-furred mice is allowed to divide four times, until becoming a 16-cell cluster. A similar, 16-cell embryo of two black-furred mice parents is then put with it, the two embryos thus forming a clump of 32 cells. This clump will become a single embryo, eventually developing into a single, healthy mouse with fur that is black and white! That mouse has four parents, and the various cells of its body (those not growing in the fur) may derive their DNA from any one of the four.[5]

Of course the human embryo is a "being" in the sense that every existent thing is a being, and it is "human" in the sense that it is the product of human growth. Using the words in that way, a clipped finger nail is also a "human being" — but from this we draw no moral conclusions about its right to life. All the diverse cells of the body, all its somatic cells, have the very same DNA. A fragment of skin, alive, has DNA absolutely identical to that of the earlier zygote — but the skin fragment, like the zygote, is surely not a human being. Science does not warrant the claim that the embryo is a "human being" as that term is normally used. Conservatives who defend their fundamental premise with reasoning that is a parody of the science it purports to apply, will in the end be hoist with their own petard.

Second, *confusion*. For conservatives, abortion is a moral horror because it is the killing of a human person. But "person" is a moral category, not one of science. Genetic science (as noted above) does not warrant the claim that the embryo is a "human being" — but nothing remotely within the power of science to discover could help us to determine whether an embryo is a human *person* possessing rights. What characteristics are essential for the presence of a human person is a deep philosophical question, one whose answer cannot take the form of an empirical report. Therefore, any conservative effort to establish the presence in the embryo of a human person *on scientific grounds* badly misconceives the role that science can play in moral argument.

But from all that is known about fetal development we may confidently conclude that, whatever the essential features of personhood are held to be, credulity must be strained to suppose those features present in the embryo. During the first weeks of its development, before any brain has developed and before there is even the first firing of a synapse between two nerve cells, the clump that may become a human fetus has no capacity for any experience or any awareness of any kind. That much is known. There being no possibility of experience in it during this period of its growth, it is difficult even to understand what is being asserted when the conservative claims that the embryo is a person. For that claim there is and can be no scientific support. Indeed, for that claim there is and can be no empirical content.

In sum: The conservative argument hangs upon the truth of its fundamental premise that from its conception the fetus is a person. Reliance upon biological science to establish the truth of that premise fails, and must fail.

If science does not support the conservative view of the fetus as person, or even speak to that matter, the needed conservative premise may yet be defended with arguments of a non-scientific kind. This would amount to a partial withdrawal, true—but withdrawal to an argumentative fortress from which conservatives cannot be driven. Arguments incorporating some non-natural claims may not persuade any who do not already accept their conclusions—but intellectual integrity is more important than rhetorical effectiveness. If the personhood of the fetus is the heart of the argument, and if that personhood has no natural foundation, conservatives must be forthright about the authority beyond nature upon which they rely.

Bad arguments on both sides illuminate what good arguments require: *The moral status of the fetus is the key to the controversy over abortion.* The liberal argument fails when it assumes what needs to be proved about this moral status; the conservative argument fails when it seeks to establish conclusions about this moral status with bad science and inappropriate uses of science.

For all those between the liberal and the conservative extremes the widespread conviction that abortion is wrong must somehow be reconciled with the widespread conviction that it is in some circumstances desperately needed and justifiable. Some on both sides would be willing to compromise, to make concessions in return for concessions that would lead to more general harmony. But many of those who seek a middle way do so, not in a spirit of compromise, but because they genuinely believe that the middle way is the morally right way. Call those who seek a path between the conservative

and liberal extremes "moderates." There are moderates of conservative leaning, who detest abortions but believe that it is right to make
room for a few; and there are moderates of liberal leaning, who
defend the mother's right to choose, but who believe that some such
choices are not right. To formulate some middle path is not difficult,
but to give a consistent and rational defense of any moderate position proves to be very difficult indeed.[6]

### 3. Conservative Moderation: The Burden of Consistency

Conservative moderates retain the conviction that killing the fetus
is a great moral wrong—but they believe that some exceptional
circumstances may justify it. Thus conservative moderates often
hold that abortion is permissible not only when the mother's life is
endangered by the pregnancy, but also when the pregnancy is the
outcome of incest, or of rape. Pregnancy thus caused, say they in
effect, is so cruelly unfair to the mother that to compel her to bring
the fetus to term in such circumstances is unconscionable. In a small
set of uncommon cases—but only in these—the abortion, evil in
itself, may be the least of the evils open to us.

The argument is as bad as it is common. If abortion is morally
wrong because it is the killing of an innocent human person, it
remains wrong and unjustifiable no matter how that innocent person came to be. If the fetus is an innocent person it cannot be justly
killed because of any misconduct by either of its parents, including
the rapacity of its father.[7]

Sensitive conservatives have always understood that the obligation to bring pregnancy to term may impose a very great burden
upon the mother, especially if she is unmarried and impoverished.
But some burdens cannot be escaped. The longed-for middle way is
precluded, for conservatives, by their own most fundamental conviction: that the fetus is a human person. That is the rock upon
which the entire conservative position is built, and if that premise be
true no weighing of the burdens of the mother, no compassion for
her, could possibly justify killing it. The fetus either is a human
person or it is not. The conservative holds that it is, and (for him)
that must end the matter if no other life is at stake; even very great
burdens do not justify the killing of persons who innocently cause
them. The only defensible exception (and even this is disputable)
would be that of a killing that is necessary to save the life of the
mother.

## 4. Liberal Moderation: The Demand for Relevance

Liberal moderates believe that the fetus is not a person, at least not always or not fully; therefore they can defend a middle course without abandoning fundamental convictions. To do so coherently they must either a) give a plausible account of the *intermediate moral nature* of the fetus, or b) give an account of some *change in the moral status of the fetus* during its development that renders a different set of moral rules applicable to it after that change.

In formulating a moderate solution it is common among liberals to segment the period of pregnancy. A temporal point during gestation is identified before which some specifiable reasons justify termination of the fetus, or before which only the mother is entitled to decide which reasons justify termination, but after which the protection of the fetus is morally appropriate or required. The foremost liberal solution of this kind, that based upon the viability of the fetus, goes essentially like this:

> During the late-middle of the nine-month period of gestation there comes a time after which, with very intense care, the fetus can be kept alive even if the umbilical connection to its mother has been severed. From that point on the fetus is called "viable" — and thereafter the moral rules pertaining to it change. Before the fetus is viable the mother has the authority to decide upon its disposition; after viability the fetus acquires a moral status that renders its termination a great evil. Therefore, once the fetus is viable, abortion is permissible only for the most extraordinary reasons, usually reasons pertaining to the danger in which the mother lies.

Such a middle path, carefully formulated in the landmark case of *Roe v. Wade* [410 U.S. 113, (1973)], has long been the keystone of American law in this arena. In this case the U.S. Supreme Court held that subsequent to viability it is permissible (but not obligatory) under the U.S. Constitution for a state to regulate, and even to proscribe, abortion "in promoting its interest in the potentiality of human life." Before viability, said the Court, two earlier phases of the pregnancy may be distinguished. For the first of these (approximately the first third of the pregnancy, during which abortion is safer for the mother than childbirth), the choice of termination is solely a matter for mother and physician to make. For the second phase before viability (approximately the second third of the pregnancy, during which abortion may pose substantial risk to the mother) the state may lawfully regulate the abortion procedure, but may do so only in ways "that are reasonably related to maternal health." Thus, the regulation of abortion for the sake of the fetus is permissible, under this Supreme Court decision, only after viability.

Viability, for very many liberals, has thus become a moral watershed, but the reasoning that underlies its use in segmentation is often muddled. To defend it liberals need to explain what it is about being "viable" that gives to the life of the fetus a moral status it did not have before it was viable. After it is viable we can do certain things for the fetus that we could not do before that time. But what follows from this? Why has our ability to sustain it outside of the mother's womb altered its moral status? The moral relevance of viability remains to be explained.

One common reply is that only after viability is the fetus *independent*, and this newly-acquired independence is what gives to the fetus its enhanced moral status. This surely cannot serve. The independence of a moral agent may have some bearing on the duties owed to it — but the fetus does not become independent at the time of viability, any more than the baby becomes independent at birth. Without great care and attention both will surely die, and that is true also for normal infants after normal birth. No developing human in its earliest days is independent, or can live without care for more than a matter of hours. Viability does not change that. Since viability does not mark the independence of the fetus, independence cannot be the quality that gives viability moral relevance.

But after it is viable (the liberal might respond) the fetus may receive life support from a source other than its mother. True; that is what viability means. This leaves the central question unanswered: why does its capacity to receive such external support make a moral difference to *it*? Why is its separability from its mother a morally relevant consideration?

The thoughtful liberal may answer:

> A change in our abilities can sometimes alter our duties, and that is the case here. Before viability we could protect the fetus, but only by forbidding abortion, unjustly restricting the mother's control over what could not be separated from her. After viability we can protect the fetus without that degree of restriction upon her, since the fetus is now separable from her. This change alters our obligations to the fetus.

But if this is so, it cannot be so because the rights of the fetus have been enhanced. Whether it is viable or not the fetus can be protected by law. Viability effects no change in society's capacity to do (or seek to do) that. Protection of the fetus may be more feasible after viability, or it may oppress the mother less after viability because mother and baby are separable — but a change in the impact of societal protection upon the mother's freedom of action has no bearing upon any rights the fetus itself may possess. Can changes in *our* capacities change *its* rights? If it is of such a nature that it is entitled to protection when separable, it is of such a nature as to deserve that protection when not separable. Viability may be very important for the mother, but if it is to account for a change in the duties owed to the fetus, some other explanation must be offered.

There is, moreover, an independent reason to believe that viability does not mark a morally significant change in the fetus. The age (from conception) at which a fetus becomes viable has been declining at about one week per decade for some decades. Now (in 1990) the age of viability is about 24 weeks. A fetus viable today may well not have been viable (if in that precise biological condition) ten years ago. If viability depends upon the state of technology (which it does), and moral status depends upon viability (as alleged), then the moral status of the fetus would appear to change with technological advance.

This would be difficult to explain. If a fetus in a given biological condition has a right to protection, and it can be protected in some way, it surely must have had that right before technological advance made that protection easier. If the obligation to protect the fetus flows from its rights, it must be based upon *what the fetus is*, and not from *what we can do*.

The liberal may reply:

> If technology gives us new powers, it may give others new rights. Patients, for example, may become entitled by right, as a result of technology, to treatments that did not even exist a decade before. In this way technological advance may expand moral rights for the fetus also, and this explains how it can be that fetuses may acquire rights at younger and younger gestational ages.

This reasoning is faulty. Entitlements brought on by new technology are the entitlements of existing moral agents to the benefits of machines (or therapies, etc.) that are available now but were not available earlier. A person gravely ill may be entitled now to the benefit of some new machine that he would have been equally entitled to ten years ago had that machine existed. But it did not exist then, although it does now, and in that sense mere technology may expand the rightful claims of persons like him. This is true of *persons*, whose moral status before the new machine became available is not in doubt.

But even if technology can enlarge the right of existing claimants, it cannot alter the nature of a claimant. Regarding fetuses, for whom technology lowers the age of viability, the case is very different from that of pre-existing patients. The decrease in the age of viability flowing from technical advance appears here (for the liberal) to call into existence now moral agents who, had there been only a fetus in that same condition a decade before, would not have existed then. This cannot be. Technology cannot create persons in whom rights inhere.

But if a lowering of the age of viability cannot create new moral agents, then a viable fetus of a given age that has rights now would, at the same age, have had rights then, before the techniques for achieving viability had developed. And in that case the non-viable fetus of a decade ago must also have been a moral agent deserving the same protection. There are no morally relevant features of the 24-week-old 1990 fetus that the 24-week-old 1970 fetus lacked; their moral claims on us (if they have any) are identical, even if the former be viable while the latter was not. How then could it be possible that terminating the 1970 fetus was right then and that terminating the equivalent 1990 fetus is wrong now?[8]

A last line of defense for the role of viability may be presented by the liberal moderate as follows:

> Viability is a morally significant point in the pregnancy, but not because it changes the rights of the fetus; of course separability cannot have that consequence. What gives moral significance to viability does not lie in *changes in* the fetus, but in the *changed relation* of the fetus to the mother. The fetus is not a person. But it is a being that deserves moral consideration, it is *morally considerable*, worthy of respect and concern. Now the degree of its considerability is such that, not being a person and having no human rights, it cannot prevail over the mother in the event of conflict; that is why the mother's concerns often do render abortion fully justified. But viability brings separability; after viability the rights of the mother can be protected while at the same time our due consideration of the special moral status of the fetus justifies us in protecting it as well. In other words, what is important about viability is not that it changes the fetus's inherent moral claims but that *it marks a change in the balance of*

*competing moral claims* that were already in force. Sheer technology can affect that balance. The morally considerable fetus may now be protectable while the rights of the mother are considered and protected as well. This is the crux of the matter. If we can protect both we are obliged to do so, because both the rights of the mother and the special consideration that is due to the fetus (even though it is not a person) make legitimate claims upon us; after viability both sets of claims can be met.

This argument may prove tenable, but it is highly problematic at best. It can succeed only if the liberal is able to give some account of the moral nature of the fetus as less than a person but still morally considerable, such that viability will have precisely that middling result. The moral account of the fetus given, however, must provide an *independent* explanation of the fetus's quasi-human moral stature. Liberals cannot simply say that the fetus is morally considerable to such a degree that, after viability, it deserves protection. That is what was to be shown — and here again the liberal must avoid the temptation to beg the question. If viability is to be defended as the fulcrum of liberal argument, some plausible account of the fetus's moral nature must be shown to give to viability its critical importance. What that account might be heaven only knows.

If this path leads to stymie, the liberal must return to the moral changes *in* the fetus during its growth, and viability as the critical point must be abandoned. Some date in the development of the fetus must be identified after which its right to life might reasonably be protected, but before which the fetus has no rights against the mother. That there is such a date is surely possible — but its key role in the compromise must make sense *morally*. The change must be such that what was justifiable before the change becomes unjustifiable after it. Some characteristic or capacity of the fetus, a feature that arises during pregnancy and whose presence can be objectively ascertained, must be identified — something that gives to the fetus a moral status it did not earlier possess. If that development can be identified, and if its rise can be known with confidence to take place no earlier than a given gestational age, liberal moderates may plausibly argue that after it develops abortion is wrong or at least morally problematic, but that before it develops abortion is morally permissible.

What features might liberals plausibly identify to serve this purpose? Viability, as we have seen, cannot serve. Some have argued that the morally relevant change in early human growth is the development of consciousness of self, and of self-conscious desires.[9] But this, of course, would not yield a middle path.

Upon what other features might liberal moderates rely? They may focus upon the development of those capacities of the central nervous system that make experience possible, and are thus the necessary condition of all awareness. The earliest growth of the brain can be traced. Before even the possibility of any experience has arisen in the fetus (such moderates may contend) it can have no naturally grounded moral interests. And if this possibility of experience never can arise before a certain known stage of the pregnancy, we can know the period during which, on this intermediate liberal view, abortion can do the fetus no wrong. The premises upon which such argument relies would need to be established; evidence would be needed, and the position defended as neither arbitrary nor question-begging — and all that might not be easy. But such an enterprise would at least be morally coherent.

## 5. How to Argue About Abortion

To argue effectively in defense of their respective positions, the several controversialists must fully grasp and fairly state what their opponents contend, and must meet those claims with argument and evidence. That much is true for all.

For full-blooded liberals, the task is to confront the moral issue that has been typically evaded by insisting upon the mother's right to choose. She has a right to choose only if the fetus has the moral status that leaves open room for her choice. Whether the fetus has that status (as we saw) is the very point at issue, and it must not be begged. So liberals, in arguing about abortion, must face up to the difficult moral core of the controversy; they must come to grips with the question of what the fetus is, and what its moral status is, and why.

For full-blooded conservatives the task is very great: their central claim, that the fetus is a person, must be defended. Their resort to science cannot possibly succeed, (as we saw); pseudo-scientific defenses of the personhood of the embryo from conception, based upon misconstrued genetic reports, must be eschewed. What renders abortion morally wrong (on the conservative view) cannot be any feature of the fetus determinable by science. Resort to some convictions having a non-empirical foundation is therefore inescapable for conservatives; that inevitability should be recognized, and the non-empirical foundation claimed should be forthrightly identified.

The conservative premise, that the fetus is a human person from conception, precludes any middle path that would involve killing it when the unfairness of the pregnancy is very great. The deliberate sacrifice of the life of one innocent person for the sake of another — however agonizing the mother's burdens — cannot be justified. Conservatives must therefore come to see that a middle path is not open to them.

Liberals who seek to defend a middle path may be rationally hopeful, but their task also remains great. They must either: a) give an independent account of the moral considerability of the fetus such that, after viability, its life deserves protection, while before viability its life may be sacrificed to the interests of the mother; or b) identify and defend some morally relevant change in the fetus during pregnancy (a change which, unlike viability, is not merely in us or in our capacities) that renders some or most abortions justifiable before that change, and some or most abortions less justifiable or unjustifiable after that change.

Thinking about how argument goes wrong helps us to see how to make it go right.

## NOTES

[1]Here is an archetypical presentation of the argument, in recent testimony before the Judiciary Committee of the Connecticut legislature, by Paul A. Byrne, M. D.:

> Half the DNA [of a new human life] is provided by the ovum, the other half by the sperm, to form new DNA. The new DNA, the new set of chromosomes, is different from the DNA or the chromosomes of the father, different from the DNA or the chromosomes of the mother. The DNA is the genetic material present and duplicated in each and every cell of the body; it has the biochemical identity of a particular human being subsequently duplicated in the nucleus of every cell of that particular individual . . . . At all stages of development from conception to adulthood, biochemical identity is present in the nucleus of each and every cell. At all stages of development there is structure that is wholly and only human . . . . Thus, from conception, the new human being has a particular identity, oneness, structure . . . . These are the basic elements of the human structure essential to human life, and their presence clearly establishes the existence of human life . . . . [I]t is my expert medical opinion that it is a fact that human life begins at conception. (*ALL About Issues*, American Life League, April, 1990.)

[2]See L. Wolpert and W. D. Stein, "Positional Information and Pattern Formation," in *Pattern Formation: A Primer in Developmental Biology*, ed. G. M. Malacinski and S. V. Bryam (London: Macmillan, 1984), pp. 3–21.

[3]A detailed account of the development of the fertilized human egg may be found in C. A. Bedate and R. C. Cefalo, "The Zygote: To Be or Not to Be a Person," *The Journal of Medicine and Philosophy*, Vol. 14, pp. 641–645, 1989. The authors of this account, a molecular biologist and a specialist in fetal medicine, conclude: "The development of a zygote depends at each moment on several factors: the progressive actualization of its own genetically coded information, the actualization of pieces of information that originate *de novo* during the embryonic process, and exogenous information independent of the control of the zygote . . . . [T]he zygote makes possible the existence of a human being but does not in and of itself possess sufficient information to form it . . . . The zygote does possess sufficient information to produce exclusively human tissue but not to become an individual human being."

[4]For a detailed account of recent research into the critical role of morphogens in the development of the embryo, see P. M. Brickell and C. Tickle, "Morphogens in Chick Limb Development," *BioEssays*, Vol. 11, No. 5, November 1989; and J. Lee and C. Tickle, "Retinoic Acid and Pattern Formation in the Developing Chick Wing," *Journal of Embryology and Experimental Morphology*, 90, pp. 139–169.

[5]A more detailed account of the growth of the embryo, and experiments illuminating that growth, may be found in C. A. Gardner, "Is an Embryo a Person?", *The Nation*, November 13, 1989. This geneticist concludes: "[T]here does not seem to be any blueprint for embryonic development. Each step toward greater complexity depends instead upon the pattern of cells and molecules just reached in the preceding step. The information required to make an eye or a finger does not exist in the fertilized egg."

[6]See Martin Benjamin, *Splitting the Difference: Compromise and Integrity in Ethics and Politics*, (University Press of Kansas, 1990), pp. 139–174. Controversy over abortion is used by Benjamin (pp. 151–171) as an excellent example of the distinction between compromising and defending a morally right middle path.

[7]Some have argued that a fetus arising from rape, even if it is a person and has a "right to life," may be viewed as a threatening parasite, never welcomed or entitled to entry, and may therefore be rightly ejected from a woman's body, even if doing so results in its death, if its continued presence seriously conflicts with the rights of its maternal host. See Judith Jarvis Thomson, "A Defense of Abortion," *Philosophy and Public Affairs*, Vol. 1, No. 1, Fall, 1971, pp. 47–66. "[H]aving a right to life does not guarantee having either a right to be given the use of or a right to be allowed continued use of another person's body — even if one needs it for life itself." (p.56)

[8]The changing date of fetal viability may have a paradoxical consequence if it is one day pushed to a very early gestational age. We may never achieve the capacity to do it, but if at some future date it were to become possible to nurture the fetus in an artificial uterine environment from its earliest days, what had been the keystone of liberal moderation may become a devastating conservative weapon. Leaning upon the reed of viability is dangerous for liberals. If *Roe v. Wade* is eventually overturned, the consequent need of liberals to re-think the grounds of a middle course may prove highly salutary for them.

[9]This position is thoughtfully defended by Michael Tooley in a well-known essay, "Abortion and Infanticide," in *Philosophy and Public Affairs*, Vol 2, No. 1, Fall, 1972. If self-consciousness arises only days or weeks after birth, as Tooley notes, this approach might lead to the consideration of infanticide as sometimes morally permissible. In any event, if the feature(s) essential for personhood do(es) not arise until birth or thereafter, it (or they) can be no ground for a moderate liberal position regarding the pre-natal period during which abortion should be prohibited, because there would be no such period.

ANDREA DWORKIN

# IN OCTOBER 1973 (AGE 27)

There's a basketball court next to where I live, not a court exactly, a
hoop high up, and broken cement, rocks, broken glass; there's boys
that play, the game ain't ballet like on television, it's malice, they
smash the ball like they're smashing heads and you don't want to
distract them, you want their eyes on the ball, always on the ball,
you want them playing ball; so you get small and quiet walking by,
you don't let nothing rattle or shake, you just blend, into the sidewalk, into the air, get gray like the fence, it's wire, shaky, partly
walling the place in, you walk quiet and soft and hope your heart
don't beat too loud; and there's a parking lot for cops right next to
the basketball, not the official vehicles but the cars they come to
work in, the banged up Chevys and Fords they drive in from the
suburbs because most of them don't live here no more but still, even
though they got more money than they make you don't see nothing
smart and sleek, there's just this old metal, bulky, heavy, discolored.
The young cops are tight and you don't want to see them spring
loose, their muscles are all screwed together real tight and their lips
are tight, sewed tight, and they stand straight and tight and they
look ahead, not around, their pupils are tight in the dead center of
their eyes staring straight ahead; and the older ones wear cheap
sports jackets too big for them, gray, brown, sort of plaid, nearly
tweed, wrinkled, and their shoulders sag, and they are morose men,
and their cars can barely hold them, their legs fall out loose and
disorganized and then they move their bodies around to be in the
same direction as the legs that fell down, they move the trunks of
their bodies from behind the steering wheels against gravity and
disregarding common sense and the air moves out of the way, slug-
gish and slow, displaced by their hanging bellies, and they are tired

This is an excerpt from the novel *Mercy*, published in England in September 1990 by Secker & Warburg.

men, and they see everything, they have eyes that circle the globe,
insect eyes and third eyes, they see in front and behind and on each
side, their eyes spin without moving, and they see you no matter
how blank and quiet you are, they see you sneaking by, and they
wonder why you are sneaking and what you have to hide, they note
that you are trash, they have the view that anything female on this
street is a piece of gash, an open wound inviting you in for a few
pennies, and that you especially who are walking by them now have
committed innumerable evils for which you must pay and you want
to argue except for the fact that they are not far from wrong, it is not
an argument you can win, and that makes you angrier against them
and fearful, and you try to disappear but they see you, they always
see you; and you learn not to think they are fools; they will get
around to you; today, tomorrow, someday soon; and they see the
boys playing basketball and they want to smash them, smash their
fucking heads in, but they're too old to smash them and they can't
use their guns, not yet, not now; even the young cops couldn't smash
them fair, they're too rigid, too slow up against the driving rage of
the boys with the ball; so you see them noting it, noting that they got
a grudge, and the cars are parked on gravel and broken glass and
rocks and they should have better and they know it but they don't
and they won't and later they get to use the guns, somewhere, the
city's full of fast black boys who get separated from the pack; and
you hear the fuck, shit, asshole, of the basketball players as a counterpoint to the solitary fuck, shit, asshole, of the lone cops as they
emerge from their cars, they put down their heavy legs and their
heavy feet in their bad old shoes, all worn, chewed leather, and they
pull themselves out of their old cars, and they're tired men, over-
weight, there ain't many young ones at all, and there's a peculiar
sadness to them, the fascists are melancholy in Gotham, they say
fuck, shit, asshole, like it's soliloquies, like it's prayers, like it's amen,
like it's exegesis on existence, like it's unanswered questions, urgent,
eloquent, articulated to God; lonely, tired old Nazis, more like
Hamlet, though, than like Lear, introspective from exhaustion, not
grand or arrogant or merciless in delusion; and the boys hurl the ball
like it's bombs, like it's rocks and stones, like it's bullets and they're
the machines of delivery, the weapons of death, machine guns of
flesh, bang bang bang, each round so fast, so hard, as the ball hits
the ground and the boy moves with it, a weapon with speed up its
ass; and they're a choir of fuck, shit, asshole, voices still on the far
edge of an adolescent high, not the raspy, cigarette-ruined voices of

the lonely, sad men; the boys run, the boys sing the three words they
know, a percussive lyric, they breathe deep, skin and viscera
breathe, everything inside and outside breathes, there's a convul-
sion, then another one, they exhale as if it's some sublime soprano
aria at the Met, supreme art, simple, new each time, the air comes
out urgent and organized and with enough volume to fill a concert
hall, it's exhilarating, a human voice, all the words they don't know;
and the cops, old, young, it don't matter, barely breathe at all, they
breathe so high up in the throat that the air barely gets out, it's thin
and depressed and somber, it's old and it's stale and it's pale and it's
flat, there's no words to it and no music, it's a thin, empty sound, a
flat despair, Hamlet so old and dead and tired he can't even get up a
stage whisper. The cops look at the boys, each cop does, and there's
this second when the cop wants to explode, he'd unleash a grenade
in his own hand if he had one, he'd take himself with it if it meant
offing them, fuck them black boys' heads off, there's this tangible
second, and then they turn away, each one, young, old, tight, sagging, each one, every day, and they pull themselves up, and they
kick the rocks, the broken glass, the gravel, and they got a hand
folded into a fist, and they leave the parking lot, they walk big, they
walk heavy, they walk like John Wayne, young John, old John, big
John, they walk slow and heavy and wide, deliberate, like they got
six-shooters riding on each hip; while the boys move fast, mad,
mean, speeding, cold fury in hot motion. You want them on each
other; not on you. It ain't honorable but it's real. You want them
caught up in the urban hate of generations, in wild west battles on
city streets, you want them so manly against each other they don't
have time for girlish trash like you, you want them fighting each
other cock to cock so it all gets used up on each other. You take the
view that women are for recreation, fun, when the battle's over; and
this battle has about another hundred years to go. You figure they
can dig you up out of the ground when they're ready. You figure
they probably will. You figure it don't matter to them one way or
the other. You figure it don't matter to you either; just so it ain't
today, now, tonight, tomorrow; just so you ain't conscious; just so
you ain't alive the next time; just so you are good and dead; just so
you don't know what it is and who's doing it. If you're buying milk
or bread or things you have to go past them, walk down them
streets, go in front of them, the boys, the cops, and you practice
disappearing; you practice pulling the air over you like a blanket;
you practice being nothing and no one; you practice not making a

sound and barely breathing; you practice making your eyes go blank and never looking at anyone but seeing where they are, hearing a shadow move; you practice being a ghost on cement; and you don't let nothing rattle or make noise, not the groceries, not your shoes hitting the ground, not your arms, you don't let them move or rub, you don't make no spontaneous gestures, you don't even raise your arm to scratch your nose, you keep your arms still and you put the milk in the bag so it stays still and you go so far as to make sure the bag ain't a stupid bag, one of them plastic ones that makes sounds every time something touches it; you have to get a quiet bag; if it's a brown paper bag you have to perfect the skill of carrying it so nothing moves inside it and so you don't have to change arms or hands, acts which can catch the eye of someone, acts which can call attention to you, you don't shift the bag because your hand gets tired or your arm, you just let it hurt because it hurts quiet, and if it's a plastic bag it's got to be laminated good so it don't make any rustling noise or scratching sound, and you have to walk faster, silent, fast, because plastic bags stand out more, sometimes they have bright colors and the flash of color going by can catch someone's attention, the bag's real money, it costs a dime, it's a luxury item, you got change to spare, you're a classy shopper so who knows what else you got; and if it's not colorful it's likely to be a shiny white, a bright white, the kind light flashes off of like it's a mirror sending signals and there's only one signal widely comprehended on cement: get me. The light can catch someone's eye so you have to walk like Zen himself, walk and not walk, you are a master in the urban Olympics for girls, an athlete of girlish survival, it's a survival game for the world's best. You get past them and you celebrate, you celebrate in your heart, you thank the Lord, in your heart you say a prayer of gratitude and forgiveness, you forgive Him, it's sincere, and you hope He don't take it as a challenge, razor-sharp temper He's got, no do unto others for Him; and if you hear someone behind you you beg, in half a second you are on your knees in your heart begging Him to let you off, you promise a humility this time that will last, it will begin right now and last a long, long time, you promise no more liturgical sacrilege, and your prayer stops and your heart stops and you wait and the most joyous sound on God's earth is that the man's feet just stomp by. Either he will hurt you or he will not; either He will hurt you or He will not. Truth's so simple and so severe, you don't be stupid enough to embellish it. I myself live inside now. I don't take my chances resting only in the arms of God. I put myself

inside four walls and then I let Him rock me, rock me, baby, rock
me. I lived outside a lot; and this last summer I was tired, disori-
ented. I was too tired, really, to find a bed, too nervous, maybe too
old, maybe I got old, it happens pretty fast past eighteen like they
always warned; get yourself one boy when you're eighteen and get
yourself one bed. It got on my nerves to think about it every night, I
don't really like to be in a bed per se. I stayed in the lot behind where
the police park their cars, there's a big, big dirt lot, there's a fence
behind the police cars and then there's empty dirt, trash, some rats,
we made fires, there's broken glass, there's liquor to stay warm, I
never once saw what it was, it's bottles in bags with hands on the
bags that tilt in your direction, new love, anti-genital love, polymor-
phous perverse, a bottle in a bag. You got to lift your skirt sometimes
but it doesn't matter and I have sores on me, my legs is so dirty I just
really don't look. You don't have to look. There's many mirrors to be
used but you need not use them. I got too worn out to find some bed
each new night, it got on my nerves so I was edgy and anxious in
anticipation, a dread that it would be hard to find or hard to stay or
hard to pay, if I just stayed on the dirt lot I didn't have to worry so
much, there's nothing trapping you in. Life's a long, quiet rumble,
and you just shake as even as you can so you don't get too worn out.
When I lifted up my skirt there was blood and dirt in drips, all
dried, down my legs, and I had sores. I felt quiet inside. I felt okay. I
didn't worry too much. I didn't go see movies or go on dates. I just
curled up to sleep and I'd drink whatever there was that someone
give me because there's generous men too; I see saliva; I see it close
up; if I was an artist I would paint it except I don't know how you
make it glisten, the brown and the gold in it; I saw many a face close
up and I saw many a man close up and I'd lift my skirt and it was
dirty, my legs, and there was dried blood. I was pretty dirty. I didn't
worry too much. Then I got money because my friend thought I
should go inside. I had this friend. I knew her when I was young.
She was a pacifist. She hated war and she held signs against the
Vietnam War and I did too. She let me sleep in her apartment but
enough's enough; there's places you don't go back to. So now I was
too dirty and she gave me money to go inside definitively; which I
had wanted, except it was hard to express. I thought about walls all
the time. I thought about how easy they should be, really, to have;
how you could fit them almost anywhere, on a street corner, in an
alley, on a patch of dirt, you must make walls and a person can go
inside with a bed, a small cot, just to lie down and it's a house, as

much of a house as any other house. I thought about walls pretty much all the time. You should be able to just put up walls, it should be possible. There's literally no end to the places walls could go without inconveniencing anyone, except they would have to walk around. They say a roof over your head but it's walls really that are the issue; you can just think about them, all their corners touching or all lined up thin like pancakes, painted a pretty color, a light color because you don't want it to look too small, or you can make it more than one color but you run the risk of looking busy, somewhat vulgar, and you don't want it to look gray or brown like outside or you could get sad. There's got to be some place in heaven where God stores walls, there's just walls, stacked or standing up straight like the pages of a book, miles high and miles wide running in pale colors above the clouds, a storage place, and God sees someone lost and He just sends them down four at a time. Guess He don't. There's people take them for granted and people who dream about them — literally, dream how nice they would be, pretty and painted, serene. I wouldn't mind living outside all the time if it didn't get cold or wet and there wasn't men. A roof over your head is more conceptual in a sense; it's sort of an advanced idea. In life you can cover your head with a piece of wood or with cardboard or newspapers or a side of a crate you pull apart, but walls aren't really spontaneous in any sense; they need to be built, with purpose, with intention. Someone has to plan it if you want them to come together the right way, the whole four of them with edges so delicate, it has to be balanced and solid and upright and it's very delicate because if it's not right it falls, you can't take it for granted; and there's wind that can knock it down; and you will feel sad, remorseful, you will feel full of grief. You can't sustain the loss. A roof over your head is a sort of suburban idea, I think; like that if you have some long, flat, big house with furniture in it that's all matching you surely also will have a roof so they make it a synonym for all the rest but it's walls that make the difference between outside and not. It's a well-kept secret, arcane knowledge, a mystery not often explained. You don't see it written down but initiates know. I type and sometimes I steal but I'm stopping as much as I can. I live inside now. I have an apartment in a building. It's a genuine building, a tenement, which is a famous kind of building in which many have lived in history. Maybe not Trotsky but Emma Goldman for certain. I don't go near men really. Sometimes I do. I get a certain forgetfulness that comes on me, a dark shadow over my brain, I get took up in a certain feeling, a wandering feeling to run from existence, all restless, perpetual motion. It drives me with an ache and I go find one. I get a smile on my face and my hips move a little back and forth and I turn into a greedy little fool; I want the glass all empty. I grab some change and I hit the cement and I get one. I am writing a certain very serious book about life itself. I go to bars for food during happy hours when my nerves aren't too bad, too loaded down with pain, but I keep to myself so I can't get enough to eat because bartenders and managers keep watch and you are supposed to be there for the men which is why they let you in, there ain't no such thing as a solitary woman brooding poetically to be left alone, it don't happen or she don't eat, and mostly I don't want men so I'm hungry most of the time, I'm almost always hungry, I eat potatoes, you can buy a bag of potatoes that is almost too heavy to carry and you can just boil them one at a time and you can eat them and they fill you up for a while. My book is a very big book about existence but I can't find any plot for it. It's going to be a very big book once I get past the initial slow beginning. I want to get it published but you get afraid you will die before it's finished, not after when it can be found and it's testimony and then they say you were a great one; you don't want to die before you wrote it so you have to learn to sustain your writing, you take it serious, you do it every day and you don't fail to write words down and to think sentences. It's hard to find words. It's about some woman but I can't think of what happens. I can say where she is. It's pretty barren. I always see a woman on a rock, calling out. But that's not a story per se. You could have someone dying of tuberculosis like Mann or someone who is suffering—for instance, someone who is lovesick like Mann. Or there's best-sellers, all these stories where women do all these things and say all these things but I don't think I can write about that because I only seen it in the movies. There's marriage stories but it's so boring, a couple in the suburbs and the man on the train becoming unfaithful and how bored she is because she's too intelligent or something about how angry she is but I can't remember why. A love story's so stupid in these modern times. I can't have it be about my life because number one I don't remember very much and number two it's against the rules, you're supposed to make things up. The best thing that ever happened to me is these walls and I don't think you could turn that into a story per se or even a novel of ideas that people would grasp as philosophical: for instance, that you can just sit and they provide a framework of dignity because no one's watching and I have had too many see too much, they see you when they do things to you that you don't want, they look, and the problem is there's no walls keeping you sacred; nor that if you stand up they are solid which makes you seem real too, a real figure in a room with real walls, a touchstone of authenticity, a standard for real existence, you are real or you feel real, you don't have to touch them to feel real, you just have to be able to touch them. My pacifist friend gave me money to live here. She saw me on the street one day, I guess, after I didn't go back to her apartment no more. She said come with me and she got a newspaper and she found an apartment and she called the landlord and she put the money in my hand and she sent me to the landlord which scared me because I never met one before, a real one, but also she wasn't going to let the cash go elsewhere which there was a fair chance it would, because I would have liked some coke or something or some dinner or some drinks and a movie and a book or something more real than being inside which seemed impossible — it seemed not really available and it seemed impossible to sustain so it made more sense to me to use the cash for something real that I knew I could get, something I knew how to use. I started sending her money back as soon as I got some, I'd put some in an envelope and mail it back even if it was just five dollars but she said I was stupid because she only said it was a loan but it wasn't and I didn't need to pay it back and everyone knew that which is my weakness, how everyone got to know things but I don't know them. I can't think of any stories about pacifists that aren't true. There's nothing imaginary about walls, or eating, nothing fictive as it were, but more especially there's nothing imaginary about them when they're missing. My walls are thin; yeah I wish they were mine. Nothing's yours. God hurts you if you think they're yours. In one second of a bad thought you can bring evil down on you. The walls are thin. I dream there's holes in them and I get scared as if it's not really inside. There's not much food and I know it ain't mine in any meaningful sense. You're supposed to make things up, not just write down true things, or sincere things, or some things that happened. My mother who you can't make up either because there's nothing so real as one named me Andrea as if I was someone: distinct, in particular. She made a fiction. I'm her book, a made-up story written down on a birth certificate. You could also say she's a liar on such a deep level she should be shot by all that's fair; deep justice. If I was famous and my name was published all over the world, in Italy and in Israel and in Africa and in India, on continents and subcontinents, in deserts, in ancient cities, it would still be cunt to every fucking asshole drunk on every street in the world; and to them that's not drunk too, the sober ones who say it to you like they're calling a dog: fetch, cunt. If I won the Nobel Prize and walked to the corner for milk it would still be cunt. And when you got someone inside you who is loving you it's still cunt and the ones who'd die if they wasn't in you, you, you in particular, at least that night, at least then, that time, that place, to them it's still cunt and they whisper it up close and chill the blood that's burning in you; and if you love them it's still cunt and you can love them so strong you'd die for them and it's still cunt; and your heart-beat and his heartbeat can be the same heartbeat and it's still cunt. It's behind your back and it's to your face; the ones you know, the ones you don't. It's like as if nigger was a term of intimate endear-ment, not just used in lynching and insult but whispered in lovema-king, the truth under the truth, the name under the name, love's name for you and it's the same as what hate calls you; he's in you whispering nigger. It's thugs, it's citizens, it's cops, it's strangers, it's the ones you want and the ones you deplore, you ain't allowed indifference, you have to decide on a relationship then and there on the spot because each one that passes pisses on you to let you know he's there. There's some few you made love with and you're still breathing tight with them, you can still feel their muscles swelling through their skin and bearing down on you and you can still feel their weight on you, an urgent concentration of blood and bone, hot muscle, spread over you, the burden of it sinking into you, a stone cliff into a wet shore, and you're still tangled up in them, good judgment aside, and it's physical, it's a physical memory, in the body, not just in the brain, barely in the brain at all, you got their sweat on you as part of your sweat and their smell's part of your smell and you have an ache for them that's deep and gnawing and hurtful in more than your heart and you still feel as if it's real and current, now: how his body moves against you in convulsions that are awesome like mountains moving, slow, burdensome, big, and how you move against him as if you could move through him, he's the ocean, you're the tide, and it's still cunt, he says cunt. He's indelibly in you and you don't want redemption so much as you want him and still it's cunt. It's what's true; Andrea's the lie. It's a lie we got to tell, Jane and Judith and Ellen and whomever. It's our most desperate lie. My mother named me Andrea. It means man-hood or courage. It means not-cunt. She specifically said: not-cunt. This one ain't cunt, she declared, after blood spilled and there was the pain of labor so intense that God couldn't live through it and wouldn't which is why all the pain's with us and still she brought herself to a point of concentration and she said: not-cunt. This one's someone, she probably had in mind; a wish; a hope; let her, let her, something. Something. Let her something. Don't, not with this one. Just let this one through. Just don't do it to this one. She wrote: not-cunt, a fiction, and it failed, and the failure defeated her and turned her cold to me, because before I was even ten some man had wrote "this one's cunt," he took his fingers and he wrote it down on me and inside me, his fingers carved it in me with a pain that stayed half buried and there wasn't words I had for what he did, he wrote I was cunt, this sweet little one who was what's called a child but a female one which changes it all. My mama showed that fiction was delusion, hallucination, it was a long, deranged lie designed to last past your own lifetime. The man, on the other hand, was a pragmatist, a maker of reality, a shaper of history, an orchestrator of events. He used life, not paper, bodies, not ink. The Nazis, of course, synthesized the two: bodies and ink. You can't even say it would solve the problem to have numbers on us, inked on. Numbers is as singular as names unless we are all zero, 0, we could all be 0; Pauline Réage already suggested it, of course, but she's a demagogue and a utopian, a kind of Stalinist of female equality, she wants us all equal on the bottom of anything that's mean enough to be on top; it has a certain documentary quality. Unlike Réage, my mother just made it up, and her fiction was a lie, almost without precedent, not recognized as original or great, a voyage of imagination; it was just a fucking lie. I don't want to tell lies, not for moral reasons but it's my idea of pride, you name it, I can take it. I was born in a city where the walls were falling down; I didn't see many solid walls. The streets were right next to you it seemed because you could always hear the buzz, the hum, the call, as if drums were beckoning you to the tribal dance; you could see the freedom. Inside was small and constrained with rules designed to make you some kind of trained cockroach and outside was forever, a path straight to the heart of the world; there were no limits, it spread out in front of you to anywhere, with anyone. Limits were another lie, a social fiction all the zombies got together to tell. The destination was always the street because the destination was always freedom; out from under; no rule on top of you. You could almost look through the brick, which was crumbling, and you had this sense that every building had holes in it, a transparency, and that no walls were ever finished or ever lasted; and the cement outside was gray, cracked, streaked with blood from where they threw you down to have fun with you on hot nights and cold nights, the boys with their cars and knives; I knew some of those boys; I loved Nino who said "make love" as if it was something real special and real nice and so fine, so precious and kind and urgent, his eyes burned and his voice was low and soft and silk, it wrapped itself around you, he didn't reach out, he didn't move towards you, you had to let him know, you had to; I could still fucking die for what he promised with his brilliant seduction, a poor, uneducated boy, but when he did it I got used to being hurt from behind, he used his knife, he made fine lines of blood, delicate, and you didn't dare move except for your ass as he wanted and you didn't know if you'd die and you got to love danger if you loved the boy and danger never forsakes you; the boy leaves but danger is faithful. You knew the cement under you and the brick around you and the sound of the boys speeding by in their cars and the sudden silence, which meant they were stalking you. I was born in Camden down the street from where Walt Whitman lived, Mickle Street, he was the great gray poet, the prophetic hero of oceanic verse; also not-cunt. Great poet; not-cunt. It's like a mathematical equation but no one learns it in school by heart; it ain't written down plain on the blackboard. It's algebra for girls but no one's going to teach you. You get brought down or throwed down and you learn for yourself. There's no mother on earth can bear to explain it. I can't write down what happened and I can't tell lies. There's no words for what happened and there's barely words for the lies. If I was a man I would say something about fishing and it would be a story, a perfectly fine one too; the bait, the hook, the lake, the wind, the shore, and then everything else is the manly stuff. If I was a man at least I'd know what to say, or I'd say it so grand it wouldn't matter if it was true or not; anyone'd recognize it and say it was art. I could think of something important, probably; recognizably so. If I was a man and something happened I could write it down and probably it would pass as a story even if it was true. Of course, that's just speculation. I'd swagger, too, if I was a man; I'm not proud to say it but I'm sure it's true. I would take big steps, loud ones, down the street; I could be the Zen master of fuck you. I would spread myself out and take up all the space and spread my legs wide open in the subway to take up three seats with just my knees like they do. I would be very bold and very cool. I'd be smarter than I am now, I'm sure, because what I knew might matter and I'd remember more, I'm sure. I don't think

I'd go near women though because I wouldn't want to hurt them. I know how everything feels. I think if I was a man my heart would not hurt so much and I wouldn't have this terror I am driven by but cannot name. I think I could write a poem about it, perhaps. I think it could probably make a very long poem and I could keep rewriting it to get every nuance right and chart it as it changed over time; song of himself, perhaps, a sequel. Ginsberg says he chased Whitman through supermarkets; I fucking was him; I embraced all the generations without distinctions and it failed because of this awfulness that there is no name for, this great meanness at the heart of what they mean when they stick it in; I just don't know a remedy, because it is a sick and hostile thing. Even if there were no wars I think I could say some perceptions I had about life, I wouldn't need the Civil War or the Vietnam War to hang my literary hat on as it were, and I could be loud, which I would try, I'm sure, I could call attention to myself as if I mattered or what happened did or as if I knew something, even about suffering or even about life; and, frankly, then it might count. I could stop thinking every minute about where each sound is coming from and where the shadows are each minute. I can't even close my eyes now frankly but I think it's because I'm this whatever it is, you can have sophisticated words for it but the fact is you can be sleeping inside with everything locked and they get in and do it to you no matter how bad it hurts. In magazines they say women's got allure, or so they call it, but it's more like being some dumb wriggling thing that God holds out before them on a stick with a string, a fisher of men. The allure's there even if you got open sores on you; I know. The formal writing problem, frankly, is that the bait can't write the story. The bait ain't even barely alive. There's a weird German tradition that the fish turned the tables and rewrote the story to punish the fisherman but you know it's a lie and it's some writer of fiction being what became known as a modernist but before that was called outright a smartass; and the fish still ain't bait unless it's eviscerated and bleeding. I just can't risk it now but if I was a man I could close my eyes, I'm sure; at night, I'd close them, I'm sure. I don't think my hands would shake. I don't think so; or not so much; or not all the time; or not without reason; there's no reason now anyone can see. My breasts wouldn't bleed as if God put a sign on me; blessing or curse, it draws flies. Tears of blood fall from them; they weep blood for me, because I'm whatever it is: the girl, as they say politely; the girl. You're supposed to make things up for books but I am afraid to make things up because in life everything evaporates, it's gone in mist, just disappears, there's no sign left, except on you, and you are a fucking invisible ghost, they look right through you, you can have bruises so bad the skin's pulled off you and they don't see nothing; you bet women had the vapors, still fucking do, it means it all goes away in the air, whatever happened, whatever he did and however he did it, and you're left feeling sick and weak and no one's going to say why; it's just women, they faint all the time, they're sick all the time, fragile things, delicate things, delicate like the best punching bags you ever seen. They say it's lies even if they just did it, or maybe especially then. I don't know really. There's nothing to it, no one ever heard of it before or ever saw it or not here or not now; in all history it never happened, or if it happened it was the Nazis, the exact, particular Nazis in Germany in the thirties and forties, the literal Nazis in uniform; when they were out of uniform they were just guys, you know, they loved their families, they paid off their whores, just regular guys. No one else ever did anything, certainly no one now in this fine world we have here; certainly not the things I think happened, although I don't know what to call them in any serious way. You just crawl into a cave of silence and die; why are there no great women artists? Some people got nerve. Blood on cement, which is all we got in my experience, ain't esthetic, although I think boys some day will do very well with it; they'll put it in museums and get a fine price. Won't be their blood. It would be some cunt's they whispered to the night before; a girl; and then it'd be art, you see; or you could put it on walls, make murals, be political, a democratic art outside the museums for the people, Diego Rivera without any conscience whatsoever instead of the very tenuous one he had with respect to women, and then it'd be extremely major for all the radicals who would discover the expressive value of someone else's blood and I want to tell you they'd stop making paint but such things do not happen and such things cannot occur, any more than the rape so-called can happen or occur or the being beaten so bad can happen or occur and there are no words for what cannot happen or occur and if you think something happened or occurred and there are no words for it you are at a dead end. There's nothing where they force you; there's nothing where you hurt so much; there's nothing where it matters, there's nothing like it anywhere. So it doesn't feel right to make things up, as you must do to write fiction, to lie, to elaborate, to elongate, to exaggerate, to distort, to get tangled up in moderations or modifications or deviations or compromises of mixing this with that or combining this one with that one because the problem is finding words for the truth, especially if no one will believe it, and they will not. I can't make things up because I wouldn't know after a while what's blood, what's ink. I barely know any words for what happened to me yesterday, which doesn't make tomorrow something I can conceive of in my mind; I mean words I say to myself in my own head; not social words you use to explain to someone else. I barely know anything and if I deviate I am lost; I have to be literal, if I can remember, which mostly I cannot. No one will acknowledge that some things happen and probably at this point in time there is no way to say they do in a broad sweep; you describe the man forcing you but you can't say he forced you. If I was a man I could probably say it; I could say I did it and everyone would think I made it up even though I'd just be remembering what I did last night or twenty minutes ago or once, long ago, but it probably wouldn't matter. The rapist has words, even though there's no rapist, he just keeps inventing rape; in his mind; sure. He remembers, even though it never happened; it's fine fiction when he writes it down. Whereas my mind is getting worn away; it's being eroded, experience keeps washing over it and there's no sea wall of words to keep it intact, to keep it from being washed away, carried out to sea, layer by layer, fine grains washed away, a thin surface washed away, then some more, washed away. I am fairly worn away in my mind, washed out to sea. It probably doesn't matter anyway. People lead their little lives. There's not much dignity to go around. There's lies in abundance, and silence for girls who don't tell them. I don't want to tell them. A lie's for when he's on top of you and you got to survive him being there until he goes; Malcolm X tried to stop saying a certain lie, and maybe I should change from Andrea because it's a lie. It's just that it's a precious thing from my mother that she tried to give me; she didn't want it to be such an awful lie, I don't think. So I have to be the writer she tried to be — Andrea; not-cunt — only I have to do it so it ain't a lie. I ain't fabricating stories. I'm making a different kind of story. I'm writing as truthful as the man with his fingers, if only I can remember and say; but I ain't on his side. I'm on some different side. I'm telling the truth but from a different angle. I'm the one he done it to.

DARCY GRIMALDO GRIGSBY

# DILEMMAS OF VISIBILITY:
# CONTEMPORARY WOMEN ARTISTS'
# REPRESENTATIONS OF FEMALE BODIES

A curator's essay is customarily an argument for the criteria of selection. One argues, for example, that the aggregation of objects under inspection can be composed into a cohesive whole. This is organization by the criterion of sameness. If, however, the curator's charge is to produce a portfolio of different artists representing the female body, then the attempt to find some consistent practice or *body* of works threatens not only to level diverse artistic projects but also to totalize the female body by some kind of (aesthetic) consensus.

While the criterion of difference may be construed as a positive value in opposition to sameness, it poses other dangers. The unconstrained ("free") association of aesthetic objects participates in the liberal ideology of pluralism. If different artists depict different bodies, there is a pretense to a field of representation free of conflict. That is to say that each work is autonomous and abstains from a critical and contentious dialogue with other representations. A pluralist account not only removes contention from the field of representation but also effaces the parameters of the field itself. Denied are the shared issues, problems, and motivations that impel — and circumscribe — the representation of female bodies.

As curator, I have attempted to assemble a collection of works which simultaneously resists totalization *and* describes the politics and debates, the high stakes, characterizing the representation of female bodies. My project does not produce *one* female body nor is it a set of female bodies that bear no relation to each other. The artists selected for this portfolio share a number of things. They are women. Their work has been produced during and since the women's movement of the 1970s. Because of their relationship to concomitant (and related) art-historical phenomena (conceptual and performance art), these artists work in non-traditional media. Indeed, most utilize their own bodies as their primary material. They also share the conviction that women's bodies are sites of negotiation and struggle within history. As they produce their art, these women assume the responsiblity of entering a critical exchange, not only within history and against dominant androcentric practices, but also within feminism. Consequently, this visual art takes on the character of research, of feminist theory and practice, and the artists represented here are each other's most vigilant critics. The subsequent portfolio and essay intend to facilitate such critical interchange.

*     *     *

Virginia Maksymowicz's ongoing work, *The History of Art*, deliberately confuses art history and the strip tease, art viewing and voyeurism (Fig. 1). The contact sheet provides a narrative of undress, but the unbuttoning of the blouse surprises. Instead of luxuriant nakedness, unveiling reveals a history of pictorial images from the caves of Lascaux to the classical vase painting of Euphronios to the paint splatters of Jackson Pollock to the graffiti art of Keith Haring. Rather than an imaginative reconstruction of "herstory" as in Judy Chicago's *Dinner Party*, the paper cast of Maksymowicz's body is inscribed by the hand of the male artist. Moreover, art painted on a woman's torso becomes fashion, the stuff in museum gift shops as well as department stores, the Op look and Mondrian T-shirt. Continually deferred, the female body cannot be seen except as it is inscribed by the history of art and style. Taking away the veil of clothing only reveals the cultural construction of another skin. As the successive styles of the western canon are traced on Maksymo-wicz's person (or rather that indexical representation of her torso), her tease not only reproduces the authority of male authorship on her own recast self but underscores the impossibility of retrieving or representing a naked (natural and unacculturated) female body. If, however, nakedness is continually deferred, the form of the female body is delivered; in its consistent shape, the woman's torso can be interpreted as the permanent vessel upon which man's passing culture is recorded. Even in a humorous portrayal of the female body's cultural inscription by (male-authored) art and fashion, the artist is unable to entirely circumvent a reading of woman as timeless nature to man's historical culture.

Cindy Sherman and Millie Wilson are choreographers of duplicity, orchestraters of deferral. Skillful and compelling liars, Sherman and Wilson offer a woman's presence only to underscore her perpetual absence in representation. Cindy Sherman's work consists of series of photographs of herself, here represented by one of her early untitled film stills (Fig. 2). Yet Sherman does not produce self-portraits. Rather, her person functions as a constituent element of a *mise-en-scène*. Moreover, her body appears to be endlessly pliant before the camera. The way she looks is determined by photographic conventions, costume, setting, and lighting. Long-shot of an unhappy blonde in a bedroom, distant view of a pensive brunette on a flight of stairs — this is the prosaic repertory of a highly conventionalized idiom.

Sherman, however, wields camera *and* "dresses up"; she is both director and actress. There is pleasure in the woman's simultaneous usurpation of the camera's omnipotence and her compliant flexibility before it. Through her own volition and skill, she can, it seems, become anyone. But the photographs also invoke frustration and a sense of loss. The images which seem so familiar and full are ultimately insufficient and opaque. The represented woman seems to anticipate or respond to something outside the stilled moment of the frame, but her expression — apparently so significant — is either impassive and illegible or exaggerated like a mask. The woman remains an orchestrated "look," a surface which hides as much as it reveals. "Woman" represented is but a series of impersonations. Furthermore, if femininity is the prescription and disciplining of female subjects by fashion and deportment in public and private spaces, it must be constantly reenacted. Only a continued and consistent performance produces a unified and consenting female subject. While Sherman consents to perform female, she refuses to sustain a single performance that would naturalize "femininity."

Millie Wilson's installation *Fauve Semblant. Peter (A Young English Girl)* purports to disclose the identity of a lesbian artist (Fig. 3). Peter, a supposedly forgotten early twentieth-century lesbian painter, is reconstructed from the few artifacts which survive her. Photographs of the artist, one painting, and various possessions are accompanied by texts which describe her habits and personality. The fragments fail to cohere, however. The cross-dressing artist is repeatedly described in contradictory terms:

She was a woman. She dressed as a man. She was authoritative and uncompromising. She was romantic and domestic. She was born working-class. She was acclaimed in stylish circles. She became famous. She withdrew from the public. She was a mannish renegade. She wanted to marry the love of her life. She was a flawless technician. She neglected to paint for years at a time. She risked everything to be an artist. She gave up her art for love.

Millie Wilson produces a list of typical biographical statements. Each sentence provides definitive information, but each unit of information is compromised by the statement that follows it. The sentences are not contradictions as much as they are insufficient. The more one knows, the less one is sure about who "Peter" was. While biographical exhibits normatively provide viewers with the satisfaction of building a composite person through the presentation of a series of facts and truisms, here the desultory list frustrates such closure. Indeed, it is "she" to whom the reader/spectator seems to have no access. Fauve Semblant/Faux Semblant, the lesbian artist, like the exhibition, is a sham, a masquerade, a fiction.

But Wilson's masquerade is of a highly polished and professional kind. Wilson is deploying a deconstructionist strategy to parody the museum exhibition which "mythologizes a particular artist through the use of a few dramatically positioned works" and elegant display.[1] If Sherman designs female subjects through affects, pose and setting, Wilson uses the procedures by which the institutional authority and wealth of the museum canonize a masculinist, heterosexist, and racist history of art. By constructing an exhibition devoted to a fictitious lesbian artist, Wilson simultaneously underscores exclusionary institutional practices and the ease with which the museum can manipulate a few artifacts in order to *create* canonized artists. *Fauve Semblant* demonstrates that the authority of art-historical narratives lies in typeface as much as historical artifacts; Peter's single extant painting provides a pretext for the orchestration of the biographical narrative upon which canonicity depends.

Wilson refuses to provide a "convincing" biography of a unified and idealized lesbian heroine, but the understated humor she embeds in the banal texts addresses and thereby constitutes a (specific) group of lesbian viewers privy to a set of in-jokes. The dominant culture's exclusionary language is replaced by the exclusionary language of a marginalized group. *Fauve Semblant* does not offer "the lesbian woman" to its diverse audience; instead, it allows individual lesbian spectators to constitute themselves as members of a lesbian art-viewing public with a shared culture.

Actual women are the materials of performance artist Suzanne Lacy's work, which is not to claim that these women are transparent signs of "womanhood" appropriated by the artist. Rather, artist and female collaborators perform particular representations of women. A committed feminist and artist-activist, Lacy has long been interested in representing older women. Two performances separated by eleven years reveal the continuities and discontinuities of her work (Figs. 4 and 5). In her 1976 performance, *Inevitable Associations*, Lacy sat in the lobby of the Los Angeles Biltmore Hotel for four hours while a makeup artist transformed her appearance into that of an old woman. Subsequently, three elderly friends of Lacy dressed her in black clothes similar to their own. The four women then continued to sit in the lobby of the hotel quietly talking (in the photograph, Lacy is the second woman from the right).

In May 1987, *The Crystal Quilt* was performed in Minneapolis, Minnesota. As several thousand people looked down from balconies, four hundred and thirty elderly women walked into a vast space filled with tables organized in a grid pattern. Sitting at tables in groups of four, the women removed black tablecloths to reveal red and yellow cloths; the quilt-like pattern of colored squares was further elaborated by the women's slowly choreographed hand movements on the tables. While the women spoke among themselves, their pre-recorded discussions regarding aging, death and life histories were broadcast over loudspeakers. Eventually, the audience was invited to join the women participants on the floor.

*Inevitable Associations* and *The Crystal Quilt* differ not only in scale but intention. While both designate a social activity — sitting in a lobby, quilting — as "Art," the earlier performance is a modestly understated enactment of invisibility. The young woman artist who claims public attention in the display of her transformation — the make-over — subsequently disappears into a social configuration to which the voyeuristic gaze is all but indifferent. The power of this performance resides in the fact that Lacy will (in all likelihood) become an old woman. Rather than attempting to "identify" with a marginalized group to which she bears no relation, Lacy performs her "inevitable" future. In so doing, she predicts her disappearance from view but also describes her future community.

If *Inevitable Associations* was a performance of invisibility and dissimulation, *The Crystal Quilt* is a grand pageant of collective visibility. While the earlier work valorized the artist's personal transformation, the later performance removes the artist from the tableau and attempts to represent a collective presence. Perhaps the greatest difference between the two performances lies in the conception of their purpose and duration. *The Crystal Quilt* was the culmination of a three year collective labor on the part of a wide coalition of elderly women and community organizations as well as businesses. Lacy describes three criteria by which she measures the success of her work: 1) the quality of experience for participants and audience; 2) the performance's efficacy as a model that can be applied to other issues and circumstances; and 3) the lifespan of the collective actions initiated by the performance.[2] Rather than a personal exercise in transformation and imaginative identification, Lacy's performance art becomes a vehicle for the mobilization of women and community agencies in relation to particular issues, in this case the needs of elderly women (Lacy's 1980 *River Meetings*, for example, was catalyzed by Louisiana's nonratification of the ERA).

Performance artist Adrian Piper also conceives of her art as a form of social intervention. However, while Lacy orchestrates spectacular events as symbolic collective gestures, Piper produces a work which is at once intimate in scale and coolly confrontational in tenor. Piper is black and the material of her art is difference rather than commonality. Highly educated and light-skinned, Piper repeatedly encounters racism by white persons who assume she is white, and that they are figuratively "alone" in the room, that is, alone among themselves. Piper's "reactive guerilla performance," *Calling Card #1*, functions as a confrontational but politely impersonal response. Deploying the language of conflict management — the rhetorical style of public information — Piper addresses the individual as a social pattern (Fig. 6). The calling card's printed message converts the personal confrontation into a statistical probability: some white people make racist remarks; some white people agree with or laugh at racist remarks. Piper's calling card is an anticipation of a likelihood.

Enacted at dinners and cocktail parties, academic meetings and art openings, Piper's guerilla performance constitutes her self-portrayal; her card represents her body as black. A social act — handing out the card — and a text — the card's message — together redefine the way her body is read. The recipient of the card must contend with her assertion and regard her — see her — differently.

What is particularly interesting is the fact that Piper's self-representation is initiated by the racist remark. If white people did not make racist remarks, she would not be compelled to produce herself as Other: she would not hand out the card. Adrian Piper produces herself in order to arrest racist conversation. Her calling-card simultaneously confronts people with their own, often unacknowledged, racism and requests a modification of their behavior, at least in her presence. Do not feel free to be racist in front of me; I am black. Furthermore, if I am black, you cannot assume you know who is white. You cannot be confident that you are alone among yourselves. So modify — edit — your behavior (even if your beliefs do not change). In the end, interpersonal behavior functions as the locus of Piper's political intervention. She has stated that she is "interested in acceptance of cultural and ethnic others as a social norm of etiquette, not just a moral or political norm."[3]

As a black woman who can "pass" as white, Piper occupies a position in-between classificatory categories and the boundaries of stereotypes. Her ambiguous status subjects her to racism of a particular sort: not only is she forced to be an "unwilling witness" to "confidential" racist remarks, "the hostile underside of the system of norms," but she is also subjected to callous scrutiny (where is the "blackness"?) and hostility (why does she insist she's black, anyway?). Piper makes the confusion and anger elicited by her very person the material of her art. The power of her work lies precisely in its capacity to make people uncomfortable and unsure, to not only provoke but sustain the audience's confusion.

If *Calling Card #1* is a reactive performance, a self-disclosure initiated by racist behavior, Piper's video installation, *Cornered*, is an aggressive and impressively bewildering provocation of the art gallery viewer (Fig. 7). From a video monitor mounted on a table pushed up against the room's corner and blocked by another upturned table, Piper quietly addresses the viewer in an archly formal, sometimes sardonic tone. On the video screen, a discreetly attired Piper clasps her hands in front of her and directly faces the camera in the manner of a newscaster. Calmly and deliberately, she begins with a confrontation:

> I'm black. Now let's deal with the social fact of the fact of my stating it together. Maybe you don't see why we have to deal with it together. Maybe you think this is just my problem and that I should deal with it by myself, but it's not just my problem. It's our problem. For

example, it's our problem if you think I'm making an unnecessary fuss about my racial identity, if you don't see why I have to announce it this way . . . but the larger problem would be your feeling antagonized and turned-off at all. Why does my telling you who I am have this effect? Do you feel affronted or embarrassed or accused? I think we need to look more closely at why my identifying myself as black seems to you to be making a fuss. I think we need to keep in mind that it's only a fuss if it disturbs your presumption that I'm white. So perhaps the solution is for you not to make that presumption. That certainly would be better for me because I don't look forward to your confusion and hostility at all. I really would prefer not to disturb you. But you see I have no choice. I'm cornered. If I tell you who I am, you become nervous and uncomfortable or antagonized. But if I don't tell you who I am then I have to pass for white and why should I have to do that?

Identity here is polarized into black and white. The black speaker presumes her audience is white; only a few subsequent clauses, such as "if you consider yourself white," recognize the possibility that the art gallery viewer might also be black — or Native American or Chinese. Piper exclusively confronts white persons, but the opposition is subsequently obfuscated. Through a startling series of logical deductions based on "statistical facts," Piper asserts that most purportedly white persons in the United States share black ancestry and hence are actually black "according to entrenched conventions of social classification." A biologically essentialist conception of race unfurls an ethical and political problem. If, like Piper, most white Americans are light-skinned blacks, why does she announce her identity while others choose not to? Piper concludes, "Now that you have this information about your black ancestry, you have some difficult choices to make." The camera closes in on Piper's face and she asks, "What are you going to do?"

Piper's installation corners the addressee in a discomforting way. There is no absorption in a voyeuristic fiction, no safe withdrawal to a detached contemplation of a representation. The talking head bears the mimetic force of an actual person's presence, an unblinking, unrelenting returned gaze of admonishment. Moreover, the lecture is confrontational and patronizing, the racial categories inflexible and exclusionary, the argument's premises fundamentally and disturbingly essentialist, the artist's intention difficult to assess. It is entirely possible to feel manipulated, misrepresented, and irritated without being certain why. This is what is troubling and effective. Piper undoes complacent assumptions regarding the categories of race and racial identity at the same time that she further entrenches them. Rather than discarding the categories in a gesture that would conform to her own shifting bodily status (is she white or black?), she reinscribes that terminology onto her own body and implicates the addressee's body as well (I am black but probably you are too). Race, according to Piper, is intellectually, politically and personally confusing, but to ignore it is a privilege no one should be allowed.

Mary Kelly's recently completed work, *Interim*, focuses on an under-represented age group of women, the middle-aged woman, the woman stranded "between two conditions referred to as young and old" (Figs. 8 and 9). Ignored yet pathologized by Freud, Dora's mother epitomizes for Mary Kelly,

> the dilemma for the older woman of representing her femininity, her sexuality, her desire when she is no longer desirable. She can neither look forward, as the young girl does, to being a woman, that is, having the fantasized body of maturity; nor can she return to the ideal moment of maternity — ideal in that it allows her to occupy the position of actively desiring subject without transgressing the socially acceptable definition of woman as mother. She is looking back at something lost, acknowledging perhaps that 'being a woman' was only a brief moment in her life.[4]

Composed of four parts *Corpus* (Body), *Pecunia* (Money), *Historia* (History), and *Potestas* (Power), *Interim* is a highly self-conscious and ambitious essay on the female subject's continual construction of self/ves within history, particularly the recent history of psychoanalytic theory and the women's movement. Part I, *Corpus*, arrays three narrative and image panels in five groups entitled *Menacé*, *Appel*, *Supplication*, *Erotisme*, and *Extase* after nineteenth-century French neuropathologist J. M. Charcot's classification of the stages of hysteria. While Charcot's photographic records of women's bodily performances of illness were integral to his specularization of madness, Kelly replaces these *attitudes passionelles* with the poses of "emblematic articles of clothing" and handwritten first-person accounts. At once sarcastic and melancholic, melodramatic and aloof, the photographed items of clothing impersonate the expressivity accorded women's (staged) bodies. Leather jacket, handbag, white dress, boots, and black nightgown simultaneously function as objects of the medical gaze, fetish substitutes for women's bodies, subjects of romantic elaboration and fantasy, fashion commodities bought, sold and desired.

Juxtaposed to the contrived gestures of the articles of clothing, the first-person narratives function as figurations of an historical shift in the conceptualization of mental illness, the shift from Charcot's visual theater to the linguistic one of Freud and Lacan. In addition, the diaristic stories allude to the pivotal role of consciousness-raising groups in the women's movement. Eliminating images of the female body, Kelly insists that the gallery patron *listen*, not look.

Women rather than Woman provide *Corpus* with its enunciative subjects. Based on an archive of (overheard and shared) conversations compiled over a three-year period, the voices of *Corpus* are multiple and fragmentary. Prosaic yet tantalizing, these first-person narratives are the stuff of private self-disclosure, confessions of forlorn attempts to represent the body to oneself through the discourses of medicine, fashion, mass media, and romantic fiction. However, if Kelly carefully describes women's continual construction of bodies and selves *within* culture and history, she nonetheless evokes a body unmarked and unmapped in terms of racial and ethnic categories. Within dominant cultural institutions, to be unmarked is to be read as "white." As Piper's art demonstrates, within this (white) context, to not specify is to enjoy the privilege of whiteness. Kelly's multiplicity of voices maintains the cohesion of a specific milieu. The narratives of *Corpus* afford the reader glimpses of the privileged "lifestyle" of certain relatively affluent white middle-aged women. The work's successful dispersal of a unified female identity must, therefore, be explicitly qualified in these terms (a qualification critics seldom make).

In contrast to Kelly, the body is reintroduced in the work of British photographer Jo Spence, and it is, moreover, the body of the artist herself. Spence has repeatedly represented herself in collaborative projects with another person. In *Remodelling Photo History* (1981–2), Spence and male collaborator Terry Dennett attempt to denaturalize photographic conventions of representing the female body (Figs. reproduced in text). Conceived as a pedagogical project, the series of photographs demonstrates the ways the female body is differentially produced and disciplined by various photographic genres — medical, ethnographic, police, documentary realist, journalistic, advertising, high art surrealist, and so forth. This may sound similar to Cindy Sherman's enterprise, but there are crucial differences. While Sherman produces a prolonged series of images within a particular "glamorous" style, Spence and Dennett juxtapose a wide variety of genres in labelled pairs. For instance, the

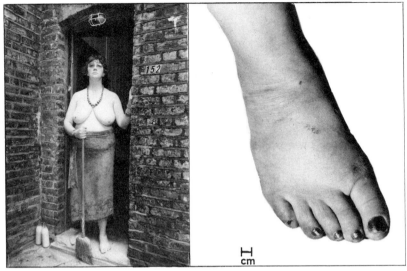

COLONIZATION

Jo Spence and Terry Dennett, *Remodelling Photo History*, 1982. Black and white photographs. 8″ × 10″. Photo: Courtesy of Jo Spence.

ethnographic and medical photograph are placed side by side and are titled "Colonization." A documentary realist image of hands washing clothes is paired with a sensationalist journalistic photograph of a prone naked woman next to an automobile; the pair is labelled "Victimization." The juxtaposition of images accompanied by text not only exposes the formal conventions particular to each genre but also correlates their classificatory functions.

Moreover, in contrast to Sherman's art, the particular resonance of *Remodelling Photo History* resides in the way Spence's body *resists* malleable re-making. Partly this is due to a decison on the photographers' parts to render their images crude paraphrases rather than convincing duplications of conventional styles. Partly this results from the discrepancy between Spence's body and the smaller body-type traditionally constituted as the neutral, anonymous, pliant and thereby ideal female body. In contrast to Sherman's chameleon make-overs, Spence's corporeal visibility functions as a constant term inserted into photographic idioms which differently enframe her. In the obstinant persistence of her body, its refusal of transformation, the photographs dramatize the violence of the body's subjection to the medium's coercive powers. The recalcitrant body underscores the conventionality, artifice and violence of photographic styles. Unlike Sherman's work, these images do not inspire fascination with the ease and magical capacity of photography to make women anew.

This is not to say that *Remodelling Photo History* is an iconoclastic gesture. Rather, the series itself proposes various modes of intervention, not only the unmasking of photographic convention but also parody, ridicule and the appropriation of the camera for the exercise of personal fantasy. If photography acts powerfully, often coercively, upon the woman-model-object, its power can nonetheless be usurped and wielded, even if awkwardly, by the woman-photographer. Underlying all of Spence's work is a deeply-felt conviction that "Anybody can do it" with the implication that the disempowered should do it. Spence states:

> I'm claiming that the camera can be reappropriated. Most people have a camera in the family, yet the way most women are encouraged to use it in the dominant photographic press is utterly banal. At the most they are encouraged to photograph their children—but only in an idealized way. When you talk to women's groups about amateur photography, you find it is difficult for them to give themselves permission to even listen to the fact they don't have to limit themselves to naturalistic photography of the family, that they can actually stage things for the camera or attempt a dialogue with themselves or take different sorts of photographs.[5]

While one could argue that Spence's project is limited by a liberal concern for individual transformation, she envisages the contestation of dominant modes of representation as a political and social enterprise. Unlike Kelly, Spence believes in the political efficacy of women's picturing of their unpictured selves. Intervention here is the *production* of visual images, the attempt to construct new genres somehow between or among pre-existent ones.

Spence's collaborative project, *Carcinoma Excision. Part I: Narratives of Dis-ease*, begins a (re)picturing of her body subsequent to breast cancer and a lumpectomy (Figs. 10 and 11). Rather than speaking from a privileged position as autonomous artistic subject, Spence chooses to collaborate with a doctor, Tim Sheard. Subjectivity, she suggests, is produced within an interactive exchange and within a set of power relations. Woman artist and male doctor collaborate in the production of images which lie uneasily between medical, artistic and mass media discourses and iconographies. If

Kelly's work maps social, scientific and psychoanalytic discourses onto textual and symbolic figurations of the body, Spence's photographic representation of her corporeal self is the outcome of a decidedly social practice. While Kelly attempts to disengage the female subject from its objectification in sight, Spence is compelled to render the tabooed body repeatedly and variously visible.

Combining prostitutes' testimonies and statistical sociological "facts," Carol Jacobsen's *Prostitution Project* attempts to harness public support for the abolition of all laws against prostitution (Fig. 12). Jacobsen, a white Michigan artist, began the project in 1987 by transcribing the statements of prostitutes who worked the streets of Detroit. Thus far, the work consists of three videotapes: *Street Sex*, *Night Voices*, and *Cheryl*, as well as video and photo-text installations, textual and photo-essays and a "Fact Sheet on Prostitution." *Street Sex* intersperses a series of (paid) interviews with prostitutes just released from jail with footage of women walking the streets at night. During the interviews, the women hold the microphone, look at the camera and describe their arrest, their nights in jail, the reasons they work the streets, and the dangers they encounter there.

Jacobsen perceives her project as a documentary and activist enterprise. Her explicitly stated goal is to educate women regarding prostitution in order to eradicate stereotypical views which alienate women into two groups, Good Women (virgins/ wives/ feminists) and Bad Women (whores/ victims). Jacobsen attempts to place the issue of prostitution within the larger feminist discourse regarding women's rights to control their bodies. Given that the women's movement has been dominated by middle-class white women, it is not surprising that freedom of choice regarding abortion has been a central feminist concern while the rights of prostitutes have not. Jacobsen emphasizes that the criminalization of prostitution targets only certain women: the poor, non-white female prostitute is most often subjected to the economic, physical and psychological harassment of the police and courts. Prostitutes are oppressed not because of their sexual activity but because of their race and class. This is Jacobsen's "Fact Sheet":

* 10–20% of all prostitutes are street workers.
* 85–90% of prostitutes who are arrested work on the streets.
* 40% of all street prostitutes are women of color.
* 85% of prostitutes who are jailed are women of color.

The prostitute's body is the volatile site of discourses of sexuality, political order, forensic and medical technologies, race, class and gender. Jacobsen's activist art competes, therefore, with the technologies of public information. In response, the artist chooses to deploy its materials: statistical facts, video documentation, dissemination beyond high art venues. Jacobsen's work communicates the values of urgency and expediency rather than self-reflexivity; clearly, this is not an art which situates itself within an autonomous aesthetic discourse. Instead, the woman artist usurps the authority of the documentary style as an efficacious political tool.

One cannot minimize the risks inherent to such a project. Even while attempting to allow the poor, black prostitute to speak for herself, the middle-class white woman controls her representation. If activist commitments deem the risks worth taking, representing the disenfranchised nonetheless remains a project fraught with problems. In contrast to Jacobsen's tactics of social documentary, the photography of black artist Lorna Simpson is catalyzed by an angry dissatisfaction with the documentary enterprise (Fig. 13). While both artists wish to disrupt stereotypical views of the socio-political Other, Simpson attempts to thwart and thereby deconstruct the ideological operations of an "objective" documentary style.

Most of Simpson's work consists of serial arrangements of polaroid images accompanied by texts. In *Gestures/Reenactments* (1985), for instance, seven photographs depict the torso of a black man in T-shirt and pants, his arms crossed. Each image is accompanied by a text, among them, "prisoner, orderly, cook, some non-professional laborer," "Sometimes Sam stands like his mother," and "So who's your hero? Me and my running buddy. How his running buddy was standing when they thought he had a gun. How Larry was standing when he found out." By interjecting a multiplicity of connotations, the artist short-circuits a conventional reading of the black man as anonymous representative of the black race, the poor man, the working man and so forth. The same pose and the same man provide figurations of a prisoner, Sam, his mother, Larry upon hearing the news, Larry's presumably misread running buddy. Refusing to individuate the sitter through the conventions of the portrait, Simpson, like Sherman, emphasizes that the legibility of the photographic image conventionally relies on the inexorable power of stereotypes. Imagining a prisoner, one might be startled to see Sam's mother traced upon a black man's body.

While *Gestures/Reenactments* appends discrete narratives to dif-

ferent photographs, *Guarded Conditions*, 1989, produces two oscil-
lating readings of the same woman's body. "Sex Attacks, Skin
Attacks," the text describes her dual oppression. The black woman's
body is alternately impinged by her gender and race. Her visibility
requires guarded conditions to protect her from racial and sexual
violence; indeed, the woman must be guarded from the viewer as
well. Simpson distances the viewer through a number of means:
seriality, segmented images, the back view. In so doing, she disal-
lows conceits integral to the ideological function of much documentary photography: the privileged viewer's empathetic identification
with the sitter, the pretense of mutual conversation, the reassurance
of a "shared humanity." If the insidious naturalizing mechanisms of
one idiom are thereby avoided, others are encountered. *Guarded
Conditions* moves the black woman's body into the high art context,
but her glossy containment, her aloof removal, may house her there
all too easily — it is difficult to create an art which doesn't aestheti-
cize and thereby commodify the body. Lorna Simpson's self-imposed
task is not an easy one.

In Cindy Sherman's recent untitled work, (Fig. 14), imposture
continues, but now within the field of high art. If Sherman appropriated the phallic camera of the film industry in her early work (see
Fig. 2), she now assumes the position of great "master" painters.
Indeed, by producing a pastiche of Raphael's *La Fornarina*, Sherman not only impersonates Raphael, but the sons who paid homage
to him, Ingres and Picasso. Moreover, *La Fornarina* is purportedly
the portrait of Raphael's mistress and thus epitomizes an androcentric fantasy which conflates visual and carnal possession (Picasso's
obsessive elaborations depicted the artist and model in coitus). Pur-
posefully clumsy, overbearing, and ridiculous, Sherman's molded
body parts exaggerate the impositions of the male painter's brush as
it (sh)apes the female body.

Carmelita Tropicana is the persona of a Cuban lesbian performance artist (Fig. 15). In this role, Tropicana delivers the hack-
neyed trappings of Latina femininity. Tropicana first gained notori-
ety in the Manhattan lesbian community that attended her ongoing
parodic talk show staged at the WOW Cafe (1984). Tropicana's
mock femininity can be understood as a form of distancing from
gender identification. Her hyperbolic femininity underscores gender
as a performative construction, an assumed stance as artificial as
feathered boas and wigs. Another Tropicana imposture, her alter-
(gendered)ego Julio Iglesia further travesties the construction of ster-

eotypic Latin heterosexual roles. This alternation of masquerades is the grotesque theatricalization of the confines of gender and ethnic identification in a heterosexist society. To sing, "for all the girls I've loved," the lesbian adopts an insipidly patronizing male voice. Nevertheless, if heterosexist culture's clichés are confining, lesbian appropriation at least undermines their univocality with irreverent humor.

But humor requires a shared culture. In Tropicana's performances, the excessive foregrounding of a staged femininity and masculinity derives its significance from its particular social context. It has been argued that the recuperation of lesbian camp and butch-femme bar culture functions as a form of resistance to cultural conformity and disciplined norms of sexual decorum.[6] This is not to say that the meaning of this performance is read uniformly by a particular constituency. Tropicana cannot speak to or for a singular, coherent spectator. As the work constitutes an audience, it also represents the tensions among members of that audience. The potential and limitations of the stratagem of gender *as drag* are presently the subject of important heated debates among lesbian/feminist theorists.[7] Suffice it to say, performances like Tropicana's generate contradictory claims regarding the possibility of representing a lesbian desire that is *not* an impersonation of male heterosexual desire. Tropicana's "oppositional appropriation" may be criticized as a repetition of heterosexual positions, but I would argue that the debate provoked by her abuse of available dominant materials is itself constitutive of a commmunity and set of concerns.

Since the early important work of performance artist Carolee Schneeman, many women performance artists like Tropicana have explicitly addressed desire, sexuality and violence in their work. In the 1980s, Karen Finley, for example, undressed, rubbed food over her body and enacted various male and female personae who scream narratives of sexual abuse, rape and violence. Porno-film star and former prostitute Annie Sprinkle combines self-display (asking a member of the audience to describe her labia) and formal slide shows attesting to the pleasures and displeasures, advantages and disadvantages, of working in the "sex industry." These women's performances provide one context within which to see the work of West-Coast artist, Johanna Went. In contrast to Finley and Sprinkle, however, Went does not make her body the singular locus of her art.

In Went's imaginative extravaganzas, there is no fixed image of her body (Fig. 16). Indeed, there are few discrete female or male bodies. Rather there is a constellation of scatological figures, vaginal and phallic masquerades. Her kaleidoscope of hallucinatory puppets and masked characters creates a series of projections—"turds" and raw eggs, breasts and zombies, "sewage demons" and "compassion containers," toilet water and "Geraldo's evil children." In Went's performances, corporeal dramas are orchestrated as the actions of a set of characters. Toilet water chases after the turd; the giant mouth-box must be continually fed shovel-size spoonfuls of food; the gargantuan penis is contained by the condom; the expansive egg billows like a sail across the stage; the giant vagina pulses violently clamoring for attention. To the pounding rhythm of music, every orifice enacts its desire; the containment of the passions requires tremendous energy and some violence. The drama is also, however, a comedy; the frenzy a form of slapstick. The excesses of Went's performances suggest carnival as well as infantile sexuality. Certainly, this choreographed chaos can be read as a nostalgia for the Bahktinian unbounded body as well as the polymorphously perverse stages of infancy. While the regressed infantilism of Finley's performances renders the body vulnerable, subject to abuse and violence, Went's dispersed anatomical organs are powerfully lustful and seemingly insensate to pain; they are monsters of a sort but they are monsters which collaboratively perform Went's undisciplined fantasies. Dispersed as specular object, her desiring female body is enacted by an ensemble of imaginative projections.

The feminist commitment to redefine the terms of representing women is merely twenty years old. This portfolio attests to a dual heritage: the critique or suppression of misrepresentations as well as the claims for producing or reclaiming (self)representations. The binary—critique and production—is misleading, however. A representation always operates within a field of other representations; to represent the female body in a certain way is to enter into a dialogue with other works, to assert allegiances as well as competing claims. The production of images of female bodies cannot be seen to be antithetical to the critical deconstruction of dominant modes of representation. Rather, the efficacy of different representational strategies is intensely debated; the question is as much *how* to represent female bodies as it is *why* to represent them.

For the feminist artist representing female bodies, one dilemma is the role of visibility itself. After all, the history of women's visibility is predominantly the history of women's objectification and oppression. To produce images of women, to perform female, is, therefore, to take responsibility for what it is to make bodies visible. Some artists, such as Mary Kelly, have refused to offer the female body to sight. But if visibility continually risks perpetuating the objectification of women, invisibility in itself provides no simple or easy answers. Rather, the burden of resistance is displaced onto the written and emblematic substitutes. Whether textual or visual (or both), the feminist representation of female bodies must contend with dominant society's all too easy conflation of the generality Woman with ideologically prescriptive "norms": Woman as white, middle-class, heterosexual, youthful, and untouched by disease. If, in contrast to Kelly, other artists have risked repeating various specular regimes, from aesthetic to forensic, from cinematic to burlesque, they have done so not only to deconstruct those regimes but also to make often marginalized women visible both within society at large and for and among other women. The embodied female spectators addressed and constituted by these works have, perhaps, been underplayed in this essay. To represent is always, of course, to exclude.

## NOTES

[1]Millie Wilson, unpublished artist's statement, 1989.

[2]Suzanne Lacy, "Speak-Easy," *New Art Examiner*, October 1982.

[3]Quoted in Lowery S. Sims, "Mimicry, Xenophobia, Etiquette and Other Social Manifestations: Adrian Piper's Observations from the Margins," in *Adrian Piper. Reflections 1967–1987* (New York: Alternative Museum, 1987), n.p.

[4]Mary Kelly, E. Cowie and N. Bryson, "Invisible Bodies: Mary Kelly's INTERIM," *New Formations*, Summer 1987, p. 11.

[5]Jo Spence, *Putting Myself in the Picture. A Political, Personal and Photographic Autobiography* (Seattle: The Real Comet Press, 1988), p. 209.

[6]See Sue-Ellen Case, "Towards a Butch-Femme Aesthetic," in *Feminist Perspectives on Contemporary Women's Drama*, ed. Lynda Hart (Ann Arbor: University of Michigan Press), forthcoming.

[7]See, for example, Teresa de Lauretis, "Sexual Indifference and Lesbian Representation," *Theatre Journal*, May 1988, and Jill Dolan, "The Dynamics of Desire: Sexuality and Gender in Pornography and Performance," *Theatre Journal*, May 1987, and Jill Dolan, "Desire Cloaked in a Trenchcoat," *The Drama Review*, Spring 1989.

# Contemporary Representations of Women's Bodies

Fig. 1. Virginia Maksymowicz, *History of Art*, ongoing series. Cast paper and acrylic. Life-size. Photo: Blaise Tobia.

Fig. 2. Cindy Sherman, *Untitled Film Still*, 1978. Black and white photograph. 8″ x 10″. Photo: Courtesy of Metro Pictures, N.Y., N.Y.

Fig. 3. Millie Wilson, *Fauve Semblant. Peter (A Young English Girl)*, 1989. Installation. Photo: Courtesy of the artist.

Fig. 4. Suzanne Lacy, *Inevitable Associations*, 1976. Performance. Photo: Susan Mogul.

Fig. 5. Suzanne Lacy, *The Crystal Quilt*, 1987. Performance. Photo: Peter Latner.

Fig. 6. Adrian Piper, *Calling Card #1*, 1986. Guerilla performance with calling card, 3.5″ x 2″ (for dinners and parties). Photo: Courtesy of John Weber Gallery, N.Y., N.Y.

Fig. 7. Adrian Piper, *Cornered*, 1988. Video, table, lighting, birth certificates, size variable (17 minutes). Photo: Courtesy of John Weber Gallery, N.Y., N.Y.

Figs. 8 and 9. Mary Kelly, *Corpus* (Part I *Interim*), 1984–85. Preliminary artwork for *Extase*. Black and white photograph and chinagraph. 36″ x 48″. Photo: Courtesy of artist.

Figs. 10 and 11. Jo Spence and Tim Sheard, *Carcinoma Excision. Part I: Narratives of Dis-Ease*, 1990. Color photographs. 24″ x 36″. Photo: Courtesy of Jo Spence.

Fig. 12. Carol Jacobsen, *Prostitution Project: Street Sex*, 1989. Videotape. Photo: Courtesy of artist.

Fig. 13. Lorna Simpson, *Guarded Conditions*, 1989. 18 color polaroid prints with 21 plastic plaques. 131″ x 91″. Photo: Courtesy of Josh Baer Gallery, N.Y., N.Y.

Fig. 14. Cindy Sherman, *Untitled*, 1989. Color photographs. 48.25″ x 61.5″. Photo: Courtesy of Metro Pictures, N.Y., N.Y.

Fig. 15. Carmelita Tropicana, The Songbird of Cuba, Untitled, 1990. Performance. Photo: Dona Ann McAdams.

Fig. 16. Johanna Went, Untitled, 1983. Performance. Photo: Anna Barrado.

1

FAUVE SEMBLANT
Peter (A Young English Girl)

3

4

Dear Friend,

I am black.

I am sure you did not realize this when you made/laughed at/agreed with that racist remark. In the past, I have attempted to alert white people to my racial identity in advance. Unfortunately, this invariably causes them to react to me as pushy, manipulative, or socially inappropriate. Therefore, my policy is to assume that white people do not make these remarks, even when they believe there are no black people present, and to distribute this card when they do.

I regret any discomfort my presence is causing you, just as I am sure you regret the discomfort your racism is causing me.

Sincerely yours,
Adrian Margaret Smith Piper

*Extase*

The white dress is part of a plot to escape. From what I'm not quite sure, but all through the cold, dark and different winter I have been planning it. Learned academic by day, and by night, secret reader of holiday brochures and eater of maple sugar candy, planning how the three of us would meet in Miami, happy family reunited - father, mother, child, against a backdrop of blue sky and pounding surf of course. I have told no one. Finally, the day arrives. I pack the suitcase with devotion, the way a bride would do her trousseau: no jeans, no boots, no leather jacket or coat of any kind and nothing black, only brightly colored blouses, loosely fitting trousers, shorts, halters, high-heeled shoes and all the jewelry I ever wanted to wear and didn't have a chance to. And the dress. I refuse to wear a coat even to the airport in anticipation of the happy metamorphosis that will inevitably take place when I emerge eight hours later. And it does. The air is hot and thick. I feel it soldering the bits and pieces of my body into something tangible, entire. I can be seen, imagine men are looking at me, even look at them sometimes. Soon, they arrive, seem much shorter, fatter, whiter than I had remembered, but it doesn't matter. We are together, I am glad. What's more, today is Easter Sunday. Naturally, I'm wearing the white dress - simple, silk, embroidered bodice, gathered at the waist, full skirt falling just below my knee, and thinking, thank god no one will see me, (I mean everyone is in New York) and wonder who am I wearing this for anyway. Not him, he doesn't notice and the prospect of negotiating Disneyland has already given him a headache. Then my angelic son tells everyone, "Look at my Mommy." The riddle solved. I am transported in a halo of fluorescent light to the land of "good-enough-mothers." The motel manager waves his magic wand and says, "Please come with me into the dining room where you will feast on champagne, strawberries and cream, the Seven Dwarfs will play the Brandenburg Concertos and I'm quite sure you will live happily ever after." And we do.

10

11

SEX ATTACKS | SKIN ATTACKS | SEX ATTACKS | SKIN ATTACKS | SEX ATTACKS | SKIN ATTACKS | SEX ATTACKS | SKIN ATTACKS | SEX ATTACKS

13

**15**

LOIS-ANN YAMANAKA

# KALA GAVE ME ANYKINE ADVICE
# ESPECIALLY ABOUT FILIPINOS
# WHEN I MOVED TO PAHALA

Don't whistle in the dark
or you call the Filipino man
from the old folks home across your house
who peek at you already from behind
the marungay tree, the long beans
in front of his face;

he will cut across your backyard
from the papaya tree side
when you whistle the Filipino love call,
then take you when you leave your house
to buy jar mayonnaise for your mother
from the superette.

Then he going drag you to his house
and tie you to the vinyl chair,
the one he sit on outside all day,
and smile at you with the yellow teeth
and cut off your bi-lot with the cane knife.
He going fry um in crisco for dinner.
That's what Kala told me.

Don't sleep with your feet to the door.
Don't sleep with your hair wet,
Kala said, or you going be like Darlene Ebanez
who run around her house naked
and nobody can stop her when she like that.
She take her two fingers

and put um up her bi-lot.
That's what you not supposed to do, Kala said,
the Bible said so that's why.

Don't clip your toenails at night.
And no wear tight jeans or
Felix going follow you home with his blue Valiant
when you go plantation camp side past
the big banyan tree, past the sugar mill,
past the pile of bagasse, down your dirt road.
Kala said he rape our classmate Abby already
and our classmate Nancy even if he get one
girlfriend senior in high school
and his father one cop.

Kala told me no use somebody's deodorant
or I going catch their b.o.
No make ugly faces or my nose going be pig
and my eyes Japanee.
And no tell nobody the words she tell me.
Nobody. Especially the word she told me today.
Ok. Ok. The word is cremation.

The graveyard man he sew all the holes
on your body shut with dental floss, Kala said;
your eyes, your nose, your mouth,
your belly button, your okole hole
and yea, even your bi-lot so the gas
cannot escape when he shove you in the brick oven.

Watch out for the Filipino man, Kala said,
he eyeing my black dog, Melba,
he eyeing my baby goat
that my father caught for me up Mauna Kea,
the small green papayas on my tree.

MARGE PIERCY

# HEEL SHOULD NOT BE AN INSULT

The true humility of heels:
pale, battered, wrinkled, swollen.
We may paint our toes, but naked
heels are dumb as cows' behinds.

Patient, stubborn, vulnerable
they follow us looking back
like children in cars making faces
through the rearview window.

In undressing a lover, even
foot fetishists must blink:
the sock, the stocking peeled,
the unappetizing bony fruit.

We are always landing on them
slamming them into pavement,
jumping out of trucks, forcing
them into stirrups and pedals.

Cats walk on their toes like ballerinas
but we, ape cousins, go shuffling
and what we leave in the sand
is the imprint of our heels coming home.

They are the periods under the leaping
exclamation point, gravity's mooring,
our anchor to earth, the callused
blind familiar of soil, rock, root.

Let me rub your angular barnacled
hull with unguents and massage you
tenderly, my little flatiron shaped
heroes, my hard laboring heels.

SUSAN BORDO

# "MATERIAL GIRL":
# THE EFFACEMENTS OF
# POSTMODERN CULTURE

## 1. Plasticity as Postmodern Paradigm

In a culture in which organ transplants, life-extension machinery, microsurgery and artificial organs have entered everyday medicine, we seem on the verge of practical realization of the seventeenth-century imagination of the body as machine. But if we seem to have technically and technologically realized that conception, it can also be argued that metaphysically we have deconstructed it. In the early modern era, machine imagery helped to articulate a totally determined human body whose basic functionings the human being was helpless to alter. The then dominant metaphors for this body — clocks, watches, collections of springs — imagined a system that is set, wound up, whether by nature or God the watchmaker, ticking away in predictable, orderly manner, regulated by laws over which the human being has no control. Understanding the system, we can help it to perform efficiently, and intervene when it malfunctions. But we cannot radically alter the configuration of things.

Pursuing this modern, determinist fantasy to its limits, fed by the currents of consumer capitalism, modern ideologies of the self, and their crystallization in the dominance of "American" mass culture, Western science and technology have now arrived, paradoxically but predictably (for it was a submerged, illicit element in the mechanist conception all along) at a new, "postmodern" imagination of human freedom from bodily determination. Gradually and surely, a technology that was first aimed at the replacement of malfunctioning parts has generated an industry and an ideology fueled by fantasies of re-arranging, transforming, and correcting, an ideology of limitless improvement and change, defying the historicity, the mortality, and indeed the very materiality of the body. In place of that

106

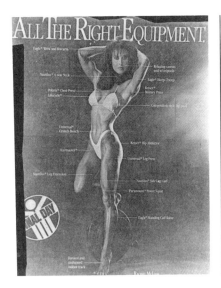

**Phyllis Diller's Resumé**

- Hard contact lenses. 1960.
- Soft contact lenses. 1970.
- Teeth straightened. 1970. Dr. Budd Rubin (San Diego)
- Complete face-lift: nose job (rhinoplasty), eyes (above and below), neck job. 1971. Dr. Franklin L. Ashley (Los Angeles)
- Breast reduction. 1974. Dr. Franklin L. Ashley
- Tummy tuck. 1976. Dr. Franklin L. Ashley
- Teeth bonded. 1980. Dr. Ronald Goldstein (Atlanta)
- Mini-lift (face). 1981. Dr. Franklin L. Ashley
- Teeth bonded. 1984. Dr. Alfred Menzies (Los Angeles)
- Teeth bonded. 1985. Dr. John Lake (Palm Springs)
- Brow-lift. 1985. Dr. Michael Elam,
                   Dr. Frederick Berkowitz (Newport Beach)
- Nose job. 1985. Dr. Michael Elam,
                  Dr. Frederick Berkowitz
- Under-eye lift. 1985. Dr. Michael Elam,
                        Dr. Frederick Berkowitz
- Cheek implants. 1985. Dr. Michael Elam,
                        Dr. Frederick Berkowitz
- Eyeliner tattoo. 1985. Dr. Warren Katz (Dallas)
- Chemical peel. 1986. Dr. Michael Elam,
                       Dr. Frederick Berkowitz
- Fat liposuctioned from stomach and injected into deep vertical wrinkles around mouth. 1987. Dr. Steven M. Hoefflin, F.A.C.S. (Santa Monica)

FIG. 1                              FIG. 2

materiality, we now have what I will call "cultural plastic." In place of God the watchmaker, we now have ourselves, the master sculptors of that plastic. This disdain for material limits, and intoxication with freedom, change, and self-determination, is enacted not only on the level of the contemporary technology of the body but in a wide range of contexts, including much of contemporary discourse on the body, both casual and theoretical, popular and academic. In this essay, looking at a variety of these discursive contexts, I will attempt to describe key elements of this paradigm of plasticity, and expose some of its effacements — the material and social realities that it denies or renders invisible.

## 2. Plastic Bodies
(Fig. 1)

"Create a masterpiece, sculpt your body into a work of art," urges *Fit* magazine. "You visualize what you want to look like, and then you create that form." "The challenge presents itself: to rearrange things." "It's up to you to do the chiseling. You become the master sculptress."[1] The precision technology of body-sculpting, once the secret of the Arnold Schwarzeneggers and Rachel McLishes of the professional body-building world, has now become available to anyone who can afford the price of membership in a gym. "I now look

at bodies," (says John Travolta, after training for the movie *Staying
Alive*) "almost like pieces of clay that can be molded."[2] On the medical front, plastic surgery, whose repeated and purely cosmetic
employment has been legitimated by Michael Jackson, Cher and
others, has become a fabulously expanding industry, extending its
domain from nose jobs, face lifts, tummy tucks and breast augmen-
tations to collagen-plumped lips and liposuction-shaped ankles,
calves and buttocks. In 1989, 681,000 procedures were done, up
80% over 1981; over half of these were performed on patients
between the ages of eighteen and thirty-five.[3] The trendy *Details*
magazine describes "surgical stretching, tucking and sucking [as]
another fabulous [fashion] accessory," and invites readers to share
their cosmetic surgery experiences in their monthly column "Knife-
styles of the Rich and Famous" (Fig. 2). In that column, the trans-
portation of fat from one part of the body to another is described as
breezily as changing hats:

> Dr. Brown is an artist. He doesn't just pull and tuck and forget about
> you . . . . He did liposuction on my neck, did the nose job and
> tightened up my forehead to give it a better line. Then he took some
> fat from the side of my waist and injected it into my hands. It goes in

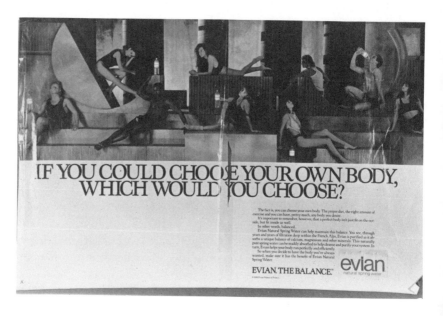

FIG. 3

as a lump, and then he smooths it out with his hands to where it looks good. I'll tell you something, the nose and neck made a big change, but nothing in comparison to how fabulous my hands look. The fat just smoothed out all the lines, the veins don't stick up anymore, the skin actually looks soft and great. [But] you have to be careful not to bang your hands.[4]

Popular culture does not apply any brakes to these fantasies of re-arrangement and self-transformation. Rather, we are constantly told that we can "choose" our own bodies (Fig. 3). "The proper diet, the right amount of exercise and you can have, pretty much, any body you desire," claims Evian. Of course, the rhetoric of choice and self-determination and the breezy analogies comparing cosmetic surgery to fashion accessorizing are deeply mystifying. They efface, not only the inequalities of privilege, money, and time that prohibit most people from indulging in these practices, but the desperation that characterizes the lives of those who do. "I will do anything, *anything*, to make myself look and feel better" says Tina Lizardi (whose "Knifestyle" experience I quoted from above). Medical sci-ence has now designated a new category of "polysurgical addicts" (or, as more casually referred to, "scalpel slaves") who return for

FIG. 4 FIG. 5

operation after operation, in perpetual quest of the elusive yet ruthlessly normalizing goal, the "perfect" body.[5] The dark underside of the practices of body transformation and re-arrangement reveals botched and sometimes fatal operations, exercise addictions, eating disorders. And of course, despite the claims of the Evian ad, one cannot have *any* body that one wants — for not every body will *do*. The very advertisements whose copy speaks of choice and self-determination visually legislate the effacement of individual and cultural difference and circumscribe our choices (Fig. 4).

That we are surrounded by homogenizing and normalizing images — images whose content is far from arbitrary, but instead suffused with the dominance of gendered, racial, class, and other cultural iconography — seems so obvious as to be almost embarrassing to be arguing here. Yet contemporary understandings of the behaviors I have been describing not only construct the situation very differently, but in terms that preempt precisely such a critique of cultural imagery. Moreover, they reproduce, on the level of discourse and interpretation, the same conditions which postmodern bodies enact on the level of cultural practice: a construction of life as plastic possibility and weightless choice, undetermined by history, social location, or even individual biography. A recent *Donahue* show offers my first illustration.

The show's focus was a series of television commercials for Dura-Soft colored contact lenses. In these commercials (as they were originally aired), a woman was shown in a dreamlike, romantic fantasy — for example, parachuting slowly and gracefully from the heavens. The male voiceover then described the woman in soft, lush terms: "If I believed in angels, I'd say that's what she was — an angel, dropped from the sky like an answer to a prayer, with eyes as brown as bark." [significant pause] "No . . . I *don't think so*." [At this point, the tape would be rewound to return us to:] "With eyes as violet as the colors of a child's imagination." The commercial concludes: "DuraSoft colored contact lenses. Get brown eyes a second look" (Fig. 5).

The question posed by Donahue: Is this ad racist? Donahue clearly thought there was controversy to be stirred up here, for he stocked his audience full of women of color and white women to discuss the implications of the ad. But Donahue, apparently, was living in a different decade than most of his audience, who found nothing "wrong" with the ad, and everything "wrong" with any inclinations to "make it a political question." Here are some comments taken from the transcript of the show:

"Why does it have to be a political question? I mean, people perm their hair. It's just because they like the way it looks. It's not something sociological. Maybe black women like the way they look with green contacts. It's to be more attractive. It's not something that makes them — I mean, why do punk rockers have purple hair? Because they feel it makes them feel better." [white woman]

"What's the fuss? When I put on my blue lenses, it makes me feel good. It makes me feel sexy, different, the other woman, so to speak, which is like fun." [black woman]

"I perm my hair, you're wearing makeup, what's the difference?" [ww]

"I want to be versatile . . . having different looks, being able to change from one look to the other." [bw model]

"We all do the same thing, when we're feeling good we wear new makeup, hairstyles, we buy new clothes. So now it's contact lenses. What difference does it make?" [ww]

"It goes both ways . . . Bo Derek puts her hair in cornstalks, or corn . . . or whatever that thing is called. White women try to get tan." [ww]

"She's not trying to be white, she's trying to be different." [about a black woman with blue contact lenses]

"It's fashion, women are never happy with themselves."

"I put them in as toys, just for fun, change. Nothing too serious, and I really enjoy them." [bw][6]

Some things to note here: First, making up, fixing one's hair and so forth are conceived only as free *play*, fun, a matter of creative expression. The one comment that hints at women's (by now depressingly well-documented) dissatisfaction with their appearance trivializes that dissatisfaction and puts it beyond the pale of cultural critique: "It's fashion." What she means is: "It's *only* fashion," whose whimsical and politically neutral vicissitudes supply endless amusement for woman's eternally superficial values. ("Women are never happy with themselves.") If we are never happy with ourselves, it is implied, that is due to our female nature, not to be taken too seriously or made into a "political question." Second, the "contents" of fashion, the specific ideals that women are drawn to embody (ideals that vary historically, racially, and along class and other lines) are seen as arbitrary, without meaning; interpretation is neither required nor even appropriate. Rather, all motivation and value comes from the interest and allure — the "sexiness" — of change and difference itself. Blue contact lenses for black women, it is admitted, make one "other" ("the other woman"). But that "other" is not a racial or cultural "other"; she is "sexy" because of the piquancy, the novelty, the erotics of putting on a different self. *Any* different self would do, it is implied. Closely connected to this is the construction of *all* cosmetic changes as the same: perms for white women, corn rows on Bo Derek, tanning, makeup, changing hairstyles, blue contacts for black women — all are seen as having equal political valance (which is to say *no* political valance) and the same cultural meaning (which is to say *no* cultural meaning) in the heterogeneous yet undifferentiated context of "the things women do" "to look better, be more attractive." The one woman in the audience who offered a different construction of things, who insisted that the styles we aspire to do not simply reflect the free play of fashion or female nature — who went as far, indeed, as to claim that we "are brainwashed to think blond hair and blue eyes is the most beautiful of all," was regarded with hostile silence. Then, a few moments later, someone challenged: "Is there anything *wrong* with blue eyes and blond hair?" The audience enthusiastically applauded this defender of democratic values.

This "conversation" — a paradigmatically postmodern conversation, as I will argue shortly — effaces the same general elements as the rhetoric of body-transformation discussed earlier. First, it effaces the inequalities of social position and the historical origins which, for example, render Bo Derek's corn rows and black women's hair-straightening utterly non-commensurate. On the one hand we have Bo Derek's privilege, not only as so unimpeachably white as to afford an exotic touch of Otherness with no danger of racial contamination, but her trend-setting position as a famous movie star. Contrasting to this, and mediating a black woman's "choice" to straighten her hair, is a cultural history of racist body-discriminations such as the nineteenth-century comb-test, which allowed admission to churches and clubs only to those blacks who could pass through their hair without snagging a fine-tooth comb hanging outside the door. (A variety of comparable tests — the pine-slab test, the brown bag test — determined whether or not one's skin was adequately light to pass muster.)[7]

Second, and following from these historical practices, there is a "disciplinary" reality that is effaced in the construction of all self-transformation as equally arbitrary, all variants of the same trivial

FIG. 6 FIG. 7

game, without differing cultural valance. I use the term "disciplinary" here in the Foucauldian sense, as pointing to practices which do not merely transform, but *normalize* the subject. That is, and to repeat a point made earlier, not every body will do. A recent poll of *Essence* magazine readers revealed that 68% of those who responded wear their hair straightened chemically or by hot comb.[8] "Just 'for fun'?" The kick of being "different"? Looking at the pursuit of beauty as a normalizing discipline, it is clear that not all body-transformations are "the same." The general tyranny of fashion — perpetual, elusive, and instructing the female body in a pedagogy of personal inadequacy and lack — is a powerful discipline for the normalization of *all* women in this culture. But even as we are all normalized to the requirements of appropriate feminine insecurity and preoccupation with appearance, more specific requirements emerge in different cultural and historical contexts, and for different groups. When Bo Derek put her hair in corn rows, she was engaging in normalizing feminine practice. But when Oprah Winfrey admitted on her show that all her life she has desperately longed to have "hair that swings from side to side" when she shakes her head (Fig. 6), she revealed the power of racial as well as gender normal-

FIG. 8                                    FIG. 9

ization, normalization not only to "femininity," but to the Caucasian standards of beauty that still dominate on television, in movies, in popular magazines. Neither Oprah nor the *Essence* readers have creatively or playfully invented themselves here.

DuraSoft knows this, even if Donahue's audience does not. Since the campaign first began, the company has replaced the original, upfront magazine advertisement with a more euphemistic variant, from which the word "brown" has been tastefully effaced. (In case it had become too subtle for the average reader, the model now is black.) [Fig. 7] In the television commercial, a comparable "brownwash" was effected; here "eyes as brown as . . ." was retained, but the derogatory nouns—"brown as boots," "brown as bark"—were eliminated. The announcer simply was left speechless: "eyes as brown as . . . brown as . . .," and then, presumably having been unable to come up with an enticing simile, shifted to "violet." As in the expurgated magazine ad, the television commercial ended: "Get *your* eyes a second look."

When I showed my students these ads, many of them were as dismissive as the Donahue audience, convinced that I was once again turning innocent images and practices into "political issues." I persisted: if racial standards of beauty are not at work here, then why no brown contacts for blue-eyed people? A month later, two of my students triumphantly produced a DuraSoft ad for brown contacts (Fig. 8), from *Essence* magazine, and with an advertising campaign directed solely at black consumers, offering the promise *not* of "getting blue eyes a second look" by becoming excitingly darker, but of "subtly enhancing" already dark eyes, by making them *lighter* brown. The creators of the DuraSoft campaign clearly know that not all "differences" are the same in our culture, and they continue, albeit in ever more mystified form, to exploit and perpetuate that fact.

## 3. Plastic Discourse

The Donahue-DuraSoft show (and indeed, any talk show one might happen to tune to) provides a perfect example of what we might call a postmodern conversation. All sense of history and all ability (or inclination) to sustain cultural criticism, to make the distinctions and discriminations which would permit such criticism, have disappeared. Rather, in this conversation, "anything goes" — and any positioned social critique (for example, the woman who, speaking clearly from consciousness of racial oppression, insisted that the attraction of blond hair and blue eyes has a cultural meaning significantly different from that of purple hair) is immediately de-stabilized. Instead of distinctions, endless *differences* reign — an undifferentiated pastiche of differences, a grab-bag in which no items are assigned any more importance or centrality than any others. Television is, of course, the great teacher here, our prime modeler of plastic pluralism: if one Donahue show features a feminist talking about battered wives, the next day a show will feature mistreated husbands. Incest, exercise addictions, women who love too much, the sex habits of priests, disturbed children of psychiatrists, male strippers — all have their day, all are given equal weight by the great leveler: the frame of the television screen.

This spectacle of difference defeats the ability to sustain coherent political critique. Everything is the same in its unvalanced difference. ("I perm my hair. You're wearing makeup. What's the difference?") Particulars reign, and generality — which collects, organizes and prioritizes, suspending attention to particularity in the interests of connection, emphasis and criticism — is suspect. So, whenever some critically charged generalization was suggested on the Donahue-DuraSoft show, someone else would invariably offer a counter-example—e.g. "I have blue eyes, and I'm a black woman," "Bo Derek wears corn rows"—to fragment the critique. What is remarkable is that people accept these examples *as* "refutations" of social critique. They almost invariably back down, utterly confused as to how to maintain their critical generalization in the face of the de-stabilizing example. Sometimes they qualify, claiming they meant "some" people, not all. But of course, they neither meant all, nor some. They meant *most*—that is, they were trying to make a claim about social or cultural *patterns*—and that is a stance that is increasingly difficult to sustain in a postmodern context, where we are surrounded by endlessly displaced images and no orienting context to make discriminations.

Those who insist on an orienting context (and who therefore do not permit particulars to reign in all their absolute "difference") are seen as "totalizing," that is, as constructing a falsely coherent and morally coercive universe that marginalizes and effaces the experiences and values of others. ("What's *wrong* with blond hair and blue eyes?") As someone who is frequently interviewed by local television and newspaper reporters, I have often found my feminist arguments framed in this way, as they were in a recent article on breast augmentation surgery. After several pages of "expert" recommendations from plastic surgeons, my cautions about the politics of female body transformation (none of them directed against individuals contemplating plastic surgery, all of them of a "cultural" nature) were briefly quoted by the reporter, who then went on to end the piece with a comment on *my* critique—from the director of communications for the American Society of Plastic and Reconstructive Surgery:

> Those not considering plastic surgery shouldn't be too critical of those who do. It's the hardest thing for people to understand. What's important is if it's a problem to that person. We're all different, but we all want to look better. We're just different in what extent we'll go to. But none of us can say we don't want to look the best we can.[9]

With this tolerant, egalitarian stroke, the media liaison of the most powerful plastic surgery lobby in the country presents herself as the protector of "difference" against the homogenizing and stifling regime of the feminist dictator.

\* \* \* \* \* \* \* \* \* \*

Academics do not usually like to think of themselves as embodying the values and preoccupations of popular culture on the plane of high theory or intellectual discourse. We prefer to see ourselves as the de-mystifyers of popular discourse, bringers-to-consciousness-and-clarity rather than unconscious reproducers of culture. Despite what we would *like* to believe of ourselves, however, we are always within the society that we criticize, and never so strikingly as at the present postmodern moment. All the elements of what I have here called "postmodern conversation"—intoxication with individual choice and creative *jouissance*, delight with the piquancy of particularity and mistrust of pattern and seeming coherence, celebration of "difference" along with an absence of critical perspective differentiating and weighting "differences," suspicion of the totalitarian nature of generalization along with a rush to protect difference from its homogenizing abuses—all have become recognizable and familiar elements of much of contemporary intellectual discourse. Within this theoretically self-conscious universe, moreover, these elements are not merely embodied (as in the Donahue/DuraSoft conversation) but are explicitly thematized and *celebrated*—as inaugurating new constructions of the self, no longer caught in the mythology of the unified subject, embracing of multiplicity, challenging the dreary and moralizing generalizations about gender, race, and so forth that have so preoccupied liberal and left humanism.

For this celebratory, academic postmodernism, it has become highly unfashionable—and "totalizing"—to talk about the grip of culture on the body. Such a perspective, it is argued, casts active and creative subjects as "cultural dopes," "passive dupes" of ideology; it gives too much to dominant ideology, imagining it as seamless and univocal, overlooking both the gaps which are continually allowing for the eruption of "difference" and the polysemous, unstable, open nature of all cultural texts. To talk about the grip of culture on the body (as, for example, in "old" feminist discourse about the objectification and sexualization of the female body) is to fail to acknowledge, as one theorist put it, "the cultural work by which nomadic, fragmented, active subjects confound dominant discourse."[10]

So, for example, contemporary culture critic John Fiske is harshly critical of what he describes as the view of television as a "dominating monster" with "homogenizing power" over the perceptions of viewers. Such a view, he argues, imagines the audience as "power-less and undiscriminating," and overlooks the fact that:

> Pleasure results from a particular relationship between meanings and power . . . . There is no pleasure in being a "cultural dope" . . . . Pleasure results from the production of meanings of the world and of self that are felt to serve the interests of the reader rather than those of the dominant. The subordinate may be disempowered, but they are not powerless. There is a power in resisting power, there is a power in maintaining one's social identity in opposition to that proposed by the dominant ideology, there is a power in asserting one's own subcultural values against the dominant ones. There is, in short, a power in being different.[11]

Fiske then goes on to produce numerous examples of how *Dallas*, *Hart to Hart*, and so forth have been read (or so he argues) by various subcultures to make their own "socially pertinent" and empowering meanings out of "the semiotic resources provided by television."

Note, in Fiske's insistent, repetitive invocation of the category of "power," a characteristically postmodern flattening of the terrain of power-relations, a lack of differentiation between, for example, the "power" involved in creative *reading* in the isolation of one's own home and the "power" held by those who control the material production of television shows, or the "power" involved in public protest and action against the conditions of that production, or the dominant meanings — e.g., racist and sexist images and messages — therein produced. For Fiske, of course, there *are* no such dominant meanings, that is, no elements whose ability to grip the imagination of the viewer is greater than the viewer's ability to "just say no," through resistant reading of the text. That ethnic and subcultural meaning *may* be wrested from *Dallas* and *Hart to Hart* becomes proof that dominating images and messages are only in the mind of those totalitarian critics who would condescendingly "rescue" the disempowered from those forces that are in fact the very medium of their creative freedom and resistance ("the semiotic resources of television").

Fiske's conception of "power" — a terrain without hills and valleys, where all "forces" have become "resources" — reflects a very common postmodern misappropriation of Foucault. Fiske conceives of power as the *possession* of individuals or groups, something they "have" — a conception Foucault takes great pains to criticize — rather than (as in Foucault's reconstruction) a dynamic of non-centralized forces, its dominant historical forms attaining their hegemony, not from magisterial design or decree, but through multiple "processes, of different origin and scattered location," regulating and normalizing the most intimate and minute elements of the construction of time, space, desire, embodiment.[12] This conception of power does *not* entail that there are no dominant positions, social structures or ideologies emerging from the play of forces; the fact that power is not held by any *one* does not entail that it is equally held by *all*. It is "held" by no one; rather, people and groups are positioned differentially within it. This model is particularly useful to the analysis of male dominance and female subordination, so much of which is reproduced "voluntarily," through our self-normalization to everyday habits of masculinity and femininity. (Fiske calls this being a "cultural dope.") Within such a model, one can acknowledge that women may indeed contribute to the perpetuation of female subordination (for example, by embracing, taking "pleasure" in, and even feeling empowered by the cultural objectification and sexualization of the female body) without this entailing that they have "power" in the production and reproduction of sexist culture.

Foucault does insist on the *instability* of modern power relations — that is, that resistance is perpetual and unpredictable, and hegemony precarious. This notion is transformed by Fiske (perhaps under the influence of a more deconstructionist brand of postmodernism) into a notion of resistance as *jouissance*, a creative and pleasurable eruption of cultural "difference" through the "seams" of the text. What this celebration of creative-reading-as-resistance effaces is the arduous and frequently frustrated historical struggle that is required for the subordinate to articulate and assert the value of their "difference" in the face of dominant meanings — meanings which often offer a pedagogy directed at the reinforcement of feelings of inferiority, marginality, ugliness. During the *Brown v. the Board of Education* trials, as a demonstration of the destructive psychological effects of segregation, black children were asked to look at two baby dolls, identical in all respects except color. The children were asked a series of questions: which is the nice doll? which is the bad doll? which doll would you like to play with? The majority of black children, Kenneth Clark reports, attributed the positive characteristics to the white doll, and negative characteristics to the black. When Clark asked one final question — "which doll is like you?" — they looked at him, as he says, "as though he were the devil himself" for putting them in that predicament, for forcing them to face the inexorable and hideous logical implications of their situation. Northern children often ran out of the room; southern children tended to answer the question in shamed embarrassment. Clark recalls one little boy who laughed, "Who am I like? That doll! It's a nigger and I'm a nigger!"[13]

Not acknowledging the hegemonic power of normalizing imagery can be just as effacing of people's experiences as lack of attentiveness to cultural and ethnic differences, and just as implicated in racial bias — as postmodern critics sometimes seem to forget. A recent article in *Essence* described the experience of a young black woman who had struggled with compulsive overeating and dieting for years and who had finally gone to seek advice from her high-school guidance counselor, only to be told that she didn't have to worry about managing her weight because "black women can go beyond the stereotype of woman as sex object" and "fat is more acceptable in the black community." Saddled with the white woman's projection onto her of the stereotype of the asexual, maternal Mammy, the young woman was left to struggle with an eating disorder that she wasn't "supposed" to have.[14]

None of this is to *deny* what Fiske calls "the power of being different," but rather to insist that it is won through ongoing political *struggle* rather than through an act of creative interpretation. Here, once again, although many postmodern academics may claim Foucault as their guiding light, they differ from him in significant and revealing ways. For Foucault, the metaphorical terrain of resistance is explicitly that of the "battle"; the "points of confrontation" may be "innumerable" and "instable," but they involve a serious, often deadly struggle of embodied (that is, historically situated and shaped) forces.[15] Barbara Kruger exemplifies this conception of resistance in a poster which represents the contemporary contest over reproductive control via the metaphor of the body as battleground (Fig. 9). The metaphor of the body as battleground (rather than postmodern playground) more adequately captures, as well, the *practical* difficulties involved in the political struggle to empower "difference." *Essence* magazine consciously and strenuously has tried to promote images of black strength, beauty, and self-acceptance. Beauty features celebrate the glory of black skin and lush lips; other departments feature interviews with accomplished black women writers, activists, teachers, many of whom model styles of body and dress that challenge the hegemony of white

FIG. 10          FIG. 11

Anglo-Saxon standards. The magazine's advertisers, however, continually elicit and perpetuate consumers' feelings of inadequacy and
insecurity over their racial bodies. They insist that hair must be
straightened (and eyes lightened) in order to be beautiful; they
almost always employ models with fair skin, Anglo-Saxon features
and "hair that moves," ensuring associations of their products with
fantasies of becoming what white culture most prizes and rewards.
This ongoing battle over the black woman's body and the "power" of
its "difference" is made manifest in the recent 20th anniversary
issue, where a feature celebrating "The beauty of black" *faced* an
advertisement visually legislating virtually the opposite (and offering, significantly, "escape"). [Figs. 10 and 11] This invitation to
cognitive dissonance reveals what *Essence* must grapple with, in
every issue, as it tries to keep its message clear and dominant, while
submitting to economic necessities on which its survival depends. It
also reveals the conditions which make it difficult for black women
(particularly dark-skinned black women) to *believe* that they are
beautiful. This terrain, clearly, is not a playground, but a field of
dangerous mines threatening to *literally* (and not merely literarily)
deconstruct "difference" at every turn.

### 4. "Material Girl": Madonna as Postmodern Heroine

(Fig. 12)

John Fiske's conception of "difference," in the section quoted above, at least imagines resistance as challenging specifiable historical forms of dominance. Women, he argues, connect with subversive "feminine" values leaking through the patriarchal plot of soap operas; blacks laugh to themselves at the glossy, materialist-cowboy culture of *Dallas*. Such examples suggest a resistance directed against *particular* historical forms of power and subjectivity. For some postmodern theorists, however, resistance is imagined as the refusal to embody *any* positioned subjectivity at all; what is celebrated is continual creative escape from location, containment and definition. So, as Susan Rubin Suleiman advises, we must move beyond the valorization of historically suppressed values (for example, those values that have been culturally constructed as belonging to an inferior, female domain and generally expunged from Western science, philosophy, religion), and toward "endless complication" and a "dizzying accumulation of narratives."[16] She appreciatively (and perhaps misleadingly) invokes Derrida's metaphor of "incalculable choreographies" to capture the dancing, elusive, continually changing subjectivity that she envisions, a subjectivity without gender, without history, without location. From this perspective, the truly resistant female body is not the body that wages war against feminine sexualization and objectification, but the body that, as Cathy Schwichtenberg has put it, "uses simulation strategically in ways that challenge the stable notion of gender as the edifice of sexual difference . . . [in] an erotic politics in which the female body can be refashioned in the flux of identities that speak in plural styles."[17] For this erotic politics, the new postmodern heroine is Madonna.

The celebration of Madonna as postmodern heroine is not the first time that Madonna has been portrayed as a subversive culture-figure. Until recently, however, Madonna's resistance has been seen along "Body as Battleground" lines, as deriving from her refusal to allow herself to be constructed as an object of patriarchal desire. John Fiske, for example, argues that this was a large part of Madonna's original appeal to her "wanna-bes" — those hoards of largely white, middle-class sub-teeners who emulated and mimicked Madonna's moves and costumes. For the "wanna-bes," Madonna modeled the possibility of a female heterosexuality that was inde-

FIG. 12                    FIG. 13

pendent of patriarchal control, a sexuality that defied rather than
rejected the male gaze, teasing it with her *own* gaze, deliberately
trashy and vulgar, challenging anyone to call her a whore, and
ultimately not giving a damn what judgements might be made of
her. Madonna's rebellious sexuality, in this reading, offered itself,
not as coming into being through the look of the Other, but as self-
defining and in love with, happy with itself — something that is
rather difficult for women to achieve in this culture — and which
helps to explain, as Fiske argues, her enormous appeal to teenage
girls.[18] "I like the way she handles herself, sort of take it or leave it;
she's sexy but she doesn't need men . . . she's kind of there all by
herself," says one. "She gives us ideas. It's really women's lib, not
being afraid of what guys think," says another.[19]

Madonna herself, significantly and unlike most "sex symbols," has
never advertised herself as disdainful of feminism, or constructed
feminists as "man-haters." Rather, in a 1985 *Time* interview, she
suggests that her lack of inhibition in "being herself," and her "luxuriant" expression of "strong" sexuality, is her *own* brand of feminist
celebration.[20] Some feminist theorists would agree: Molly Hite, for
example, argues that ". . . asserting female desire in a culture in

which female sexuality is viewed as so inextricably conjoined with passivity" is "transgressive":

> Implied in this strategy is the old paradox of the speaking statue, the created thing that magically begins to create, for when a woman writes—self-consciously from her muted position as a woman and not as an honorary man—about female desire, female sexuality, female sensuous experience generally, her performance has the effect of giving voice to pure corporeality, of turning a product of the dominant meaning-system into a producer of meanings. A woman, conventionally identified with her body, writes about that identification, and as a consequence, femininity—silent and inert by definition—erupts into patriarchy as an impossible discourse.[21]

Not all feminists would agree with this, of course. For the sake of the contrast I want to draw here, however, let us grant it, and note, as well, that a similar argument to Fiske's can be made concerning Madonna's refusal to be obedient to dominant and normalizing standards of female *beauty*. I'm now talking, of course, about Madonna in her more fleshy days. In those days, Madonna saw herself as willfully out-of-step with the times. "Back in the fifties [she says in the *Time* interview] women weren't ashamed of their bodies." (The fact that she is dead wrong is not relevant here.) Identifying herself with that time and what she calls its lack of "suppression" of femininity, she turns her nose down at the "androgynous" clothes of our own time, and speaks warmly of her own stomach, "not really flat" but "round and the skin is smooth and I like it." Contrasting herself to anorexics, whom she sees as self-denying and self-hating, completely in the thrall of externally imposed standards of worthiness, Madonna (as she saw herself) stood for self-definition through the assertion of her own (traditionally "female" and now anachronistic) body-type (Fig. 13).

Of course, this is no longer Madonna's body type. Over the last year or so she has gone on a strenuous reducing and exercise program, runs several miles a day, lifts weights and now has developed, in obedience to dominant contemporary norms, a tight, slender, muscular body. Why did she decide to shape up? "I didn't have a flat stomach anymore," she has said. "I had become well-rounded." Please note the sharp about-face here, from pride to embarrassment. My point, however, is not to construct Madonna's formerly voluptuous body as a non-alienated, freely expressive body, in contrast with the constricted, culturally-imposed ideal that she now strives for.

FIG. 14

The voluptuous female body is a cultural form, too (as are all bodies), and was a coercive ideal in the '50s. It seems clear, however, that in terms of Madonna's *own* former lexicon of meanings — within which feminine voluptuousness and the choice to be round in a culture of the lean was clearly connected to spontaneity, self-definition, and defiance of the cultural gaze — the terms set by that gaze have now triumphed. Madonna has been normalized; more precisely, she has self-normalized (Fig. 14). Her "wanna-bes" are following suit. Studies suggest that as many as 80% of nine-year-old suburban girls (the majority of whom are far from overweight) are making rigorous dieting and exercise the organizing discipline of their lives.[22] They don't require Madonna's example, of course, to believe that they must be thin to be acceptable. But Madonna clearly no longer provides a model of resistance or "difference" for them.

None of this "materiality" — that is, the obsessive body-praxis that regulates and disciplines Madonna's life and the lives of the young (and not-so-young) women who emulate her—makes its way into the representation of Madonna as postmodern heroine. In the terms of this representation (in both its popular and scholarly instantiations) Madonna is "in control of her image, not trapped by it"; the proof is her ironic and chameleon-like approach to the construction of her identity, her ability to "slip in and out of character at will,"[23] to defy definition, to keep them guessing. In this coding of things, as in the fantasies of the polysurgical addict (and, as I have argued elsewhere, the eating-disordered woman[24]) "control" and "power"— words that are invoked over and over in discussions of Madonna— have become equivalent to "self-creation." Madonna's new body has no material history; it conceals its praxis, it does not reveal its pain. It is merely another creative transformation of an ever-elusive subjectivity. "More Dazzling and Determined Not to Stop Changing," *Cosmopolitan* describes Madonna: ". . . whether in looks or career, this multitalented dazzler will never be trapped in *any* mold!"[25] The plasticity of Madonna's subjectivity is emphasized again and again in the popular press, particularly by Madonna herself. It is how she tells the story of her "power" in the industry. "In pop music, generally, people have one image. You get pigeonholed. I'm lucky enough to be able to change and still be accepted . . . play a part, change characters, looks, attitudes."[26]

Madonna claims that her creative work, too, is meant to escape definition. "Everything I do is meant to have several meanings, to be ambiguous," she says. She resists, however (and in true postmodern fashion), the attribution of serious artistic intent; rather (as she recently told *Cosmo*) she favors irony and ambiguity "to entertain myself" and (as she told *Vanity Fair*) out of "rebelliousness and a desire to fuck with people."[27] It is the postmodern nature of her music and videos that has most entranced academic critics, whose accolades reproduce in highly theoretical language the same notions emphasized in the popular press. Susan McClary writes:

> Madonna's art itself repeatedly deconstructs the traditional notion of the unified subject with finite ego boundaries. Her pieces explore . . . various ways of constituting identities that refuse stability, that remain fluid, that resist definition. This tendency in her work has become increasingly pronounced; for instance, in her recent controversial video 'Express Yourself' . . . she slips in and out of every subject position offered within the video's narrative context . . . refusing more

than ever to deliver the security of a clear, unambiguous message or an 'authentic' self.[28]

Later in the same piece, McClary describes "Open Your Heart to Me," which features Madonna as a porn star in a peep-show, as creating "an image of open-ended *jouissance* — an erotic energy that continually escapes containment."[29] Now, to many feminist viewers, this particular video may be quite disturbing, for a number of reasons. First, unlike many of Madonna's older videos, and like most of her more recent ones, "Open My Heart" does not visually emphasize Madonna's subjectivity or desire — through, for example, frequent shots of Madonna's face and eyes, flirting with and controlling the reactions of the viewer. Rather, it places the viewer in the position of the voyeur, by presenting Madonna's body-as-object, now perfectly, plasticly taut and tightly managed, for display. To be sure, we do not identify with the slimy men depicted *in* the video, drooling over Madonna's performance; but, as E. Ann Kaplan has pointed out, the way men view women *in* the filmic world is only one species of objectifying "gaze." There is also *our* (that is, the viewer's) gaze, which may be encouraged by the director to be either more or less objectifying.[30] In "Open Your Heart," as in virtually all rock videos, the female body is offered to the viewer purely as a spectacle, an object of sight, a visual commodity to be consumed. Madonna's weight loss and dazzling shaping-up job make the spectacle of her body all the more compelling; we are riveted to her body, fascinated by it. Many men and women may experience the primary reality of the video as the elicitation of desire *for* that perfect body; women, however, may also be gripped by the desire (and likely impossibility) of *becoming* that perfect body.

These elements can be effaced, of course, by a deliberate abstraction of the video from the cultural context in which it is historically embedded (the continuing containment, sexualization and objectification of the female body) and in which the viewer is implicated as well, and by treating the video as a purely formal "text." Taken as such, "Open Your Heart" presents itself (along with most of Madonna's recent videos) as what E. Ann Kaplan calls a "postmodern video": it refuses to "take a clear position *vis à vis* its images" and similarly refuses a "clear position for the spectator within the filmic world . . . leaving him/her decentered, confused."[31] McClary's reading of "Open Your Heart" emphasizes precisely these postmodern elements, insisting on the ambiguous and unstable nature of the relationships depicted in the narrative of the video, and the frequent elements of parody and play. "The usual power relationship between the voyeuristic male gaze and object" is "destabilized," she claims, by the portrayal of the male patrons of the porno house as leering and pathetic. At the same time, the portrayal of Madonna as porno-queen-object is deconstructed, McClary argues, by the end of the video, which has Madonna changing her clothes to those of a little boy and tripping off playfully, leaving the manager of the house sputtering behind her. McClary reads this as an "escape to androgyny," which "refuses essentialist gender categories and turns sexual identity into a kind of play." As to the gaze of the viewer, she admits that it is "risky" to "invoke the image of porn queen in order to perform its deconstruction," but concludes that the deconstruction is successful: "In this video, Madonna confronts the most pernicious of her stereotypes and attempts to channel it into a very different realm: a realm where the feminine object need not be the object of the patriarchal gaze, where its energy can motivate play and nonsexual pleasure."[32]

I would argue, however, that despite the video's "hedging along the lines of not communicating a clear signified," there *is* a dominant position in this video and it is that of the objectifying gaze. One is not *really* decentered and confused by this video, despite the "ambiguities" it formally contains. Indeed, the video's postmodern conceits, I would suggest, facilitate rather than deconstruct the presentation of Madonna's body as an object on display. For in the absence of a coherent critical position *on* the images, the individual images themselves become preeminent, hypnotic, fixating. Indeed, I would say that ultimately this video is entirely about Madonna's body, the narrative context virtually irrelevant, an excuse to showcase the physical achievements of the star, a video centerfold. On this level, any parodic or de-stabilizing element appears as utterly, cynically, mechanically tacked on, in bad faith, a way of claiming trendy status for what is really just cheesecake — or, perhaps, pornography.

Indeed, it may be worse than that. If the playful "tag" ending of "Open Your Heart" is successful in deconstructing the notion that the objectification and sexualization of women's bodies is a serious business, then Madonna's *jouissance* may be "fucking with" her youthful viewer's perceptions in a dangerous way. Judging from the proliferation of rock lyrics celebrating the rape, abuse and humiliation of women, the message — not Madonna's responsibility alone, of course, but hers among others, surely — is getting through. The artists who perform these misogynist songs also claim to be speaking playfully, tongue-in-cheek, and to be daring and resistant transgressors of cultural structures that contain and define. Ice T, whose rap lyrics gleefully describe the gang rape of a woman — with a flashlight, to "make her tits light up" — claims that he is only "telling it like it is" among black street youth (he compares himself to Richard Wright), and scoffs at feminist humorlessness, implying, as well, that it is racist and repressive for feminists to try to deny him his indigenous "style." The fact that Richard Wright embedded his depiction of Bigger Thomas within a critique of the racist culture that shaped him, and that *Native Son* is meant to be a *tragedy*, was not, apparently, noticed in Ice T's "postmodern" reading of the book, whose critical point of view he utterly ignores. Nor does he seem concerned about what appears to be a growing fad — not only among street gangs, but in fraternity houses as well — for gang rape, often with an unconscious woman, and surrounded by male spectators. (Some of the terms popularly used to describe these rapes include "beaching" — the woman being likened to a "beached whale" — and "spectoring," to emphasize how integral a role the onlookers play.)

Turning to Madonna and the liberating postmodern subjectivity that McClary and others claim she is offering: the notion that one can play a porno house by night and regain one's androgynous innocence by day does not seem to me to be a refusal of essentialist categories about gender, but rather a new inscription of mind/body dualism. What the body does is immaterial, so long as the imagination is free. This abstract, unsituated, disembodied freedom, I have argued in this essay, celebrates itself only through the effacement of the material praxis of people's lives, the normalizing power of cultural images, and the sadly continuing social realities of dominance and subordination.

## NOTES

[1]Quotations from Trix Rosen, *Strong and Sexy* (New York: Putnam, 1983), pp. 72, 61.

[2]"Travolta: 'You Really Can Make yourself Over,'" *Syracuse Herald*, Jan. 13, 1985.

[3]"Popular Plastic Surgery," *Cosmopolitan*, May 1990, p. 96.

[4]Tina Lizardi and Martha Frankel, "Hand Job," *Details*, February 1990, p. 38.

[5]Jennet Conant, Jeanne Gordon and Jennifer Donovan, "Scalpel Slaves Just Can't Quit," *Newsweek*, January 11, 1988, pp. 58–59.

[6]Donahue Transcript # 05257, Multimedia Entertainment, Inc.

[7]Dahleen Glanton, "Racism Within a Race," *Syracuse Herald American*, September 19, 1989.

[8]*Essence* reader opinion poll, June 1989, p. 71.

[9]Linda Bien, "Building a Better Bust," *Syracuse Herald*, March 4, 1990.

[10]This was said by Janice Radway in an oral presentation of her work, Duke University, Spring 1989.

[11]John Fiske, *Television Culture* (New York: Methuen, 1987), p. 19.

[12]Michel Foucault, *Discipline and Punish* (New York: Vintage, 1979), p. 138.

[13]Related in Bill Moyers, "A Walk Through the Twentieth Century: The Second American Revolution," PBS Boston.

[14]Retha Powers, "Fat is a Black Women's Issue," *Essence*, October 1989.

[15]*Discipline and Punish*, pp. 26–27.

[16]Susan Rubin Suleiman, "(Re)Writing the Body: The Politics and Poetics of Female Eroticism," in *The Female Body in Western Culture*, ed. Susan Rubin Suleiman (Cambridge: Harvard University Press, 1986), p. 24.

[17]Cathy Schwichtenberg, "Postmodern Feminism and Madonna: Toward an Erotic Politics of the Female Body," paper presented at the University of Utah Humanities Center, National Conference on "Rewriting the (Post)Modern: (Post)Colonialism/Feminism/Late Capitalism," March 30/31, 1990.

[18]John Fiske, "British Cultural Studies and Television," in *Channels of Discourse*, ed. Robert C. Allen (Chapel Hill: The University of North Carolina Press, 1987), pp. 254–290.

[19]Quoted in John Skow, "Madonna Rocks the Land," *Time*, May 27, 1985, p. 77.

[20]*ibid.*, p. 81.

[21] Molly Hite, "Writing—and Reading—the Body: Female Sexuality and Recent Feminist Fiction," in *Feminist Studies*, 14; 1, Spring 1988, pp. 121–122.

[22] "Fat or Not, 4th Grade Girls Diet Lest They Be Teased or Unloved," *Wall Street Journal*, February 11, 1986.

[23] Catherine Texier, "Have Women Surrendered in MTV's Battle of the Sexes?," *New York Times*, April 22, 1990.

[24] Susan Bordo, "Anorexia Nervosa: Psychopathology as the Crystallization of Culture," *The Philosophical Forum*, 17; 2, Winter 1985, pp. 73–103.

[25] *Cosmopolitan*, July 1987.

[26] David Ansen, "Magnificent Maverick," *Cosmopolitan*, May 1990, p. 311.

[27] Kevin Sessums, "White Heat," *Vanity Fair*, April 1990, p. 208.

[28] Susan McClary, "Living to Tell: Madonna's Resurrection of the Fleshly," *Genders*, Number 7, Spring 1990, p. 2.

[29] *ibid.*, p. 12.

[30] E. Ann Kaplan, "Is The Gaze Male," in *Powers of Desire*, eds. Ann Snitow, Christine Stansell and Sharon Thompson (New York: Monthly Review Press, 1983), pp. 309–327.

[31] E. Ann Kaplan, *Rocking Around the Clock: Music Television, Postmodernism and Consumer Culture* (New York: Methuen, 1987), p. 63.

[32] McClary, p. 13.

BECKIAN FRITZ GOLDBERG

# LEDA

I wanted to be like blindness in the river.

That morning the tight hum of cicadas
snapped into a fine silence. I cut
my finger on a reed, sucked
the little salt of myself as I let
the garment fall. *Something in the air,*

I might have said, as old men before
a fire, a battle. I walked the mouth
of river mud, thick lips of those Nubian
boys in sleep, then turned suddenly half
expecting their wild eyes and giggles.
I had a stone. But there was only the flat

wineskin of my shadow, and one cloud
beating with light which followed me,
my hips threaded with water
as I floated back, my skull light
in the bell pull of my hair.

When the first feather struck
I remembered the slave girl's stillborn,
its melded hand, its hole for nose,
its sealed eyes. We buried him shallow
in a grove of aleppos. This
is not the god's story — it is mine.
It is not straight. It is how the swan

warped my shape in his, like the second
ring of water the first. He moved
like a way, not a thing: All
hypothetical particles, shuddering
W's and Z's. And it was breath first

I fought for through the creature's weight
heavy with the odor of musk, of cumin.
My nails sank into the tender edge
of thunder. Rabid snow. He shoved
his hard comb into my hair, and wasted
me with light. I am the leper whose heart
falls out first. But when I rose,

at last, from the river
in the thousand drops of my skin
I was boiling. I was a woman. . .

I do not want to be one with anything.

ROBERT CREELEY

# BODY

Slope of it,
hope of it —
echoes faded,
what waited

up late inside
old desires
saw through
the screwed importunities.

This regret?
Nothing's left.
Skin's old,
story's told —

but still touch,
selfed body,
wants other,
another mother

to him, her
insistent "sin"
he lets in
to hold him.

Selfish bastard,
headless catastrophe.
Sans tits, cunt,
wholly blunt —

fucked it up,
roof top, loving cup,
sweatered room,
old love's tune.

Age dies old,
both men and women cold,
hold at last no one,
die alone.

Body lasts forever,
pointless conduit,
floods in its fever,
so issues others parturient.

Through legs wide,
from common hole site,
aching information's dumb tide
rides to the far side.

KIM EDWARDS

# IN ROOMS OF WOMEN

When I lived on the East Coast of Malaysia, I used to do aerobics over a Chinese grocery store. I went there almost every afternoon, climbed up a tunnel of concrete stairs where water rose from the walls like sweat. At the top there was a beauty parlor that served as a waiting room for our classes, a narrow room infused with the perfume of hair gel and perspiration, cosmetics and worn shoes. In Malaysia, where more than half the female population drifts through the tropical days beneath layers of concealing polyester, this room was an unusual domain of women. We were relaxed here, exposed in our leotards and shorts, our determination as strong as the situation was ironic. For an hour each day we stretched and ran and sweated, devoting ourselves entirely to the care of bodies which, in the outside world, we were encouraged to hide.

I sometimes did aerobics in America, and classes in Malaysia are much the same. Certainly the music is similar, the whine of the Bee Gees, the deep thump of the Rolling Stones. The differences were in details – the stacks of fruit and burning incense on the altar that graced the entrance, the heat seeping in through the windows of slatted glass. And most of all, the differences were in the variety of faces that looked back at us from the wall of mirrors, in the many different languages that filled the room during breaks.

Malaysia is a multi-racial country, with Islamic Malays comprising 55 percent of the population. Chinese and Indians make up the rest, at 35 percent and 10 percent, respectively. Though they have shared the Malay peninsula for generations, these groups maintain distinct languages and cultural traditions. They live together in uneasy proximity, with the biggest division occurring between the Malays, who follow Islam, and the other two groups, who don't. At aerobics, though, these population demographics were reversed; most of the women were Chinese or Indian, and they called out their pulse rates in Cantonese or Hokkien, Punjabi or English. Only

135

one or two of the women in that room were Malay. Their presence
was an act of quiet daring. Outside, they didn't wear the polyester
robes and veils. Inside, they were bold enough to appear among us
in a leotard that revealed the contours of their flesh.

From the windows of the aerobics room we could see other Malay
women as they shopped or chatted, their shiny skirts brushing their
brown feet. They wore long-sleeved tunics that hung loosely to the
knees, designed to hide every flux and curve of the body. On top of
this most wore a *telicon*, a kind of polyester scarf that fastens
beneath the chin and flows down, elbow-length, hiding the hair and
curve of breasts simultaneously. Sometimes flocks of schoolgirls
went jogging past. The heat was ferocious, like the exhaled breath of
some great beast. These girls ran through it dressed in oversized
sweatsuits that fastened firmly at the wrists and ankles. *Telicons*
hugged their faces, and fluttered behind their backs. They ran
slowly, shapeless and encumbered in the stifling afternoon heat.
From where we stood two floors up, beaded with sweat before we
even started, their exercise looked like a singular form of torture.
Things were very different for the boys. They ran by in shorts and t-
shirts, the hot wind moving through their hair.

This dichotomy, this distance between what was allowed for the
men and expected of the women, was what had sent me to aerobics
classes in the first place. Walking is my favorite exercise, and one
that I imagined would be easy to pursue in Malaysia. But I was
mistaken. Aside from the heat, which stung my flesh like needles,
the walks were unpleasant because of the attention I drew as an
uncovered woman in a country that was predominantly Islamic and
Malay. There were hoots from passing cars, men that followed me
on the street, boys at the beach who hissed and clicked as I walked
by, whispering *wannakiss wannakiss wannakiss* to my receding
back. The harassment was predictable, and occurred no matter how
modestly I dressed. Neck and arms and hair, calves and toes, these
innocent parts of the body were suddenly, mysteriously, a provocation. I grew to dread walking, the exposure of it, the vulnerability.
Little by little I constrained my activities to the limited circumfer-
ence of our neighborhood, until finally I grew so restless and so
bored that I went and signed up for aerobics.

In pictures from Malaysia that are more than ten years old, very
few of the women cover their heads. Though Islam has been the
predominant religion of the area for centuries, it has traditionally

been a gentle, even tolerant force in Malaysia, tempered by the weather and the easygoing nature of the people. In the villages it is still possible to see a lifestyle shaped by its quieter influence. The call to prayer comes five times a day, but little children, both boys and girls, play naked under the fruit trees. Women sit on porches, breast-feeding children. They bathe in the river together, wearing sarongs, and the most serious head-covering is a scarf draped gracefully across the hair on formal occasions. There are separate spheres here, for men and for women, but the focus is less on rules and their enforcement than it is on the harmonious flow of life from one day to another.

By the time I went to teach in Malaysia, however, most of the country had been profoundly influenced by the Iranian revolution. The gentle religion that had thrived in the country for centuries changed rapidly as televised images of the Middle East showed a different standard of dress and practice. Malay friends said that the Islamic police had become much more active in the past few years, rounding up couples who walked together on the beach, arresting women who rode alone in cars with men they were not related to, or who went out in public with their legs or arms uncovered.

This growing conservatism invaded every aspect of life, but it was most immediately visible in the dress mandated for girls and women. It began with pressure for them to discard Western clothes or sarongs in favor of the shapeless polyester dresses known as the *baju kurung*. Idiomatically, *baju kurung* means "shirt/skirt", and is used to describe the combination of a long-sleeved tunic with a long skirt. Literally, though, *kurung* means "prison", or "confinement". By the time I reached Malaysia, the *baju kurung* and *telicon* were commonplace, and I watched the veils grow longer, heavier, and more somber during the two years I was there. For the more radical there was *purdah*, literally *curtain*, where a veil, usually black, hides the entire face, and dark gloves protect the fingers from view. When I first went to Malaysia, it was rare to glimpse a woman in *purdah*. By the time I left, I saw them almost every other day.

Yet at the same time that conservative Islam was strengthening in Malaysia, the government was sending a record number of Malay students overseas to study subjects essential to a developing country: math and science, computers and engineering. Thus, the students were caught in two opposing forces, one that dictated a life focused solely on Islam, the other that demanded they learn technology from cultures outside of Islam. The place where these two forces met was in the preparatory schools that the students attended for two years before going overseas. Here, the stated administrative goal was to provide, as much as possible, an American style of education, in hopes of reducing the culture shock students faced when going overseas. Here too the religious teachers, alarmed by what they perceived to be a decadent influence, worked hard to ensure that the students understood the terrible evil of the West.

It was in one of these schools that I taught. My college was located in the East Coast of the peninsula, in the heart of the Islamic revival, and the religious teachers, or *ustaz*, were the most powerful men in the school. Most of them had studied in Egypt or Saudi Arabia. They had come back versed in the many rules of Islam, and were determined to spread the faith. Yet belief is an insubstantial thing, difficult to pin down or measure, especially in a population of nearly a thousand students. And so it was the rules they turned to. The equation was a simple one: those who followed the rules were virtuous, and those who did not were damned.

Of these rules, the dress code was the most obvious. For boys it was easy—they had to maintain short hair and dress in Western pants and a shirt—but girls were required to wear the *baju kurung*. The *telicon* was not required, but every girl who entered the school without one was subjected to a relentless pressure to conform. In the first few days of a new year my classes were scattered with women, mostly from larger cities, whose hair was short and stylish and exposed. Surrounded by so much polyester, these heads drew a great deal of attention. Those girls who already covered exuded a condescending pity to their uncovered, and thus unenlightened, friends. The *ustaz* were more direct. They had a captive audience in the students, who were required to take religion every semester. The pressure was strong, and unrelenting, and it was applied to every woman at the school. One librarian, who was uncovered when I arrived, started wearing her hair tied up in a colorful cotton scarf. When I asked her why, she shrugged and said she'd just gotten tired of hearing about it; it was easier to give in than to fight all the time. The same must have been true for the students too, for one by one the uncovered heads disappeared from my classes. Only a very few held out against it, until, by the end of each year, our campus was a sea of polyester.

The pressure was new to me, but the *baju kurung* and the *telicon* were no surprise. I'd had Malaysian students in the United States, young women who appeared in class with tennis shoes poking out from beneath their polyester robes. I'd been assured by the people who hired me that this dress code wouldn't affect my life; that, as a Westerner, I'd be outside the rules of Islam. Moreover, though I was an English teacher, it was also part of my job to *be* American, and to expose the students to other ways of living that they'd encounter when they went overseas. At the time of that interview I was teaching in a major university, with students from dozens of countries in my classes. The idea of being different didn't seem particularly intimidating. I packed my most discreet Western clothes, and expected that I'd exist with the local teachers in a state of mutual tolerance and respect.

What I didn't fully understand, before I left America, is what it means to be different in a society where anything but conformity is greeted with unease. In Malaysia, as in many Asian cultures, there is an emphasis on the group over the individual. This focus is made stronger by Islam, which demands a structured and visible compliance to group norms, and which viewed my particular differences — American, non-Islamic, uncovered woman — as both evil and a threat. In a community of covered women, my short-sleeved blouses and calf-length skirts seemed suddenly immodest. The religious teachers made sure I understood this on my first day there, when they veered off the path — literally walking through mud — to avoid me. They couldn't keep the government from hiring me, but they could isolate me. They treated me as an unclean person, and it was effective. The most devout students and teachers soon followed their example.

What was most difficult for me, though, was the difficulty I had making connections with other women. The veils that covered them were also a kind of barrier I could not seem to cross. I suppose my skin, my hair, the obvious isolation imposed on me by the *ustaz*, seemed as unnerving to them as their veils and long skirts sometimes seemed to me. Some of the women were kind, but distant. If we talked, the subject invariably came back to Islam. Others, those who were extremely devout, were visibly unfriendly. These were the women who wore thick socks with their sandals and dressed in the most somber shades of gray and brown and black. They covered even the heads of their infant daughters, and cast disapproving glances at my exposed forearms, my calves, my toes. In this atmosphere, it was more than a year before I made any women friends at school. There were never many, and I always understood that friendship with me carried risks for them. The *ustaz* and other teachers reprimanded them often for consorting with a Westerner. One of them told me this while we were at her village, sitting on the front steps eating mangos.

"But it isn't true," she said, thinking. "It isn't true what they say. You are not Islam. But you are good."

In another situation—if I'd been a Peace Corps volunteer—I might have given in, and sought a greater harmony with this community by wearing the *baju kurung*. I might have done it, despite the fact that polyester beneath a tropical sun clings like plastic to the skin. I know this is true because I wore it once. I was in a village with my friend and I wanted to make a good impression. I remember it so clearly, the polyester slipping over my head, and the feeling of claustrophobia that accompanied it. I felt, and looked, as though I was wearing a plastic sack. My friend and her sisters were thrilled, though. They gathered around me to exclaim at how nice I looked, and they told me I should wear the *baju kurung* every day.

At the school, though, wearing the *baju kurung* would have served no purpose except to mislead the students about what they could expect to find in America. Already the *ustaz* spewed a mixed and misleading propaganda: America was evil, all the people were greedy and had no morals. Though I tried to keep a low profile, and to show through my actions that different ways of dressing had very little to do with a person's character, it was clear that the *ustaz* saw my clothes, and the body they revealed, as clear manifestations of Western decadence. They did their best to isolate me. It was more insidious than simple unfriendliness. In a society which puts its emphasis on the group, isolation is the cruelest punishment of all.

The longer I stayed in Malaysia, and the more friends I made, the more dangerous I became. It took my friend's comment, *you are not Islam, but you are good*, to make me realize this. It wasn't just moral dissonance that my Western clothes provoked. It was politics as well. Islam teaches that there is only one way. That way is strict, and tolerates no deviance. By wearing Western clothes, clothes that acknowledged waist and skin, the curve of female flesh, I was suggesting that this was not so, that there was, in fact, a choice. As long as I could be isolated, cast as a symbol of decadence and evil, the implications of my dress could be contained. But as I stayed longer, made friends, committed no evil acts, it became more difficult to cast me in the black and white terms that symbols require. I was not Islam, but neither was I evil. In essence, my presence was a kind of unspoken question, and it was seen by the devout as an act of absolute aggression. From time to time — often during moments of political tension in the Islamic world — the minimal tolerance I was granted waned, I was forcefully reminded of my isolation. At these times I became suddenly polemic, thrust out of the middle ground with all its ambiguities, once again a symbol of heresy and dissent.

There were several incidents in the two years I was there, but the one that stays most significantly in my mind occurred after the Ayatollah Khomeini called for the death of Salman Rushdie. Stirred up by the *ustaz*, the students made repeated denunciations — first against Rushdie himself, then the West in general, and finally, in a leap of logic incomprehensible to me, against America and the three American teachers at the school. At first we watched without reacting, but in the face of such anger, it was not enough to be silent. Our intentions and actions became unimportant. We were outside Islam, and our non-belief, tolerated during calmer times, now evoked strong and emotional reactions. Even teachers who had seemed indifferent before joined in the general denunciation.

One day, in the worst of this, a Malay teacher who had never covered herself arrived at the college dressed in a *baju kurung* with a long black *telicon* falling over it. I remember the stir of pleasure she caused among those already covered. I remember that she passed me on the sidewalk and shot me a beatific smile. Lost, as she was, within a frame of black, I didn't recognize her at first. When I did, I understood her message immediately: *I belong, now, and I pity you, one among the damned.* She, like the more radical women in the town who donned *purdah* veils, was using her body, the negation of it, as a means of political expression. The denial of her body was a kind of aggression, and her aggression was sanctioned and supported — in this case, even demanded — by the community. After she began to cover, the silence from the other teachers grew more solid.

I wish I could say that in the face of this I was calm and thoughtful, tolerant and patient, but it wouldn't be true. These were qualities I wanted to have, but the fact is I was often very angry. When I passed that newly-covered woman on the sidewalk, I felt a rush of anger so intense that it left me trembling for hours. It was not so much anger with this woman, who cannot pity me any more than I pity her. Instead, my anger was an accumulated emotion, layers of isolated days and small disturbing incidents, dozens of comments and disapproving glances. It was the day the *ustaz* said that women's bodies were the tool of the devil, and that women must cover themselves to save the souls of good men. It was my brightest student, a woman skilled in language and statistics, telling me that all men were innately her superiors. It was making a presentation to the faculty and watching while several male teachers studied newspapers or carried on enthusiastic conversations. And, most of all, it was having no way of response in a society that sanctioned such actions. In retrospect I see this unspoken anger as a healthy force, the thing that saved me from self-hatred in the face of all the negative attention I received. At the time, though, it didn't feel healthy. One of my most vivid memories is walking across the baked tropical earth to the classrooms or my office, teeth clenched, steaming inside, while I kept a smile on my lips and tried to act unconscious of my legs and arms, flashing out like beacons from beneath my clothes.

It is a terrible thing to hate your own body, yet in Malaysia I found that I was never far from this feeling. I was most aware of it every time I left the country, even briefly, and felt anxiety slipping from my shoulders like a heavy cloak. In Singapore I wore shorts without a stir; in Bangkok a sleeveless sundress was nothing to anyone but a sensible way of dealing with the heat. The first time it happened I was in Hong Kong, and I remember feeling light, joyously light, when the only people who followed me were the shopkeepers hoping for a sale. It is a big city, full of lovely, visible bodies. I was anonymous, and I had never felt so free.

In the end, of course, I left Malaysia for good, with an attendant vow never again to live in a country where the bodies of women were the subject of such repression and guilt. I took a job in Japan, a country where women are just beginning to demand equal rights in employment and politics, spheres of life that have been closed to them. It would be easy to argue that the Japanese are no better than Malaysians in their treatment of women—the video shops have extensive sections of pornography which include women bound hand and foot, chained to poles or balconies with expressions of ecstasy on their faces. Yet it's hard for me to reconcile those images with my daily life here, which is good. I live in a small city, but even in Tokyo I can walk alone at night without any fear of being accosted, and I can walk during the day without evoking more than a *herro, herro, herro* from passing school children. And so I do walk — to work and back, nearly an hour each day, and I don't need aerobics classes anymore.

Sometimes, at the end of a long week, I treat myself to a trip to the local hot spring. The first time I went was not long after I arrived. I remember that I felt oddly shy at the prospect of disrobing in a public area, and I realized at that moment how strongly my sense of what was appropriate had been shaped by two years in an Islamic country. Yet I made myself go. The room, at the top of an open stairway, was empty, lovely, built of pine. Moonlight flowed in through the windows and filled the wooden shelves. It was very cold. I undressed completely, as I knew was the custom, folding my clothes carefully. Wrapped in a towel, I stepped around the corner into the hot spring area.

At first I couldn't see much. Steam rose from the pool and caught the light, creating a kind of silver fog. Even with my closest friends in Malaysia, we had dressed and undressed discreetly, within sarongs, and the image of the body was never something that was shared. I still felt hesitant, standing on the smooth rocks with my towel clutched around me. Through the steam other women appeared as glimpses of pale skin, dark hair.

Just then an older woman walked near me, grand in her naked-ness, heavy breasts and stomach glowing from the effects of the spring. She went to a wooden tub where spring water bubbled up and, filling a pail with water, she squatted down and began to wash her hair. I sat next to her and began to scrub myself with soap, carefully, methodically: toes, ankles, legs; stomach, back, breasts, arms. The other women watched carefully, not because of my nakedness, but to make sure that as a foreigner I understood the importance of cleanliness *before* the bath. It was very cold. I poured warm water over me, rinsing, forgetting my shyness in my desire to get into the warmth of the spring.

The pool was made from dark gray rocks, and women floated in it here and there, resting back on their elbows, their bodies catching the light in a white and wavering contrast to the darkness below. I slid in slowly, feeling the heat envelop me up to the thighs, then the waist, then the shoulders. Except for the murmur of spring water and women's voices, it was quiet. Above, through the shifting layers of steam, I could see the crescent moon, and count the stars that fanned out around it.

I stayed for a long time, watching the movements of women all around me. They were all so different, women whose bodies plodded or strode or moved with grace, women whose breasts were rounded or sloped, pendulous or barely formed. I watched them all with appreciation, my body one among theirs, an individual collection of permutations and shapes, yet one of a set. In that spring, a foreigner and further isolated by my stumbling Japanese, I nonetheless felt a sense of community. For two years I'd carried, unwillingly, a sense of the body as something to hide, and a message that the flesh was an aggression, a sin, an evocation of the darker forces in human nature. In a Japanese hot spring, all this was washed away.

There is something wonderful in the mountain water, a combination of heat and minerals that makes the skin tingle as if breathing. That first night I stayed for a very long time, sitting on the rocks now and then to cool down, then entering the water again. Finally it got so late that there was only one other woman left. She was young, with smooth white skin and cheeks flushed red from the heat. Her hair was caught in a bun, and black strands escaped, clinging to her neck. As she left, her foot brushed against my ankle like a fish. Our eyes met as we smiled our apologies, and then I watched her go, appreciating the firmness of her step, the curved, solid flesh of her hips, the tapering of her waist and rise of her breasts. She leaned over to pick up her towel, steam lifting from her limbs into the cool night air. Then she started to the dressing room. I watched her as long as I could, until she disappeared in the steam as it rose from the spring, swirling, shifting, separating her from view like a veil.

SALLY PETERS

# FROM EROTICISM TO TRANSCENDENCE: BALLROOM DANCE AND THE FEMALE BODY

*The human body is the best picture of the soul.*
— Ludwig Wittgenstein

*Only in the dance do I know how to tell the parable of the highest things.*
— Friedrich Nietzsche

"The next dance is the waltz. Ladies and gentlemen, your partners, please."

Hearing that sedate announcement, I glided onto the palm-lined floor of the Boston hotel ballroom and into a seductive world of glamour and fantasy. Wrapped in iridescent satin, my partner suave in tails, surrounded by hundreds of plumed and sequined couples, I felt as though I had danced back in time. Like those fabled ball nights in Bath that delighted Jane Austen and Charles Dickens, here too were moments of music and beauty, elegance and fashion.

That was the scene as my first ballroom dance competition unfolded. Closer in spirit to the grand ball than the current interest in "touch dancing," such competitions are highly-structured affairs based on artistic proficiency elegantly displayed. Of the many wonders of that day — costumes glowing with surreal color, coiffeurs shimmering with glitter, packaged passions giving way to fierce rivalries — the most startling was to find myself in that hall of masquerade and mirage. It had begun modestly enough with a wedding invitation and my naive belief that a few lessons would convert my social dance into something to dazzle all those distant cousins. But there were more than a dozen dances to learn — the samba, rumba, and tango, as well as the expected fox trot and waltz — and each had

145

Dancing the tango with Jerry Parris. This dramatic—and typical—tango pause shows my exaggerated arched-back and haughty disregard of my partner, even as he frames my body and controls the step. Photo: John Wareham.

its own ambiance and endless complex of steps. At the studio I watched competition dancers rehearse, but their level of dance seemed to have no relationship to me. Then, urged by my instructor, I impulsively joined a group of dancers that traveled from Connecticut, and competed as a "Newcomer." I won my heat and ballroom dance won me. That initial encounter some seven years ago has led to gold medals at the most challenging levels of multi-state competition and exhibition dancing with Jerry Parris, the country's most gifted ballroom interpreter, coach and choreographer to world champions.

Yet despite my seemingly ineluctable trajectory into an airy and glamorous realm, at first I was ambivalent over the *idea* of ballroom dance, with its reliance on romantic fantasy and its delineation of gender relations. Though I was fascinated, a devotee despite myself, the basic commandment — the man leads and the woman follows — made me uneasy. What if the man makes a mistake? And why should I follow? But I quickly distinguished between social dance, which requires little training, and the demanding level of dance required for exhibition or competition dancing. It was one thing to social dance with the type of male who mistook a fox trot for a power trip, and quite another to study and work with supremely fine dancers. I was discovering firsthand that the roots of ballroom dance are popular and mirror views of male/female relations specific to period or culture. Ironically, this male/female dichotomy is most evident technically at an exhibition level, ironic since performance requires artistic collaboration, not mere submission as may occur in social dance. Clearly art is the point. Moreover, the theatricalized role-playing inherent in the dances — a great part of their allure for audiences — has helped me to appreciate my partner's gender-defined role. Yet the surface of the dance form seems at odds with my feminist convictions. Only by probing the deep structure of the dance can I understand the nature of its attraction for me. This, then, is a more or less personal foray into the theoretical and elusive, as well as the concrete and emotional resonances of ballroom dance. Happily, I find fertile support from philosophical approaches that I use quite differently in writing life history.

In its role-playing, ballroom dance reconstructs and reiterates courting rituals that idealize the female body. The ensuing cultural scenario is a dramatically heightened one, since the very medium in which the subject is exhibited is the human body, male and female. Uniquely, this form of dance depends on the simultaneous execution of movement by two dancers locked in intimate body contact, but how those movements are performed and where the focus lies depends entirely and absolutely on whether one is male or female. Ballroom dance thus offers a laboratory to examine certain contemporary cultural mores and ideals vested in the human body, and specifically and dramatically reveals the female body in counterpoint with the male.

J. H. Van Den Berg suggests that "We understand the *dance* only from space transformed by music or in silence. The 'past-and-futureless space' of the dance, widely differing from our daily world of utility creates the dance, inspires the dancer with new life that metamorphoses her body."[1] Nowhere is this more universally true than in the ballroom. Here fantasies are brought to life, whether I see myself gliding ethereally across a gilt and marble colonnaded room to the strains of a Strauss waltz, or stalking a tango partner to the haunting music of bandoneon and violin. Always I am in the embrace of a gallant and adoring partner. As such fantasies are metamorphosed into contemporary scenarios, the ballroom has come to be viewed as a world where men endlessly woo women, but where urbanity tempers emotion. Here where form validates life, all couples are elegantly matched, from the debonair to the exotic. All men are suave, handsome, and powerful, while all women are beautiful, desirable, and vulnerable. Violins give way to guitars and private fantasy erupts in a crescendo of public exhibition. Art intertwines with nostalgia and romance. In this cunningly-lighted world, accoutered with chandeliers and mirrors, all encounters are choreographed and set to music.

I see the ballroom functioning as what Van Den Berg calls the landscape, one of three domains from which human movement receives significance, the others being the inner self and the glance of another. By landscape Van Den Berg means the "physiognomy of the things in which [one] daily realizes, and reveals himself." It is among these "mute things" that the world makes its appeal, so that "the silently transcended body replies to it with a certain attitude or with a certain movement." The significance of the movement "lies in the situation in which the [one] who is observed performs his movements, for from this situation they receive their meaning." Thus, for example, the gracious rounded movement that is applauded by the dancing master in the drawing room makes the dissenting Balzac fear for his daughters. For in more dangerous landscapes, the rounded movement takes on another, far more seductive meaning and may be the undoing of susceptible women.[2]

Viewed in this way, the ballroom not only constitutes a singular landscape, but also the constantly emerging forms of dance establish their own landscapes of desire. These permutations depend for their larger meaning on the ballroom as world. Thus, the landscape of the waltz is all elegance, the fox trot all sophistication. The rumba is balletic seduction, the tango dramatic eroticism. Meanwhile the cha-cha, a triple mambo that is a cousin to "Dirty Dancing," is high-spirited and playfully sensual, while the swing, part fox trot, part jitterbug, is zippy and brash. In each dance landscape, my body assumes a characteristic and different look, so that individual dances can be identified from a still photograph. This mating of ballroom dance with desire, the pantomiming of love, has an existential component. More than other forms of dance, ballroom dance moves across large blocks of space. In this, it imitates the spatiality of love itself, a spatiality William A. Sadler describes as "an apparently inexhaustible and manifold fullness. The space of love is never singular but is filled with the interpenetrating presence of the other."[3]

If the landscape is varied, so too are the views of my body, views necessarily partial and idealized. The significance of my body in the "smooth" dances — those danced in closed dance position, the classic embrace — differs from that in the Latin or rhythm dances. In the smooth dances the female body is meant to convey elegance and regal bearing, giving a balletic quality to glamour and beauty. Indeed elegance, always a goal in ballroom dance, is the primary goal in dances like the waltz and the fox trot, though the former is modified by the ethereal, the latter by the urbanely hip. Here the upper body is stressed; both my partner and I strive for "a big top," accomplished through elongated necks and accentuated backs, his militarily straight, mine arched. Long skirts create sweep, veiling the legs, adding mystery and élan, and keeping the emphasis upon the upper torso, where décolletage is customary. In the waltz the fragility of the female body is emphasized by virginally pale or gauzy costumes, while in the fox trot, sophistication demands stronger colors or fabrics. It is the difference between the exquisite Audrey Hepburn dancing the Viennese waltz in *My Fair Lady* and the spirited Ginger Rogers doing the fox trot in *Top Hat*.

The tango is nominally a smooth dance by virtue of the closed dance position. In this dance of fierce eroticism and haughty demeanor, my knees are bent and my back arched to an exaggerated degree, so that the look resembles a panther about to pounce. A dance of pelvic climbs and legs darting out from under split skirts, the tango divides the focus between the exaggerated upper torso and flashing legs. Here the body, male and female, is most dramatically and erotically presented. That such drama and eroticism is a constant in our culture is suggested by the tango fever aroused by the recent Broadway performance and tour of *Tango Argentina*, a harking back to the near-hysteria early in the century that rocketed Rudolf Valentino to superstardom and led to "tango teas" in the best hotels.

Meanwhile, in the Latin dances sensuality and seductiveness combine more openly with glamour to create an entirely different look. Indeed, in the Latin dances sensuality in varying degrees underlies the interpretation and presentation of each dance. Instead of the upper body, the lower body is stressed, with Latin motion predominating — that undulating pelvic movement that is the basic element in dances like the rumba and cha-cha. When I dance, my body weight is forward, my hips thrust backward, creating a distinctive line. Were it not that my body maintains a continuous fluid motion, I would appear segmented into upper body, waist, hips, knees, the balls of my feet. These elements of Latin motion are most easily identified in the rumba/bolera, the most elegantly sensuous Latin dance. Marking its rhythm by the sultry sound of maracas, it is a slower version of the dance memorably executed by Carole Lombard and George Raft in the film *Rumba*. Its beauty lies in the way swirling arm movements and dramatic spiral turns are combined with Latin motion. However, in competition, no matter how well one dances otherwise, technical proficiency in Latin motion is paramount. One cannot escape the primacy of the lower body. Unlike the waltz where I momentarily hover as if in midair during every measure, in the rumba my body pushes earthward. Thus my body not only takes on another look, it also feels entirely different to me. Rather curiously, the difference between the smooth and Latin dances resembles the difference between classical ballet and modern dance described by Sondra Horton Fraleigh: "The grace of ballet is not primarily of the earth but of spirit and air. The grace of modern dance is born of the sensuous, life-renewing serpent spiral . . . ."[4]

Our fascination with costume and adornment verifies Maurice Merleau-Ponty's view that "the body is to be compared, not to a physical object, but rather to a work of art."[5] My partner, whether in tails, tuxedo, or spandex jumpsuit, wears clothes that reveal the line of his body, rather than his flesh, suavely or sensually accentuating his masculine bearing. In contrast, my costume reinforces the illusion of femininity, with dominant notes of either fragility or eroticism. Typically, costumes are made of yards and yards of gossamer fabric, adorned with plumes and glitter for the smooth dances, or of satin or lace, ruffled and beaded, attached to spandex bodices for the Latin dances. The shoes are high-heeled spikes, of gold or silver. Like ballet slippers, they are fragile, offer little protection to the foot, are meant, like pointe, to extend the length of the leg, and seem to defy gravity. They throw the torso forward and make balance more difficult for the woman than the man, whose footwear resembles very flat street shoes. The costumes serve as accoutrements necessary to showcase an idealized vision of male and female, so that the costumed dancers approximate living pieces of sculpture. All their movements aim to maximize this vision of perfection, of men and women with mythologically correct bodies, as if Adonis and Venus incarnate were to dedicate themselves to Terpsichore. The overall effect is one of grace and elegance. Subsidiary effects include man serving woman, chivalrously presenting her, courting her, desiring her, vanquishing her. In this landscape, the female body is a prize actively sought by the male, who uses his power, his finesse, and especially his body as lure.

This landscape, so carefully constructed to accentuate body, and powerful in its own right, is energized and embodied in the dance. It becomes part of the world of the dancers, who, in an act of reciprocity, express themselves in this stylized world by stylized encounters. Each dance reveals both the soul of the dance and the soul of the dancer through the body. The self revealed is romanticized, idealized, and more or less erotic. Here is the second domain of human movement, what Van Den Berg describes as "the exposition of [one's] inner self; of the secrecy of head and heart." For it is in the movements of the body that the "hidden inner self becomes visible."[6]

However, given the nature of ballroom dance, the exposition of the inner self is a paired venture, and more problematic for the woman than in other forms of dance. First and foremost, all movement is initiated and controlled by the man. He "leads" and she "follows." The very language surfaces the deeply-embedded core of traditional male/female roles. In fact, all dance patterns are labeled from the man's point of view. Thus the basic patterns in all the ballroom dances move forward for the man, backward for the woman. Advanced variations continue this perspective. When I execute a "twinkle," a crossing step in the fox trot, I move backward on a "forward" twinkle and forward on a "backward" twinkle. To execute an "open left turn" in the waltz means I turn to the right, my partner to the left. One is perhaps reminded of the designations "stage left" and "stage right," which reverse left and right for the actors. However those designations are not made on the basis of gender. But my gender-based part cannot be separated from the dance without loss of artistic power. Even in the most beautiful of the dances, the Viennese Waltz, the lovely and difficult "sweetheart canter" requires that I circle my partner, he the riding master, I the steed prancing in a complexly rhythmic dressage. Yet whatever regrets I may feel off the dance floor toward the resonances accruing to this particular role assignment, they are transformed by the dance.

Of course the special beauty of ballroom dance rests on the blending of two performers into one. Yet whenever the dancers are in closed dance position, it is the man into whom the woman must blend, a blending determined by the man's body. The man moves his body against the woman's body, and she, in seamless fluidity, acquiesces. The lead itself is almost entirely physical. In closed dance position, the dancers do not make eye contact — indeed they barely see one another. They are in offset position, the left sides of their bodies making no contact, the woman's head curving to the left over the man's right shoulder. The lead generates from the man's diaphragm, although in some moves, and especially in the tango, the lead generates from the pelvis and thighs. The unforgivable sin for the woman is to anticipate a move, failing to wait for the lead. Almost equally sinful is for her to hold onto the man — he holds her; she rests her hand against his without pressure. Both these interdicta ensure that control for the pair as pair remains with the man, while the woman controls her own body within the erected parameters. My partner and I sometimes practice with hands clasped behind our own backs, a challenge to me to follow his body without breaking body contact. In effect, I must sensitize myself to his body in order to increase my responsiveness to him. This creates "body memory" as we form a dyadic pair of self and other collaborating in the dance. We merge our bodies so that I can no longer easily separate my sense of being touched from my partner who touches me, a phenomenon Merleau-Ponty calls "reversibility."[7]

One of the most difficult aspects of ballroom dance for many women is not strictly technical, but seems to be gender related. In learning to follow the lead unhestitatingly, women typically encounter a stubborn problem — to move *forward* with uninterrupted vigor. "Dance *through* me," cries the male instructor over and over. But his body blocks the path and the female, reluctant to push him out of her way, hesitates ever so slightly. She must overcome this inhibition, learning to dance aggressively even as she follows the male's lead, fulfilling her prescribed, apparently passive/ feminine role. That is, ironically, she must be aggressive precisely in order to appear non-aggressive and pliable. Men do not have this problem.

The influence of the male extends subtly, but pervasively, into self-expression, since the two dancers operate as a unit. Beyond the embodiment of the style of a dance — for example, the classicism inherent in the waltz, a dance still carrying aristocratic and courtly associations — there is personal style. Dancers develop their own personal style as a way of interpreting the essence of the dance and of expressing their feelings and temperaments. However, since the dancers are perceived as a conjoined pair, there must be one overriding style only, and that style belongs to the male. Just as a flamboyant male requires flamboyance from his partner, similarly a male who is understated or athletic expects that style to be mirrored in the female. The woman is no clone, however, since she must maintain her own center of balance and be in control of her own body. Indeed she exercises a subtle influence. Just as the gestures of lovers naturally mirror one another, in this most intimate of dance forms my tender look or haughty demeanor replicates itself in my partner. The force of my presence becomes undeniably clear when we change partners, the newly-formed couples becoming quite different entities. It is also possible for my partner to allow me freer expression at appropriate junctures, a freedom important to me. However such expressive movements must be within the range considered "feminine." Similarly, there are movements my partner would never execute because they are not considered masculine, movements, perhaps, that soften the lines of a hand or an arm, and that male ballet dancers might include in their repertoire. These seemingly onerous strictures on self-expression strike me as similar to those imposed by the sonnet form. Having submitted to the demands of fourteen lines, the sonneteer finds that virtually anything is possible if one is skillful enough. Or as Igor Stravinsky puts it, "In art, as in everything else, one can build only upon a resisting foundation. . . . My freedom thus consists in my moving about within the narrow frame that I have assigned myself."[8]

The possibility of personally expressive movement adds an important aesthetic dimension for me and signifies the essence of ballroom dance — an expansion of self through another. To be continuously in close body contact while dancing is unlike any other form of dance or, really, any other experience, combining as it does the purely aesthetic with the intensely physical. I feel the dance through my partner's body, and he through mine. The meaning of the dance is intimately and inseparably bound into our pairing, even as it enhances our private perceptions of self, perceptions expressed through movement that is stylized into what our culture defines as "feminine" or "masculine." Beyond the technical demands of the form, there is a bodily dimension that strikes me as almost mystical. Not only is it outside rational thought, intellectualization prevents its occurrence. Once my body is accustomed to my partner's body, however he may move, whether or not I am familiar with the pattern, somehow my body "knows" its part. This is most striking and exhilarating under the pressure of performance when a sudden change in the dance routine could be disastrous. Similarly, his body "knows" exactly how boldly to assert itself. This special kind of intuitive knowing, grounded in the wisdom of the body, seems related to Sartre's comment that "the body is *lived* and not *known*." Sartre further emphasizes the primacy of such body knowledge in the formulation: "*J'existe mon corps: telle est sa première dimension d'etre*," using "*existe*" as a transitive verb.[9]

Ideally, the two dancers are more than compatible — they are virtually Platonic creatures, half male, half female. This emphasis on the ideal and essences is suggested by the dance itself. For the circle, symbolic of the ultimate state of oneness, dominates the dance. The paired dancers move in huge circles that mark the outer periphery of their space, encapsulating by fluid and ephemeral motion the magical ballroom itself. Their counter-clockwise movements, contrary to modern technology, recall the ancient fertility rites at the heart of dance: "With the creation of the universe the dance too came into being, which signifies the union of the elements. The round dance of the stars, the constellation of the planets in relation to the fixed stars, the beautiful order and harmony in all its movements, is a mirror of the original dance at the time of creation."[10] Lucian's words almost two millennia ago speak to us of the mysteries of divine origins.

Less cosmically, Fred Astaire and Ginger Rogers seem the

embodiment of ballroom dance because they present male and female versions of a perfectly matched insouciant elegance. The selves being expressed seem wonderfully in synch. Yet their legendary dance relationship includes some curious resonances of interest here. Many of Astaire's solo dances occur within a given film in order to win Rogers's affection and admiration, as, for example, in *Carefree* where the agile Astaire simultaneously plays the harmonica and does a tap version of the Highland Fling. During an ensuing ballroom duet, the two manage their initial kiss, set within the frame of a dream sequence. Therefore, even in a film musical, the very essence of fantasy, ballroom dance is set aside from the landscape of other events in the film. Moreover Rogers maintains her own identity only *outside* the danced duets. When she finally relinquishes her independence, it is to Astaire, to love — and to ballroom dance, the latter symbolizing and glorifying both the man and the emotion. This pattern of acquiescence is characteristic of all the Astaire-Rogers films. Indeed Astaire's mesmerizing power over Rogers is made literal in *Carefree*, where Astaire plays the role of a psychiatrist who hypnotizes Rogers, his patient. Because of Astaire's influence on Rogers as teacher, choreographer, and mentor, the Astaire-Rogers partnership has been likened to that of a Pygmalion-Galatea / Svengali-Trilby relationship. Astaire's control over the dance elements in his films was paralleled by his control of the music, and, finally, over the shooting and editing of his dance numbers.[11] This overarching control is emblematic of ballroom dance. Of course, this has also occurred in ballet, with Balanchine the premier example of the male controlling and fashioning the female into his own vision of girlish and extreme slenderness. Certainly both forms of dance reflect the larger culture.

In that ballroom landscape where I can express my inner self, there is yet another domain, one dramatically heightened in performance. There I modify my movement because it occurs under the gaze of others. Most obviously, there is the audience for whom I make certain modifications. Here is the crux of the problem for me — the public view of the dancing body, especially of the female. Though the human form occupies a central place in Western art, the cultural imagination has been captured by the female body, and historical traditions of dance itself are replete with covert or overt sexual content. These traditions combine with the specific sexual/romantic content of ballroom dance, and for most viewers, content takes precedence over form, thereby reversing the priorities of the dancers. However, the ballroom couple does not exist merely as objects for the audience, metaphorical slaves dancing to please a master's whim. Nor do I objectify my body. Rather, the dance itself is the object. In moments of great intensity, it is possible to make the dance so much my own that it is part of my pre-reflective consciousness. I no longer think about the dance but live it and express it through my body.

As I seek to embody the dance, I may dance roles that express views of gender at odds with my personal view. That is, I may act parts that lead audiences to imagine fictional worlds of fantasy and to attribute to me beliefs I do not have. In this sense I manipulate the audience, that amorphous Other seeking both the spectacle that nurtures fantasy and the ritual that underlies courting customs. Just as they see in the dances what they want to see, so the dancers become what the audience desires. Yet the relationship between my beliefs and my roles can be a tangled one. For example, the paso doble is a fiery dance that simulates a bullfight and assigns the woman two roles — alternately that of the bull (animal) or the cape (object) — and glorifies the man as the triumphant matador. On one level I reject these roles, on another I identify with them, since they seem to me so emblematic of woman's historical predicament. The passion that I bring to this dance expresses my conflicting thoughts and feelings.

My personal conflict does not extend to the audience. In the carefully structured movements of dance, the audience finds idealized and highly aesthetic versions of male/female relationships, the aesthetic nature dependent on the physical appearance and movement of the dancers' bodies. Audience members then easily imagine themselves dancing, for ballroom dance looks like something they might do, which ballet never does. They understand the meaning of ballroom dance, though only those with special training can fully recognize the complexity of the technique.

But I do not dance only for the audience. Crucially there is my dancing partner, my male mirror, for whom there is still the mystery, as Van Den Berg puts it, "that even in utter closeness he is the *other*." According to Sartre, the look, the gaze of another, alienates. However Van Den Berg believes that there is a look "that makes the world bloom and renders the body straighter and suppler." Such a look inspires: "There is a loving look that can bestow a *fiat* on my work and at the same time justifies the body that does this work." Whatever the meaning of loving — caring, admiring, appreciating —

such a look rescues my body from alienation or objectification. In that split second before the dance begins, my dancing partner, for whom dance is life, simply whispers, "make it beautiful." As we dance, glimpsing one another fleetingly from the heights of some strange and radiant realm of being, his is the look that confers meaning. It says the dance is beautiful. And how can I be inseparable from the dance? Through my dancing body, I feel the power of Nietzsche's cry: "And once I wanted to dance as I have never danced before; over all the heavens I wanted to dance . . . ."[12]

A series of concentric circles surrounds the circling couple in ballroom dance. The woman dances for the man, the man for her. Together their bodies fashion a line of living sculpture, one body the extension and complement of the other, the sum greater and more beautiful than the parts. As the man frames and displays the woman, he invokes his utmost artistry, making the woman a virtual icon of the feminine. In the process, his theatricalized efforts to win the woman elevate him to the realm of the idealized male, supremely gallant or virile, depending on the dance. As he dances for her and she for him, body speaks to body in a communion that ranges from the protective and tender to the vanquishing and erotic. The two are partners, but they have very different parts. Their parts, dramatized entirely through body, are culturally determined and emphasize the man's strength and dominance, the woman's grace and submissiveness. Meanwhile the encircling audience approves the arrangement, bringing into play the outer surrounding culture.

The hold of the ballroom on our imaginations makes it a psychic landscape and the dance within a metaphor for male/female relations in our culture. As such, the status of the body is replete with oppositions and contradictions, for I seek the ethereal and spiritual through my lived body. Strikingly, I assert my femininity through the male body. Though chaos may rage in male/female relations in the larger culture, the landscape of the ballroom is infinitely, albeit phantasmagorically, ordered. No matter how tempestuous the dance, there are no surprises. Ultimately, of course, the male wins or subdues the female. Though I may wish a very different scenario in the world outside the ballroom, finally the artistic structure of the ballroom itself elevates me. There my body, responding to the male body, but always under my own sovereignty, becomes a source of aesthetic felicity to me; as transformed by the dance, it transforms me. It is a form of *ecstasis*, the stepping aside from everyday life that is a prelude to the existential transcendence we all seek. From this vantage point, privileged and rarefied, I can answer Yeats's inscrutable question:

> O body swayed to music, O brightening glance,
> How can we know the dancer from the dance?[13]

Through my transcending body, I become the dance, weaving a joyful and celestial allegory.

## NOTES

[1]J. H. Van Den Berg, "The Human Body and the Significance of Human Movement," in *Psychoanalysis and Existential Philosophy*, ed. Hendrik M. Ruitenbeek (New York: E. P. Dutton and Co., 1962), p. 121.

[2]Van Den Berg, pp. 127–28, 120, 122–23.

[3]William A. Sadler, *Existence and Love: A New Approach in Existential Phenomenology* (New York: Charles Scribner's Sons, 1969), p. 174.

[4]Sondra Horton Fraleigh, *Dance and the Lived Body: A Descriptive Aesthetics* (Pittsburgh: University of Pittsburgh Press, 1987), p. 148.

[5]Maurice Merleau-Ponty, *Phenomenology of Perception*, trans. Colin Smith (London: Routledge & Kegan Paul, 1962), p. 150.

[6]Van Den Berg, p. 128.

[7]On this concept, see Maurice Merleau-Ponty, *The Visible and the Invisible*, trans. A. Lingis (Evanston: Northwestern University Press, 1968), pp. 133–35, 137–38, 143. See also Edward S. Casey, *Remembering* (Bloomington: Indiana University Press, 1987), pp. 144–181.

[8]Igor Stravinsky, *The Poetics of Music* (New York: Random House, 1960), p. 68.

[9]Jean-Paul Sartre, *Being and Nothingness*, trans. Hazel Barnes (New York: Philosophical Library, 1956), p. 324. Jean-Paul Sartre, *L'étre et le néant*, (Paris: Gallimard, 1949), p. 418.

[10]Lucian, *On the Dance*, quoted in Maria-Gabriele Wosien, *Sacred Dance: Encounter with the Gods* (New York: Avon Books, 1974), p. 8.

[11]See Jerome Delamater, *Dance in the Hollywood Musical* (Ann Arbor: UMI Research Press, 1981), pp. 56, 65, 67.

[12]Van Den Berg, pp. 128, 115. Friedrich Nietzsche, *Thus Spake Zarathustra*, trans. Walter Kaufman (New York: Viking Press, 1956), p. 112.

[13]"Among School Children," in *The Poems of W. B. Yeats*, ed. Richard J. Finneran (New York: Macmillan, 1983), p. 217.

GREGORY ORR

# A RED T-SHIRT WITH "POETRY"
# EMBLAZONED IN BLOCK LETTERS
# ON ITS CHEST

for Lux and Knott

No doubt Joseph's subtle
many-colored coat
is the sartorial equivalent
of prose — fitting emblem
of the world's variety
and splendor.
        But my taste
runs to this scarlet t-shirt,
intense and crude.
        A poet
gave it to a poet who
passed it on — too loud
for him, just right for me.

    *

That was ten years ago.
Now it's faded and tattered
past all repair.
        Yet
in my mind it's still
whole and of a hue
to shame a macaw's plumes.

    *

How many times she's told me
to throw it out, yet now,
against fall's chill, my wife
pulls it over her beautiful shoulders
to wear to bed.
                    Through holes
and tears in the fabric
(erotic, oracular gaps)
I see her ribs and skin;

sex and death, body
and garment — best of lyrics
where the mysteries fuse:
a memento mori peekaboo.

DEBRA BRUCE

# BEAUTY ON THE BEACH

*Free Makeup Demonstration!*

"C'mere you handsome brute, I'll soothe your lips,"
she says, and we watch his sunburned grin cool
to the mint of her circling fingertips.

"Ladies, *voilà!*" His tan chest sprigged with gold,
she lets him go — long, luscious, scuffing
off in the sand. So what if I feel old

watching him disappear? Here comes a gust
to rough up the shore, ruffle my hair,
reassuring me. My hands pushed

deep in my pelvic pockets, I'm aloof
in this female flock. I stalk, sheared, sunbleached,
my bare face and supple swimmer's arms proof

I'm not like them. So why do I let her lay
me down along her chaise-lounge, her bland,
handpicked example of "Before" and let her say

what she says, smiling, pointing to my cheek
where pores loom, lunar. "Horrors, ladies,
but goodness, easy to hide!" A chuckle breaks

into bits in the crowd, a rubble of shells
scrubbing my face. But now she smooths on swirls
of Ivory Bisque. A touch of concealer conceals

my laugh-lines as she tells us all, "You know,
some ladies just let themselves get old.
Their mouth looks like a worn-out buttonhole."

Ladies, look at me. Who knows how far
I'll go? This Plain-Jane-And-Proud-Of-It
has caught a whiff of despair Sachet de Soir

can't mask, when ozone blows across the sand,
black clouds bank, the door to Sam's Fish House
slams, and a boy mutters, "Help you, Ma'am?"

but doesn't see me. Isn't it better
when he takes quick looks as I stand and hold my hips
just so, the delicate flicks of his wrist making flitter

spark in the last bits of sun over sole
and perch and cod? Ladies, what should I do
to keep him watching me go and come and go,
cleaning his hands, leaning, smiling, rubbing his rose tattoo?

JULIE BROWN

# BEAUTY

Hazel watched in disbelief as the Mar-Don sign was taken down from the front of the shop where she had worked as a beautician for 27 years. The new sign, "Donald's of Denmark," would go up next week, after the workmen finished their renovations. The old brown, peeling paint would be scraped off and replaced by several coats of fresh new apricot. The front door would be painted lipstick red, with a new brass doorknob and a shiny brass doorknocker. Midnight blue awnings would be stretched above the windows, which would be kept cleaner from now on, because Don — Mr. Donald — was going to hire regular cleaning people from now on instead of having Marge, his wife, do the honors.

Inside, too, Mr. Donald was making changes. The old stations were pulled out and replaced with slate grey modular structures. Bulletin boards plastered with cosmetician licenses, photos of hairdressers' kids, postcards from clients, and other "eyesores" that had accumulated over the years would be yanked, too. Eileen would no longer stand on her own purple throw-rugs from home, and Hazel and Jeanie wouldn't play their own radios on different stations. Phyllis wouldn't use her own Mr. Coffee machine, and no one would bring her own magazines for women to flip through while waiting for their perms to set. Mr. Donald was updating his beauty parlor into a *salon de beauté*, and nothing old or dirty or worn would remain when he was through.

This worried Hazel.

&

"You have to suffer to be beautiful," my mother would always tell me. As a little girl I watched her preparing to go out with my father. She stood in front of the bathroom sink in her padded bra and the girdle that dug into her soft thighs — always barefoot, resting the feet

163

that throbbed from the pumps she wore to work each day. I flinched as she tweezed away eyebrow hairs, then watched her outline new brows with her sharpened pencil. She'd curl her eyelashes with the little curler that had scissors handles and pulled her eyelids tight. Then heavy black liner, which stung like acid if she slipped and dyed her eye instead. Then shadow, the colors of bruises: blue, brown, black, green. Then she'd pull the hard electric curlers out of her hair, one by one, and drop them into the sink. Some nights she slept with these curlers in her hair. Once she set my hair in curlers and all night long they pulled at my scalp and pressed into my skull whichever way I slept. Face down was the only way it didn't hurt. I ended up pulling them out halfway through the night and flinging them onto the carpet. "Julie," my mother said in the morning, trying to comb out the snarls, "you have to suffer to be beautiful."

&

In ancient Arabia, prostitutes painted their lips red. This was a sign that they would perform oral sex.

Egyptian women rimmed their eyes with black to protect them from the rays of the sun.

To keep their skin as white as flawless linen, Renaissance women ate arsenic.

Chinese mothers wrapped their baby girls' feet to keep them small, curling the toes under the sole until the foot resembled a lotus flower.

Some tribes of African women extended their necks by stacking metal collars until the vertebrae became disconnected.

Victorian women wore corsets that reduced their waists to the size of a man's neck. Corsets also reshaped the uterus and pushed it out of place.

&

Monday, Hazel decided to join a health club. Mr. Donald had given them the week off at half pay while the salon was being remodeled, and she intended to use her time constructively. She parked her car in the parking lot and smoked a cigarette before going inside. The picture window was large and clean, and Hazel could see herself, her car, and the parking lot reflected in it. A sign above the window said "Body Inspired of Milwaukee" in slim, elegant letters.

Two young women in pastel sweatpants exited the club. They blinked in the sunlight and shaded their eyes as they walked past Hazel's car. In unison, they turned to the window and checked their mirrored reflections. Slim, blonde, tan — they looked like the twins in the chewing gum ads. Side by side they floated past Hazel as though she and her Pinto were permanent fixtures.

Hazel got out of her car and tucked her keys into her purse. The window now reflected her entire self, from her short permed hair to her plaid tennis shoes, and the heavy body between. Would she, too, become slim and elegant as the newspaper ads had promised? How many weeks or months would it take?

The woman at the counter, dressed in a pink leotard and aqua sweatpants, was about Hazel's age. That was reassuring. Her red hair (Clairol: Fresh Auburn, Hazel knew the shade) was pulled back into a snappy chignon, though a few tendrils wisped around her neck. She introduced herself as Alena and explained the basic concepts of weight loss and exercise, and how the club would improve Hazel's body, health, and state of mind. Alena led Hazel on a tour of the club. She showed her the weight-lifting room, aerobics studio, swimming pool, hot tub and sauna, dressing room, and snack bar where frozen yogurt and herbal tea were served. After Hazel made out a check — she would make monthly payments according to the budget plan — Alena weighed and measured Hazel and entered all the numbers on a chart with Hazel's name. The chart was filed in a drawer with a hundred other charts.

&

The fourth graders at my church all belonged to a club called Junior Astronauts that met each week in the church's basement. Our leaders, Mr. and Mrs. Prewitt, made a big chart with each of our names on it and a picture of a steel-blue rocket at the top. It was a contest to see who could put the most gold stars between his or her name and the word "blastoff." You earned star stickers by your attendance, bringing friends, putting money in the basket, doing your lessons each week, and by memorizing Bible verses. I had a good memory, so I learned 10 verses by heart each week. When the contest ended I won first prize by a light year and a boy named Danny Gillette won a distant second.

My prize was a book called *Letters on Loveliness* that told you how to plan your beauty regime and how to put on makeup. It said things like "blue-eyed blondes look best in pink or coral lipstick, while brunettes look best in red." It said things like "always make sure your blouse is ironed and you're wearing lipstick and a hint of fragrance in case Mr. Wonderful should be walking by." At the end of each chapter were Bible verses about how Christian women should dress and behave.

Danny won a book, too. *Heroes of The Old Testament.* Stories about David killing Goliath. Daniel braving the lion's den. Noah building an ark to save humanity.

&

Hazel Stein

| | | |
|---|---|---|
| Age: 47 | Bust: 42" | Calf: 16" |
| Height: 5'6" | Waist: 36" | Up Arm: 13" |
| Weight: 145 | Hips: 45" | Neck: 15" |
| Weight Goal: 115 | Thighs: 27" | Ankle: 10" |

&

Tuesday, Hazel took Nikki out to lunch. Nikki was a new hairdresser who'd only been with them a few months. Straight out of beauty school, she knew all about the new enzymes that were now being used for coloring and all about no-smell no-fuss no-frizz perms. Nikki's station was right beside Hazel's, and they had become friends.

"You're worried for no reason," Nikki said as they cruised through the ingredients bar together. Mongolian Wok was Hazel's favorite restaurant. You filled your bowl with pork, chicken, fish, vegetables, whatever you wanted, and the Chinese man stir-fried it with a flourish on a hot wok right before your eyes. "You're a veteran," Nikki said. "A real pro. He'd be stupid to get rid of you. You have more steady clients than even Mr. Donald himself." This was all true, and Hazel knew it. They carried their steaming bowls over to a booth.

"It's all the emphasis on up-grading that troubles me," Hazel said. "It's all the emphasis on the new and clean. I'm not as stylish as the younger hairdressers. I'm thirty pounds overweight. I don't even make my face up anymore."

"He's more interested in money than anything else," Nikki said. "Anyone could see that."

"I suppose you're right. I bring in the clients. But did you hear where he's moving my station? He's putting me in the corner by the bathroom where Rita used to be."

"Really?"

"And guess where he's putting you?"

"Where?"

"Right next to the phone. They're putting in a new station right between the phone and the big window. You'll be showcased."

"I wish we could have stayed side by side," Nikki said. "It's fun to talk while we're working."

"So do I," said Hazel, finishing her stir-fried shrimp.

Then three businessmen carried their steaming bowls across the dining room to the booth beside theirs. All three men smiled at Nikki, who was quite beautiful. They didn't smile at Hazel. For Hazel it was like a cloud had passed in front of the sun, darkening their lunch together. Nikki grabbed the check when it came. She touched Hazel lightly on the wrist. "This is on me," she said. "You get it next time."

&

# GLAMOURGLAMOURGLAMOUR

&

When I was young I always loved playing beauty parlor. I had a lipstick collection with 27 tubes, all of them named after fruits: tangy tangerine, rich raspberry, cherry, passionate plum. Not that I wore lipstick, I just enjoyed twirling out the wands of color so bright I often tasted them. For my twelfth birthday I begged my mother for a vanity with a mirror that would open and close and a chair that you could swivel around. I wanted one with a seat covered with delicious pink fur like the one I saw at K-Mart.

My girlfriends would come over and I'd seat them in the chair. After small talk about the weather and a brief consultation I'd wrap a white bath towel around their necks and fasten it in the back with a safety pin.

Facials were my specialty. In Mom's blender I'd pulverize oatmeal, cucumber, eggs, margarine, toothpaste, whatever I could find. What's your facial type, I'd ask.

My what?

Your facial type. You know, oily, dry, or combination. I'd read about this in *Glamour* magazine. Also about how to massage the scalp to make hair grow faster and how to put wads of toilet paper between each toe when you painted the toe nails.

Looks like combination, I'd say, dry cheeks and oily T-zone. That way I could slather on two kinds of masks. I'd set the timer for fifteen minutes and paint their nails while we waited. I'd dry the nails with my hairdryer, all very professional. Then I'd give them magazines to read — *Seventeen*, *Glamour*, *Mademoiselle*, *Vogue* — the magazines I pored over, learning whatever I could about how to be beautiful. After I'd finished, we'd switch places.

&

(But you weren't beautiful, Julie Brown, and you knew it. Face facts. You even made a list one time, outlining your numerous faults: breasts too small, buttocks too big, teeth crooked, hair too thin, arms and legs too skinny, feet too long, four inches too tall, nose too bumpy. You learned the meaning of the word *grotesque*: disproportion, an exaggeration of the accepted. If you were wealthy, you could make the necessary corrections. If you had enough money, you could have the breast implants you needed, the braces, the nose job, the hairweaving, and with enough money the right cosmetics could be purchased, the ones you saw in the magazines, the ones that would render you flawless . . . )

&

"[Advertising] persuades us of such a transformation by showing us people who have apparently been transformed and are, as a result, enviable. The state of being envied is what constitutes glamour. And [advertising] is the process of manufacturing glamour."

"The spectator buyer is meant to envy herself as she will become if she buys the product. She is meant to imagine herself transformed by the product into an object of envy for others, an envy which will then justify her loving herself. One could put this another way: the publicity image steals her love of herself as she is, and offers it back to her for the price of the product."

(John Berger's *Ways of Seeing*)

&

&

Wednesday, Hazel shopped at a store Nikki told her about called Units. At Units Hazel bought shirts, pants, skirts, and leggings. They were all interchangeable and coordinated in shades of peacock blue, parrot green, cardinal red, and canary. Trying them on in the store she had felt a little silly, but the sales girls were encouraging — You look terrific! they'd said. With each paycheck she could go back for one or two additional pieces. She was building a new wardrobe foundation this way. Don would be pleased with the results.

At home, Hazel filled the bathtub and slipped into the warm, friendly water. Her arms, legs, stomach, and buttocks were aching from too much exercise. With her toes she turned the hot water on a trickle, then she sank down, eyes closed, into relaxation. She envisioned the body she would like to have had: younger, slimmer, firmer — and for a moment she felt weightless in the warm, buoyant water. She crossed her arms and cupped a breast in each hand. Warm, soft like suds.

The phone rang. Hazel quickly stood up in the water, reaching over for the towels. As the phone continued ringing she wrapped one towel around her dripping hair and the other around her waist. She padded down the hall to where the phone was, but before she could reach it the answering machine clicked on: "Hazel, Don. Please call me when you get home. I need to discuss something important with you."

So this was it, Hazel thought. He's going to fire me.

&

I tried out for the cheerleading squad when I was a sophomore in high school. "This isn't a beauty contest," the advisor had told us, but we all knew better than that. After school twenty-four of us sat nervously on the first bleacher, waiting for our names to be called. Behind us, the football team had shown up to watch us and applaud their favorites. Baker, Brown — naturally, I was first. We'd spent an hour in the bathroom preparing for this moment: rolling on fruit-flavored lip gloss, perfume (our favorite: Love's Baby Soft), one more coat of mascara (we'd separate our eyelashes with the tip of a safety pin), then one final spray of Aqua Net. "Ready, begin," we yelled. Pam and I went through our routine, kicking and twirling in unison, our voices fading into the huge, dusty gymnasium. At the end of the cheer we went down for the splits, or rather Pam went down and I pushed as hard as I could to go half way, hoping the skirt would hang down to cover my awkwardness. Then a deep voice boomed from the stands: "Atta girl, bird legs," he yelled. "Bird legs!" someone added. "Bird legs, bird legs, bird legs," they chanted. I smiled as I walked to the door. That night, I cried as I told my mother the story. "That only means they like you," she said.

&

Hazel had been a beautician for 27 years; she started beauty school the summer her father died. Many of her clients had become old friends over the years. She had clients who'd first come to her when they were little; it was the pixie cut for girls when she first started, then as teenagers they wore their hair long, straight, blonde as cornsilk. She bleached many heads of hair and straightened out many curls during that time. Later, it was the shag, the gypsy, the bi-level. Then came the Dorothy Hamill cut, the Farrah Fawcett cut, the Princess Di cut. Then spiked hair, which she could never get

quite right, and she didn't like working with gels. Now it was —
anything goes!

One afternoon a long-haired teenaged girl came in with her
mother. Cut it chin length, the mother said. When Hazel asked the
girl what she wanted, she didn't say a word. Hazel combed the hair
straight and took one snip with her scissors. The daughter remained
silent, though she squirmed in the chair. Sit *still*, the mother
warned. Chin length. The girl flinched with every cut of the shears.
By the time Hazel finished, big tears were rolling down the poor
girl's cheeks. It looks *terrible*, the mother said, just what you
deserve, tipping Hazel five bucks.

There were other times, of course, when the clients were pleased
with the results. Clients who trusted Hazel's judgement and asked
her to choose a style, then were happy with the way they looked.
Women walked with a special lilt when they were feeling beautiful,
Hazel noticed. Wedding hair-dos were fun — Hazel could really go
crazy with teasing and curling, a hint of spray, artificial flowers or
strings of pearls. Women had given her wallet-sized photos of their
weddings.

&

An ordinary half-ounce bottle of fingernail polish costs around
$3.00. That figures out to be $768 per gallon. A wand of mascara, at
$4.00 for one-third of an ounce, comes to $1536 per gallon. Lipstick,
$800.00 per pound. Powder blush can vary from $96.00 per pound
to $288.00 per pound. Face powder is a bargain, weighing in at only
$80.00 per pound. And we're only talking about dimestore brands.

&

After Hazel finally worked up the courage to call Don back, she
was put on hold. Her stomach tensed and burned as she waited for
Don to come back on the line. First he'd ask her to go part-time,
then he'd ask her to retire early. But on what?

"Glad you called back, Hazel," he said. "I need your help on
Saturday. We're going to have our grand re-opening and I want you
to do a beauty makeover."

"You want me to do the hair?" she asked, relieved at this unexpected request.

"No, Hazel. I want you to *be* madeover. We'll get Nikki for the hair and Eileen for the makeup. We'll sit you in the new chair by the window."

"Why me?" Hazel asked, not sure if she should be flattered or insulted.

"Why not you? A new hairdo and makeup job could do wonders for you, Hazel. You'll look terrific when the girls are through. We'll get Mimi's Boutique to donate new clothes and jewelry, and we'll have photographers here for the before and after. We're sending engraved invitations to all our clients."

So that was it, Hazel thought. It's a choice — shape up or ship out. He'd keep her on, but only if she changed her looks. What the hell — she'd already tried aerobics and new clothes, she might as well give this a shot, too.

"What time do I come in?" Hazel asked.

"8:30 sharp. And Haze — see if you can, wear something, you know, *matronly* for the before."

&

&

One of the most beautiful women I know lives alone on a ranch in Montana. Annick is 50, Jewish, of average height, a little over-weight. If you saw her driving dirt roads in her pickup you probably wouldn't look twice, unless you got a look at her hair — a curly mass that falls over her shoulders and tumbles to her waist. It's gray, the color of un-dyed wool. I've seen her on horseback and on skis. I've seen the chips fly when she takes an axe to the woodpile. I've seen her dancing in her lover's arms, voluptuous in a lace and satin dress. She is the only woman I know who is completely unselfconscious, at home in her body at all times.

&

Saturday morning Hazel drove over to the salon, wearing old jeans, a sweatshirt, and her plaid tennis shoes without socks. No makeup, and for good measure she'd put on her older pair of glasses, even though the prescription wasn't quite right any more. She was hoping she looked *matronly* enough to suit Mr. Donald of Denmark.

A roomful of ladies were in the salon, nibbling on croissants and sipping espresso. They watched, fascinated, as the photographer shot half a dozen pictures of Hazel under the florescent lights. Those glasses are perfect, Mr. Donald said to Nikki. They'll catch the glare of the flash.

&

Hazel's Beauty Makeover

1. shampoo
2. special conditioner
3. hot oil treatment
4. facial wash
5. facial mask
6. astringent
7. eyebrow tweeze and shape
8. moisturize face and neck
9. undereye concealer
10. foundation
11. contouring
12. eye liner
13. 3 part eye shadow: lid, crease, browbone
14. cream blush
15. face powder
16. mascara
17. eyebrow pencil
18. 3 part lip color: line, fill, gloss

19.   henna rinse
20.   comb out
21.   hair mousse
22.   blow dry
23.   hair gel
24.   hair styling
25.   hair spray
26.   soak cuticles
27.   file nails
28.   3 part polish: base coat, color, top coat
29.   nail buffing
30.   new black shirt
31.   new black skirt
32.   new black boots
33.   gold earrings
34.   fragrance at pulse points

&

When it was all over, Nikki asked Hazel to lunch. "You holding up OK?" Nikki asked. "That was quite a production."

"I feel great," Hazel managed to say. "Don't I look great?"

"Fabulous," Nikki said.

"I think I'll pass on lunch," Hazel said. "Thanks anyway."

Mr. Donald left the throng of clients signing up for their own makeovers and took Hazel's hand in his.

"What a transformation!" Mr. Donald said. "We're going to have the photographs enlarged — we'll hang them in the lobby."

"That oughta be real good for business," Hazel said. "Maybe we could even sponsor Makeover of the Month."

&

rabbits are used because they do not have tear ducts so cannot dilute the hair dye or permanent wave solution when it is dropped into the eye they are immobilized with their heads clamped in position metal clips or adhesive tape force the eyelids apart when the substance is a severe irritant the rabbits struggle and sometimes scream the test may continue for a week the damage is observed and recorded often in swelling discharge from the eyes blistering and destruction of the cornea in the case of astringent or depilatory the animals used are

usually guinea pigs the hair is shaved then the skin scraped a common technique if for adhesive tape to be pressed firmly down on the
skin then quickly lifted off by repeating the painful process several
layers of skin are removed the exposed tissue is sensitive to the chemical irritants then applied and eventually covered with a patch the
animal is immobilized for a day or two unable to scratch or remove
the irritant products such as lipsticks nail polish remover and face
powder may be tested by force feeding using a tube threaded into
the stomach internal organs may be blocked or ruptured in other
cases the dose may be given by injection application to the skin or
inhalation indications of suffering as the animals are poisoned are a
variety of signs such as sharp screaming tears diarrhea convulsions
bleeding from the eyes or mouth hunching of the back shivering
(after Les Brown's *Cruelty to Animals*)

&

I was white-water rafting down the Clark Fork River with three
male friends of mine, and when the sun was highest we decided to
beach the raft and have a picnic lunch. While they gathered wood
and started the fire, I decided to go for a swim. I peeled off my t-
shirt and shorts, kicked off my tennis shoes, and stood at the edge of
the river in my bikini. I tested the water: it was that certain type of
cold that you only find during spring run-off. I stepped in and stood
there with my feet in the water, debating whether or not I should
swim. I debated about the strength of the current, too, no small
factor. At any rate, I was happy for the sunshine that day and glad
that there was no wind. While thinking of these things — sun and
water, air and current, I looked up — three pairs of eyes were on me.
I panicked. My thoughts were abruptly shifted to my body: why
were they watching? did they approve or disapprove? should I put
my clothes back on? should I be afraid? Things weren't the same
after that moment. It was them, me, and my body.

&

Hazel decided to go for a walk. She needed to stretch her legs after
all that sitting. She walked along Farwell Street, wobbling a bit,
unused to the new boots she had on. As she walked she peered into
the windows of the houses she passed, wondering about the people
who lived in them. If she had found somebody to love, she would be

sharing a house like one of these. She could have had three or four children by now, and of course dogs, cats, birds, fish. A tropical aquarium, that would be nice.

A car honked at Hazel as it passed. The car slowed down and the driver stared at her. Why? No one she knew. At the intersection she crossed the road and walked over to the new mini-mall that'd been built just recently.

The mini-mall consisted of a 7–11, a dry cleaner, a toy shop, a shoe repair, a tanning booth, and a pet shop. Hazel paused in front of the toy store, straining to see her reflection in the window, but clouds were blocking the sunlight. Hazel thought it would probably rain soon, and if she walked back through it that would be the end of the beauty makeover.

Displayed in the toy shop window was a tribute to Barbie dolls— Happy Birthday Barbie! said a banner, with dozens of dolls beneath it: the original Barbie in zebra print maillot, Barbie in a wedding dress, Barbie in aerobics wear. Every Barbie the same ideal shape its owner would hope to grow into. Every Barbie with the impossibly tiny feet, painfully arched, ready to step into Cinderella shoes.

&

Q:   I'm not happy about my eyebrows. What should I do?
     —Anxious in Akron
A:   Your "natural" eyebrows probably aren't right for your facial shape. Equip yourself with a new pair of tweezers and an eyebrow pencil. First, pluck away all eyebrow hairs until the skin is bare. Then, with light feathery strokes, pencil in new eyebrows that have the shape best suited to your face.

Q:   My skin doesn't have the right color. Help!
     —Panicked in Portland
A:   You'll need to purchase liquid foundation and cream blush. First, smooth the foundation over clean skin until you have covered over your original color and lightened the tone of your skin. Then, with upward strokes, apply the blush on your cheekbones to add a rosy glow.
Note: foundation may cause "blemishes" for some people. If this happens, you may need a bit more foundation to cover them.

Q: My hair needs to be updated. What looks are "in" this fall?
— Curious in California
A: That depends on your current hair style. If your hair is long, cut it short and swingy. If it's straight, add body and curl with a perm. If it's curly, straighten it with a blow-dryer and styling brush for added "polish." Whatever you do, change the color — this fall the style will be a shade lighter or darker than your color.

&

Just then the clouds parted and Hazel became conscious of her own reflection in the toy shop window. She was surprised — the unfamiliar makeup and hair startled her. She could hardly believe it was her face. A transvestite, she thought, that's what I've become.

The women had been enthused about Hazel, daintily eating cucumber sandwiches and sipping Perrier. A new woman! they'd cheered. She looks beautiful! Wonderful! Amazing! And the photographer, encouraging Hazel to smile for the camera under the diffused lighting he'd brought with him, said, "Terrific, Babe! Super terrific!"

Nikki and Eileen and Don had been proud of the look they'd achieved with Hazel. And Hazel herself knew the feeling — it had given her satisfaction to help hundreds of women look better. In some ways, she considered herself an artist, adorning bodies with color as people had done since prehistoric times. But sitting in the chair, Hazel had thought there was something wrong with the whole process. She couldn't quite put her finger on it, but it had something to do with expectations. Otherwise, why did she feel so bad right now?

Hazel smelled dust as the first raindrops hit the asphalt parking lot. Then came the gray downpour, accompanied by lightning she could see flashing toward Lake Michigan. Hazel stepped out from the awning and held her hands out to catch the falling water. She turned her face up toward the sky: rain rinsed her hair and face, soaking the clothes and boots. She followed the sidewalk back toward the salon where her car was parked, knowing how Don would react if he could see her right now. It was best to avoid him — on weekends, at least, this body was hers.

ANNE HERRMANN


# "PASSING" WOMEN, PERFORMING MEN


On February 2, 1989, *The New York Times* reported the death of
Billy Tipton, a saxophone and piano player living in Spokane,
Washington. After performing with the Jack Teagarden, Russ
Carlyle, and Scott Cameron bands, he formed The Billy Tipton Trio
in the 1950s. Married, with three adopted sons, Tipton's death at
seventy-four revealed the secret of his life—he was a woman.
Known to his wife but unknown to his children, Tipton appeared as
a man in nightclubs throughout the West to improve her chances of
success as a jazz musician. On November 28 of the same year, the
tabloid *The Weekly World News* reported that Salvador Sanchez,
"billed as the world's toughest bullfighter and hailed by millions of
adoring fans as the bravest man alive," was gored by an angry bull
in Pamplona, Spain. The doctor discovered that he, too, was a
woman. Like Tipton, Sanchez was married and had two adopted
daughters, but unlike Tipton, only his best male friend knew that
the former choirgirl had changed her name "to conquer the world as
a man."

While assumed class differences of the two newspaper readerships
are revealed in the sexual knowledge of the wife—it's one thing if
"millions" don't know, but quite another that *she* didn't know—
gender differences are revealed as a constant. It's not sufficient to be
as good as a man; certain professions still require being a man. What
musicians and bullfighters have in common is their visibility, their
status as performers, their dependence on spectators. While knowledge of their "true" sex remains a well-kept secret, their performances on stage and in the ring have been viewed and accepted by a
mass audience. By acquiescing to the inevitability of sexual difference in "passing" as the opposite sex, these performers at the same
time suggest that gender might be no more than just that, a performative act.

"Passing" functions as one of several terms used to designate the

178

instability of gender identities and the ability to change sexes, even as gender is considered the only characteristic which remains totally invariant from birth. "Passing" relies on cross-dressing—dressing in the clothes of the opposite sex—for the purpose of convincing an "unknowing audience" that one actually is a member of that sex. When cross-dressing is done temporarily it is referred to as "transvestism," but "transvestites" are exclusively men, often married, who feel a compulsion to put on women's clothes. They do so for erotic satisfaction as well as for laying aside the male gender role. If they dress entirely in women's clothes and do so convincingly, these men will "pass" as women. While women virtually never fetishize items of male clothing, they still aspire to "passing," but for very different reasons. As in the cases of Tipton and Sanchez, they do so in order to have access to professional and economic opportunities seen as available only to men. Women are also more able to dress in men's clothes without shocking their audience, appropriating selected items to increase mobility and thus physical activity. One famous example in United States history involves Dr. Mary Walker, an assistant in the Union army in 1863, who adopted the same uniform as her fellow officers in part as a statement about dress reform.

"Passing" can be an end in itself or it can be the means to a different end—sex reassignment. For transsexuals, most of whom are male-to-female, "passing" involves a transitional stage, one which will involve "going full time"—living in every respect as a woman. Surgical intervention completes a process that begins as the conviction that a core female identity occupies a male body. Transsexuals take their own gender for granted, although they cannot assume that others will; thus they change their genitals—not their gender—in order to correct a mistake. Transsexuals differentiate themselves from transvestites in that they seek a biological sex change in order not to "pass" as women but to pass into the populace at large with an edited biography that conceals the fact that they were ever men. At the same time transsexuals and transvestites ally with each other by rejecting the parodic relation to femininity characteristic of "drag" artists. Female impersonators or "drag queens" cross-dress not for sexual pleasure in private or for public lives as women, but to earn a living within the gay community.

While transvestism and transsexualism destabilize the relation between sex and gender, they nevertheless maintain the relationship between gender identity and sexual object choice by presuming heterosexuality. The introduction of "drag" as a form of cross-dressing brings with it an explicitly homosexual identity, one which is acted out in public and imitates not women but the glamour available to women in their social construction as sexually desirable to men. Thus the women most often imitated are movie actresses such as Bette Davis. The drag performer embodies the stigma attached to homosexuality by playing a woman (something less than a man) and by doing so in relation to other men (an "unnatural" act). At the same time the role takes a theatrical form, thus exposing the seeming "naturalness" of a system that relies almost exclusively on appearance. Appearance is repeatedly unmasked as illusion when the male performer breaks the illusion of femininity by reinvoking the male body through a change in voice or the removal of a breast. The female impersonator likewise draws attention to the homosexual who must impersonate a man by appearing "straight," that is, fulfilling a male gender role based on a heterosexual object choice.

Transvestism, transsexualism and impersonation readdress the assumptions of the sex/gender system — an analytic paradigm that has dominated feminist theory for the past fifteen years — by shifting the focus from gender differentiation (differentiation necessary for biological reproduction) to gender attribution (the conditions necessary to produce an attribution of male or female). Initially introduced by anthropologist Gayle Rubin in an essay entitled "The Traffic in Women" (1975), the sex/gender system explains how and why biological sex (male and female) is transformed into cultural categories (feminine and masculine): "a 'sex/gender' system is the set of arrangements by which a society transforms biological sexuality into products of human activity, and in which these transformed sexual needs are satisfied." The assumption is that there are two and only two genders because gender follows from sex. In recent years social scientists have moved from questions about etiology (where and how sexual difference begins and develops) to questions about how and why gender becomes a "natural" fact, one which leaves the "fact" of only two genders unchallenged. On the one hand, biological sex can range from chromosomal sex (the last vestige of the other sex after transsexual surgery and of interest primarily to the arbiters of athletic competitions who use chromosome tests to determine sex) to external genitalia (almost always invisible under clothing at the moment of gender attribution).

On the other hand, (male) genitals continue to serve as the essential sign of gender whenever a new gender attribution is made.

Psychologists Suzanne Kessler and Wendy McKenna in *Gender: An Ethnomethodological Approach* (1978) address gender attribution by examining how gender is constructed from contradictory clues. By using plastic overlays to produce figures with various combinations of typically male and female physical gender characteristics, they discovered that only the penis produces an unambiguous gender attribution in the presence of conflicting clues such as long hair, breasts, and a penis. They conclude: "See someone as female only when you cannot see them as male." This is true because gender attribution is genital attribution and genital attribution is essentially penis attribution. Attribution relies not on what is visible but on what is assumed to exist, and only the penis exists as "cultural genital" — an essential sign of gender. Thus, the only sign of femaleness is an absence of male clues.

Annie Woodhouse, a sociologist, introduces the term "appearance" into the sex/gender system in *Fantastic Women: Sex, Gender and Transvestism* (1989), to consider gender attribution in the context of the transvestites she studied while attending meetings of the TV/TS (Transvestite/Transsexual) Support Group in London. "Appearance" refers to "clothes, hairstyles, accessories, mannerisms, gestures, body movements, vocal intonation, and so on," all of which are perceived and interpreted as visible signals in the process of assigning gender. Woodhouse is less interested in how men "pass" as women than in why the reverse is not true, and why men wish to appear as women, given that it requires relinquishing a higher status role. The inferior gender status nevertheless allows the transvestite to relate to his wife through a synthetic dyad, whereby the "fantastic" feminine self responds to the desires of the masculine self. Because male deviance is read in terms of its proximity to feminine behavior, the asymmetry of transvestism can only reinforce the asymmetry of the sex/gender system by maintaining the primacy of a masculine identity and depersonalizing the position of the wife. While clothes can be used to misinform and thus produce an incorrect gender attribution, cross-dressing is only considered socially and/or sexually deviant when a man dresses as a woman; that is, when he abrogates the essential sign of gender to assume a lower status, one which connotes both femininity and effeminacy.

The relationship between sex and gender in these studies does not suggest that sex evolves into gender, but rather that gender relies on sex for its meaning. Sex itself becomes a gendered category. A "natural" sex is not established prior to culture, functioning as a neutral

surface on which culture acts without consideration to sexual politics; it is constructed retrospectively as that which justifies the production of genders as an unequal power relationship. What allows
sex to appear as "natural" is the assurance that it will not be mistaken for a performance. Even when gender is "performed" through
cross-dressing, the performance relies on the reestablishment of a
single "true" sex, whether this involves "purging" clothes from the
closet (transvestism), the surgical removal of genitals (transsexualism), or a momentary lowering of the voice (impersonation).

## II

The trope of cross-gender identification has also emerged in the
last decade in feminist film theory as a way of understanding the
position of the filmic spectator. Here the concern is not how gender
attributions are made on the basis of appearance, but how appearances are decoded in the process of watching a film. The spectator (a
*psychic* subject as opposed to the *social* subjects in the audience) is
addressed in a gender-specific way based on narrative relations of
looking. Once again the masculine gender provides the norm, since
men look at women (both in and out of movie theaters) while
women, projected onto the screen, are not assumed to be the "subjects" the film is addressing. How then do they position themselves
as spectators?
The theory of the "male gaze," first introduced by Laura Mulvey
in "Visual Pleasure and Narrative Cinema" (1975), suggests that
pleasure in looking in classic Hollywood cinema stems from the
relationship between the active male gaze (of the camera, the protagonist and the audience) and the passive female figure who connotes "to-be-looked-at-ness" in the form of an image. Although this
situation may replicate the seemingly "natural" conditions of heterosexual relations, it leaves little room for the pleasure of the female
spectator, who either must engage in masochism (over-identification
with the female image as object of the gaze) or narcissism (becoming
one's own object of desire by adopting the male gaze). Mulvey
revises this theory somewhat in "Afterthoughts on 'Visual Pleasure
and Narrative Cinema' inspired by *Duel in the Sun*" (1981), where
she suggests that women too identify with the active point of view or
look, thus producing a trans-sex identification, "a *habit* that very
easily becomes *second Nature*. However, this Nature does not sit
easily and shifts restlessly in its borrowed transvestite clothes."

Mary Ann Doane, in "Film and the Masquerade: Theorising the Female Spectator" (1982), attempts to imagine the position of the female spectator not through trans-sex identification with an active male gaze, but through over-identification with the female image, especially in relation to the "woman's film" of the 1930s and '40s. She observes that if the female spectator *is* the image, her relationship *to* the image must be characterized by closeness, resulting in an over-identification with the object of the gaze. Overidentification leads to trans-sex identification (a term Doane borrows from Mulvey) in order to establish a certain distance: the female spectator vacillates between a masculine and feminine mode of looking. Masquerade, in turn, offers a reaction-formation against this form of "transvestism" by constructing "femininity" at a distance, as a mask that can be worn or removed by the female spectator. Thus "femininity" itself becomes a kind of performance, a form of "masquerade" necessary even to women who seek to position themselves in relation to the classic cinematic image.

Against the insistence of psychoanalytic theory on the gaze as male, Carol Clover in "Her Body, Himself: Gender in the Slasher Film" (1987) asks what the appeal might be to a largely male audience of a film genre that features a female victim-hero. The answer lies in what Clover calls "gender displacement," a kind of "identificatory buffer," whereby a male viewer experiences the bodily sensations of abject terror by watching violence directed at and overcome by a member of the opposite sex. The Final Girl (the female victim-hero) in the slasher film is both boyish and sexually inactive so that her female body offers only an apparent femaleness to its male audience, enough to invoke heterosexuality. Clover breaks down the supremacy of the male gaze by shifting the discussion from theoretical spectatorship to actual audiences and by suggesting that the gaze becomes, at least temporarily, female. Through what she calls the "active investigating gaze," the Final Girl reverses the look by making a spectacle of the killer and a spectator of herself. By collapsing the categories masculine and feminine into a single character ("a physical female and a characterological androgyne"), Clover argues that the slasher film offers a visible alternative to traditional representations of gender: while masculinity remains a privileged category, it is represented by means of a female body. She avoids the notion of gender as "natural" by insisting on the "theatricalization of gender," whereby the male audience is "feminized" in the process of horror spectatorship and the Final Girl is regendered "masculine" in the process of saving herself.

All three critics agree that at least some forms of "femininity," if not also "masculinity," rely on aspects of performance. Within film theory and film reception the positions imagined or adopted for each gender take the form of a vacillation between two gendered positions rather than an either/or identification with one gender or the other. Appearance is once again emphasized as the category which undermines the sex/gender system, even as gender continues to rely on sex for its meaning. What differentiates these discourses from social scientific ones is a reluctance to rely not on sex as "natural," but on the "natural" language of film as mimetic reflection of stable gender identities. Cross-gender identifications suggest that in the very process of viewing gendered performances gender identities are adopted like roles. Rather than repressing the metaphors of performance required by scientific discourses that privilege "nature," film critics "denaturalize" gender relations by reading gender as performative.

## III

In addition to producing scientific and theoretical discourses about cross-gender identification, the 1980s also witnessed the release of an unusually large number of films which use cross-dressing as a narrative device: *Tootsie* (1982), *Victor/Victoria* (1982), *Yentl* (1983), *Liquid Sky* (1983), and *Second Serve* (1986), among others. The more successful of these focus on performers who make their living on stage, either as theater actor, cabaret singer, or fashion model. In other words, the performances involve performers who cross-dress in order to earn a living, thereby reinforcing the notion that the sex change is for money and not for sex. At the same time, by emphasizing the performative it becomes easier to reinforce the return to the single "true" sex of the performer. In two of these films (*Victor/Victoria* and *Yentl*) the narrative is also historically displaced, suggesting on the one hand that gender differences are historically specific and thus any inequality between the sexes might be read as outdated, and on the other hand that these differences are operative now as they were operative then, and thus clearly timeless.

It is generally agreed that Billy Wilder's *Some Like It Hot* (1959) is the historical precursor in classic Hollywood cinema to recent cross-dressing films. Like Wilder's film (which begins in "Chicago, 1929") *Victor/Victoria* is also set during the Depression, "Paris, 1934." While *Victor/Victoria* is a remake of both a German film *Victor und Viktoria* (1933) and its English remake *First a Girl* (1935), it nevertheless readdresses some of the same issues as its Hollywood precursor, and yet does so from the perspective of a different historical moment. In *Some Like It Hot* Joe (Tony Curtis) and Gerry (Jack Lemmon) are two musicians who lose their jobs following the raid on a speakeasy in Chicago and subsequently become unwilling witnesses to the St. Valentine's Day Massacre. In both scenes their predicament is staged as the consequence of "bad luck," a reiteration that underscores the unintentionality of their sex changes. Pursued by the mob, they dress as women in order to land a job with the "Sweet Sue and Society Syncopates" all-girl band and escape to Florida. There Josephine (Joe) redresses as Junior (heir to Shell Oil) in order to pursue one of the band members, Sugar (Marilyn Monroe), while Daphne (first Gerry then Geraldine) is being pursued by Osgood Fielding, a rich "mama's boy." In the meantime the mob continues to pursue the two cross-dressed musicians.

Victoria Grant (Julie Andrews), the protagonist of *Victor/ Victoria*, is also broke, so broke that she is ready to "compromise her virtue for a meatball." Unable to get a job as a mezzo-soprano in a gay club, Toddy (Robert Preston) — another unemployed performer — suggests that the two of them could make a lot of money if she (since she is not a "pathetic old queer" like he is) were to impersonate the female impersonator Count Grezinski. Chicago again appears as the site of the "masculine" (in contrast to "feminized" Florida and Paris) in the figure of the night club owner, King Marchand (James Garner) who visits Paris and subsequently pursues Victoria, at first because he cannot believe she's a man impersonating a woman and then because she's a woman in need of a man. Unlike Marchand, who pretends he's not a gangster even though he does business with gangsters, Victoria is not pretending to be anyone, just trying to keep down a job.

At a historical moment when "masculinity" is defined by an enormous potential for wealth which can only be produced through greed, corruption, and violence, cross-dressed characters join "effeminate" men — the "natural" heirs to family fortunes — and gay men — "natural" performers who make a living by impersonating women (since they cannot marry them). "Femininity" in both cases is represented by "natural" women, the 1950s version embodied by

Men performing as women: Tony Curtis and Jack Lemmon, with a Marilyn
stand-in, model for a publicity shot during production of *Some Like It
Hot*.

Marilyn Monroe and the 1980s version represented by Julie
Andrews, whose male impersonation provides no more than a "masculine edge" with which to increase her sexual desirability.

"Junior" and Osgood Fielding in *Some Like It Hot* are both men

whose masculine gender roles reside in wealth. As heirs to large
fortunes, their riches have been acquired neither through work nor
the illicit profits of Prohibition, thereby "feminizing" them in opposition to members of the mob. But "effeminacy" becomes recoded as
the sign of a higher social class rather than a deviant sexuality;
otherwise Sugar, "who always gets the fuzzy end of the lollipop,"
would be left without a love interest. Effeminacy approaches homosexuality only in the character of Osgood, an older man who wears a
bow tie and seems to be looking for a wife to replace his mother.
Osgood's attraction to the cross-dressed Daphne hints at homoeroti-
cism in crossing the line of homosociality created by the relations
between male "buddies" since Daphne is definitely a man in drag, a
difference Osgood seems not to notice. Junior, in addition to being
played by a man impersonating a woman dressed as a man, wears
glasses. Junior explains to Sugar that he needs them because his eyes
have become weak from reading the *Wall Street Journal* (keeping
track of Shell oil stock), while Sugar wants to understand them as
meaning that he is "gentle, sweet and helpless," that is, a man who
can provide for her without adopting the ruthless behavior of the
mob. When the two couples (Junior/Sugar and Osgood/Daphne)
drive away at the end of the film in Osgood's yacht, Daphne tries to
explain that marriage is impossible because she is an imposter: she is
not a natural blond, she smokes, she is living with a sax player, she
can't have any children, i.e. she is a man. Osgood's famous response,
"Nobody's perfect," suggests that he nevertheless is getting a better
deal since he knows what he's getting (even if a man), as opposed to
Sugar who doesn't know that "Junior" is "less than a man," only a
sax player and once again unemployed.

*Victor/Victoria* replays the "buddy film" not by having two men
dress as women and one of the "women" re-dress as a man, but by
constituting the "buddies" as a gay man and a straight woman, the
former on occasion impersonating a woman and the latter "passing"
as a female impersonator. Homosexuality replaces effeminacy as the
distinguishing characteristic between men when the "closeted" gay
man turns out to be Marchand's bodyguard. The question of masculinity shifts from the economic (how can one be a man in a world
where money is only come by either "naturally" or illegally?) to the
ontological (how can one tell what a "real" man is anymore, when
straight men are falling in love with female impersonators and All
American football players turn out to be gay?) Yet while being gay is
represented as "natural" (as natural as being a mezzo-soprano), it

Lobby poster for *Victor/Victoria* shows Julie Andrews (with James Garner)
performing the role of a cigar-smoking male.

remains "unnatural" for a woman such as Victoria to want to keep
her job after marriage if it involves compromising her husband's
sexual identity. Since "homosexuality is not an unacceptable lifestyle
to the mob," this also means compromising Marchand's level of
income, which, as in *Some Like It Hot*, serves as the essential sign of
the male gender role.

Toddy and Victoria form a "gay male couple" based on a
Pygmalion-like relationship whereby a (gay) man teaches a woman
to appear as a man. If Toddy would seem to know less about what it
means to be a man, he certainly knows more about appearances
since he is often mistaken for a woman, as both a gay man and a
female impersonator. He teaches his pupil Victoria "to convince the
audience that the illusion is real." For Marchand this lesson has a
somewhat different meaning, since he is convinced that Count Grezinski is really a woman. Although "real" women (like Marchand's
girlfriend, a parodic imitation of Marilyn Monroe) can always dis-
tinguish the "real" woman from the imposter, Marchand is determined to prove that "real" is only an "illusion." To accomplish this
he hides in the closet of Victoria's bathroom in order to catch a

glimpse before she enters her bath, thereby proving not only that the female impersonator is really a woman, but that a "real" woman is marked by an "illusion"—the lack of a penis. What brings Toddy and Victoria together is their hatred for cockroaches and their poverty—both signs of femininity (and/or effeminacy). What eventually divides them is their attraction to Marchand, not only as the sign of a different sexuality, but as the loss of a communal income. By marrying Marchand, Victoria gives up her act (which includes "being her own man"), leaving the stage to Toddy, "an aging queen," and leaving Toddy to find companionship in the other gay man. Pretending to be either a woman or a man is never as good as being the real thing.

While the last line of *Some Like It Hot* ("nobody's perfect") indicates a certain openness to the notion of same-sex relationships given that same-sex marriages have laws and conventions against them (they are simply "not done" although the Depression might make them financially advantageous), the open homosexuality in *Victor/Victoria* displays a higher level of cultural anxiety about sexuality even as it attempts to articulate a greater tolerance. Victoria (for whom there is absolutely no same-sex love interest) declares homosexuality neither unnatural nor a sin, even if still considered so by "pious clergymen and terrified heterosexuals." Nevertheless, what is now (or was in "1934") considered "unnatural" is the possibility of decidedly straight men falling for other men and of straight women dressing as men in order to "be their own man," since either scenario undermines the "natural" attraction the two "true" sexes have for each other. While the visual level of the film addresses issues of gender attribution, the narrative level reinforces gender differentiation by resolving gender contradictions through conventional heterosexual marriage. For Billie Tipton heterosexual marriage *is* the appearance, the resolution to a gender contradiction that leaves untold the years he spent living with another woman, whom Billie married in 1960 and who left him ten years before he died.

JEFFERSON HUMPHRIES

# SOUTHERN APHRODITE

"Flaccid" and "tumescent" and some others
which I shan't say here belong to Gussie
(slick oiled consonant slapping vowelbuttock),
conjure her seventy-some-odd years
precariously bikinied, leather skin all seared and basted
by the August Alabama sun until it threatens to fall off
the too small bones and short of that
careens down from the thatch of storebought hair
(for she is nearly bald in truth)
in a chaos of deep creases threatening to signify
some unspeakable thing.

She told us proudly how a bus driver in Florida
mistook her for colored and asked her to sit in the back.

Sometimes when I lie abed encumbered
by an uninvited concupiscence,
she erupts inside my mind with keys
of that used car dealer she loved
around her neck, waddling bow-leggedly
and spilling heat majestically into the air,
a great brown ruptured teat on legs,
and my desire abandons me to follow
her, a walking pleasure dome.
I may say out loud such words as "flaccid" or "tumescent"
and my blood will rush to loins in homage.
Having conjured her,
it goes back to more ordinary chores,
like lugging oxygen,
but that desire launched after her mirage
streaks endlessly at bullseye

190

framed impenetrable
in her gelatinously abstract buttocks
which, ever a-quiver,
are nothing but the body of despair.

Gussie, I must ask.
Did you in fact sunbathe *au naturel*
on the hospital lawn
and do you skinnydip and have relations
with a black man, Nubian attendant,
name of Cephus, old as you in fact
but ageless to the eye?
Did you, for instance, snare
young virgin college boys and bring them home
to drain the blood from their loins
as you feed on mine in the dark?


No — do not answer.
For if any of it should be untrue
I must believe it still —
that Venus, over seventy, sun-struck, obese,
still enters beauty contests and wins,
stricken with heart disease still spreads
jaw-dropping flesh
in the sun on the hospital lawn.

JEFFERSON HUMPHRIES

# MUSE FIGURES:
# NOTES ON GENDER DIFFERENCE
# IN POETRY

The question of whether there can be such a thing as "feminine" or "masculine" writing has worried me for some time. Language would seem to respect distinctions of gender only thematically, on the plane of content; it cannot do so linguistically. While linguistic gender—the distinction made by some languages between "masculine" and "feminine" nouns, pronouns, adjectives, etc.—does represent the inscription within language of the fact of real gender difference, it is hard to imagine how the division of "masculine" and "feminine" nouns which it establishes could be related in any meaningful way to what is male and what is female according to culture or anatomy. This is why definitions of "male" or "female" writing seem often, whether they admit it or not, to come down to a criterion based on content, rather than on any linguistic or discursive property or properties.

We may come up with various ways of sorting "male" from "female" poetry, but these usually tell us more about the content of the poems than about the gender of the poem's maker or about the way in which language is used. If we decide that a greater attention to detail, or some other rhetorical device, is what characterizes "feminine" writing, as Naomi Schor has done, we must immediately admit that such "feminine" writing has been produced at least as much by men as by women. Attempts to specify in discursive and linguistic as well as thematic terms what may be "male" and "female" in writing risk turning into self-parody, as distinctions based on nothing but anatomy and cultural tradition are arbitrarily transposed into the genderless realm of language. What, for instance, are we to make of the suggestion that the use of metaphor is "phallic" and the use of metonymy "clitoral"? [See my "Troping

192

the Body", *Diacritics*, Spring 1988, pp. 18–28] What I make of it, is that it represents a kind of fetishistic prioritization of physiological gender difference which does not at all transcend male phallocentrism, but presents a mirror-image of it.

Lately, however, and with all these risks in mind, I have begun to notice a phenomenon of perspective in poetry which seems to come close to establishing a difference of gender, or a reflection of culturally inscribed gender difference. It comes down to the poetic voice's definition of, and perspective on, its "muse." First, I will need to make clear how I understand the term, what the muse represents and has represented in poetic tradition.

The muse is "One of the nine Greek goddesses who preside over poetry, song, and the arts, traditionally invoked by poets to grant them inspiration . . . . The attribution of particular arts to each Muse is a late development, and there is some duplication of influence." [*Princeton Encyclopedia of Poetry and Poetics*] According to Robert Graves in *The Greek Myths*, Zeus fathered *three* Muses on Mnemosyne (Memory) after lying with her for nine nights. This triadic nature allies the Muse(s) to the Triple Goddess, woman as "maiden, bride, and crone." The concept of the Muse as source, inspiration, and object of poetry is one that has continued, in various guises, to modern times. Petrarchism, Dante's idealization of Beatrice, Goethe's invocation of the Eternal Feminine as that which "lures to perfection," are all ancestors of modern lyric poetry which addresses itself to an absent or uncertain object of desire. The Muse represents an object of desire which is usually unattainable, and wields great, and sometimes destructive power through inspiration or the withholding of inspiration. Particularly in the nineteenth century, the Muse becomes synonymous with Fatal Woman, Baudelaire's bloodsucking temptress, embodiment of lust and death, object of poetic horror as well as worship. In modern poetry, the Muse becomes just about indistinguishable from some real object of desire, whether the desire is requited or, even better, unrequited, or some of both. For Baudelaire, and most other nineteenth-century Western poets, love and lust can never be truly, metaphysically requited, and even in the purest love there is some corruption. This attitude toward the object and inspiration of poetry gives rise to the irony which Brooks and Warren and the New Criticism, and Paul de Man and deconstruction, diagnosed as the principal characteristic of modern literature. From the Romantics on, the Muse is no longer simply idealized, but also blamed for the poet's tragic division between love and lust, and for any poetic sterility he may suffer.

I would argue that the Muse, all Muse-like entities, have become figures for the poet's desire, for the fragmented, radical heteronomy of poetic and real desire. How a poem represents its muse will reflect the poet's sense of relation to origins, present circumstances, to desire in general, and above all, to Memory: remember Mnemosyne, mother of all the Muses. The muse is a figure made by the superimposition of desire (Zeus's desire) and Memory (Mnemosyne). Thus my own poem preceding this essay, "Southern Aphrodite," represents a Muse figure which is probably a metaphor for my Southern origins, and for the way in which I feel compelled and repulsed by those origins; she is at once compelling, comical and grotesquely horrific. Such an attitude toward origins may charge much Southern poetry with a more radical irony than that characteristic of other American poetry, and account for the excessiveness which some critics reprove in Southern letters. The Southern writer, poet particularly, feels much more divided about his/her literary vocation than any Northern, Midwestern, or generally American counterpart, because s/he comes from a region and a culture in which none of the arts has ever had a very high place and writing has never been thought of as a serious or respectable profession. You might well do poetry on the side, or at least read it, if you had enough money and time to waste on such things; certainly a classical education and a visible sense of appreciation for the arts has always been, in the South, esteemed as evidence of wealth, among the necessary accoutrements of the gentleman planter and his lady, but that is a different thing altogether. And anyway, this has only been true where there was a predominant plantation culture, and most Southern planters were very small farmers, not plantation owners. The Southern small farmer has never had *any* time for high culture of *any* sort. Paradoxically, this attitude within the culture has led to the production of a great many good writers and poets. Which may imply that ambivalence toward the muse and what she represents is not a bad thing at all, for the poet or the poetry.

There are many versions of the muse in Southern writing at least as grotesque as my own in "Southern Aphrodite." Close to my version, or I'd better say mine is close to his, is R. P. Warren's masterful "Myth on Mediterranean Beach: Aphrodite as Logos":

From left to right, she leads the eye
Across the blaze-brightness of sea and sky

That is the background of her transit.

Commanded thus, from left to right,
As by a line of print on that bright

Blankness, the eye will follow, but

There is no line, the eye follows only
That one word moving, it moves in lonely

And absolute arrogance across the blank

Page of the world, the world burns, she is
The word, all faces turn. Look! — this

Is what she is: old hunchback in bikini.[1]

Who knows, maybe Warren and I saw the same woman, he on a Mediterranean beach and I in my hometown in Alabama. In his case and mine, anyway, she has become a figure for something "gelatinously abstract" and otherwise unnameable, the heart of world or nature or spirit, toward which all poetry is a kind of expression, or admission of mad desire, that desire's song of its unrequitableness.

The Muse may just as well be represented without specific physical form, and may stand for the sculpting hand of Death itself. Reynolds Price's "The Laws of Ice" infers, without describing, an amorphous, even spectral Muse figure no less charged with irony, both maternal and deadly:

Ice has laws
(oxygen, fire,
Lord Gravity
Have laws) but loose —
A mother's call.

Human life
(Yours, mine)
Will glide down decades
Free as oil;

> Then seize on the instant,
> Rigid form —
> Your statue, mine,
> Perfected ice:
> Random pose,
> Appalling laws.[2]

Muse figures are not always female, or even humanoid: as supernatural messenger, the muse is often associated with Hermes, the postman of the gods, and may conceal herself in the guise of an animal, usually a bird, like Price's "annual heron" in his poem of the same name: "detained to alter his former message — /Endurance or death."[3] Such fierce, yet delicate inscrutability is typical, as also in Wallace Stevens's famous ornithological representation:

> The palm at the end of the mind,
> Beyond the last thought, rises
> In the bronze decor,
>
> A gold-feathered bird
> Sings in the palm, without human meaning,
> Without human feeling, a foreign song.[4]

Randall Jarrell's "The Bird of Night" provides an example in which a more explicitly delineated Muse figure than Price's in "The Laws of Ice" is synonymous with death, as it was in Price's poem:

> A shadow is floating through the moonlight.
> Its wings don't make a sound.
> Its claws are long, its beak is bright.
> Its eyes try all the corners of the night.
>
> It calls and calls: all the air swells and heaves
> And washes up and down like water.
> The ear that listens to the owl believes
> In death.[5]

These bird figures are best described as androgynous, I suppose, but Muse figures may be male as well, when they turn to Hermes, as in Randall Jarrell's Nestus Gurley, a black boy who delivers papers:

> Sometimes waking, sometimes sleeping,
> Late in the afternoon, or early
> In the morning, I hear on the lawn,
> On the walk, on the lawn, the soft quick step,
> The sound half song, half breath: a note or two

That with a note or two would be a tune.
It is Nestus Gurley.[6]

All these examples — and I could, as any reader of modern poetry knows, go on listing them indefinitely — show poetry trying to give a name to an absent, unattainable locus of desire — or fear or longing or mourning or remembrance, all of which are in fact permutated instances of positive or negative desire. Desire focused on what is entirely other and beyond, for transcendent knowledge, or perfect physical knowledge, for both of these at once, for some pure experience of truth or beauty or anything. The Muse has always been that figure for the locus of poetic desire, the goad and object of poetry.

All my examples so far have come from male poets. The time has come to ask the obvious question: since muse figures are latently, according to myth, if not in fact, female, could poetry by female poets show a different correlation between poetic desire and the Muse figure? I believe the answer is yes. If we think of a poetry like that of Marianne Moore, in which representations of this alterity, as bird, or pangolin, abound, we find that there is a subtly different relation expressed to those representations. They are still seen as inscrutable, ephemeral, but the poetry, instead of looking at them from afar, from the outside, seeks to *become* them, to enact and embody the very same pure and inscrutable otherness. Moore's poems, while they purport to describe, while addressing, "prize birds" etc., in fact overwhelm their own pretended objects, supplant the visually splendid and unnameable askesis of the animal-muse figure with a verbal enactment of inscrutability which is just as striking. The poetry here does not address the unnameable but seeks to enact, to become it. There is an identification with muse-ness which is not typical of the examples previously cited. Moore never situates, in poetry, her own desire with respect to shifting objects; it rather melds with the shifting patterns of those objects, and leaves the reader to enact the stance of poet confronted by a written muse.

'No water so still as the
dead fountains of Versailles.' No swan,
with swart blind look askance
and gondoliering legs, so fine
as the chintz china one with fawn-
brown eyes and toothed gold
collar on to show whose bird it was.

> Lodged in the Louis Fifteenth
> candelabrum-tree of cockscomb-
> tinted buttons, dahlias,
> sea-urchins, and everlastings,
> it perches on the branching foam
> of polished sculptured
> flowers — at ease and tall. The king is dead.[7]

No real swan is alluded to, but one sculpted in a Louis Fifteenth candelabrum; just as that swan is more "fine" than any real one, this written swan is even finer, even more pure in its absent, almost aphoristic inscrutability, building to a rebus at the end, than the sculpted one. This poetry seeks more to become the reader's muse than to sing about and to its own. Perhaps the reader will object that this has been a tendency and goal of poetry in general since Mallarmé, or even before. I will still contend that there is a noticeable difference. In Moore's poem "The Pangolin," there is not only a description of the animal which is pieced together, overlapping helter-skelter but with an apparently natural (linguistic) order, in mimicry of the animal's own scale-armor, but the beast itself speaks — as if it had become a poem — in an apostrophe to us: "Again the sun!"[8] Moore's poems address us as though they were the very muse or animal they affect to describe, enveloping us in gossamer dazzlement from the depths of the page.

Sure, e. e. cummings and Wallace Stevens, and many a male poet, since Mallarmé said the flower absent from all bouquets was the best one, have shown they believed that poetry should not signify, but be. But such anti-referential theoretical statements, and even enactments, are not the same as what we see in Moore: she attempts to make a bird, a pangolin out of words, one more startling, more muse-like even than any real one, more *material* and solid, though made of nothing but ink and paper, than anything at the zoo.

Kate Daniels, a fine contemporary Southern poet, gives us this apostrophe from the heart of poetry, which could be that of a muse assailed by the claims of poets, or readers, poets or readers who have become like sirens for her:

> All day I look out the window
> at the sluggish roll of the river.
> People pass by on their boats
> forgetting they're human.
> Their casual waves touch nothing in me.

They glide away easily
but the slap of their wake on the bulkhead
eats away at the stone.
I hear each little wave with clarity.
They are like hands being clapped for attention
as if I were a servant being called to my master.[9]

When Betty Adcock, another Southern woman poet, says that

There's no touch like this one
except (if you remember it) your baptism

. . .

There's just this touch that is not
like a lover's, is more
barely moth dust and sun slant . . . [10]

she is talking about memory, but the poem is talking about itself,
memory's daughter, *muse*, touching us and talking about touching
us at once.

Could it be that these women poets, in their poetry, turn into
muses, or sirens, women turned into birds (or pangolins, etc.):
"These children of Achelous or, some say, Phorcys, by either the
Muse Terpsichore, or by Sterope, Porthaon's daughter, had girl's
faces but bird's feet and feathers, and many different stories are told
to account for this peculiarity: such as that they had been playing
with Kore when Hades abducted her, and that Demeter, vexed
because they had not come to her aid, gave them wings, saying:
'Begone, and search for my daughter all over the world!' Or that
Aphrodite turned them into birds because, for pride, they would not
yield their maidenheads either to gods or men. They no longer had
the power of flight, however, since the Muses had defeated them in
a musical contest and pulled out their wing feathers to make themselves crowns. Now they sat and sang in a meadow among the
heaped bones of sailors whom they had drawn to their death."[11]
Here is the poet Maura Stanton ("A Voice for the Sirens"):

Oh they came, their eyes blank.
I pinned their souls under rocks
wanting only their shocked flesh
as the ships broke up, again, again . . .
Years now. Unlike the others I remember
a hand, some coarse hair against my cheek.
Now I stare at sea all day
singing about strange events

for I've passed through their souls
inadvertently, thinking them shadows —
their souls were particles of odd happenings
or geography or touch,
tainting my immortality with memory.

. . .

Yet I keep singing, my dangerous voice
joined in sad irresponsibility with those
on this rock who forget why
each time until the next ship crashes.
Into the haunted music I weave my warning
carefully, as if my language were decipherable.[12]

Isn't it from that meadow, among those bones, that all of Stanton's poetry speaks to us:

Each night I walk the moon, myself, strange
planet inhabited by a girl rendered backwards
by pool or mirror into the odd logic of image —
What self-deception! How could I recognize
my own ghost rising from the graveyard stream?
. . .
Here, walking this shadowless dust, I watch
a light spin dangerous across the atmosphere;
. . .
If I twined myself with greens, with weeds,
he'd never discover how deep inside my thicket
I've escaped my rare womanly blooms; or how
forever I'm only the sandswept desert,
pitiless, listening to the sphere's wild music
only I can translate, but I won't! I won't![13]

I will say it finally: the male poet listens to the muse, and brings us a report; the female poet turns into muse, or siren, and sings a music which she will not translate into theory. I could cite many more examples. Enough for a book, or God help me, a dissertation. But more examples would not prove my point, I don't think, any better than these few. What I am talking about cannot be proved.

This definition of "male" and "female" poetry is a matter of implicitly or explicitly stated relation to a muse figure. The male, by this criterion, would focus on the muse figure, while standing apart from it; the female voice *identifies* with it, tends to address us as muse. Instances in which women poets have represented muse figures — whether as male or female — and addressed them as *other* would be imitations of the male position.

I am aware that two aspects of my argument here may be criticized as weaknesses, though I do not see them as such. First, I have said that muse (or siren) may be male or androgynous, even animal or bird. In every one of these cases, however, there is the implied femininity of "muse-ness." Second, there is nothing to keep a male poet from writing female poetry, as I have defined it, and vice-versa. The wonderful thing about language is that, slipping into it, like a bath of ether, we lose our gender. Still, for whatever reason, I would guess that more women have written male poetry, by my sense of it, than the other way around. What I have described as male and female are not physiological determinations, transposed into language, but rather attitudes, roles, which may be taken up or put off, even if they usually are not.

Perhaps all attempts to define a specifically "feminine" literary discourse must break down at this point. Sandra Gilbert and Susan Gubar wish to reduce all literary discourse since women's "invasion of the public sphere" "in the late nineteenth and early twentieth centuries" to a polemical exchange between male misogynists and feminists struggling to assert themselves.[14] This theory may work quite convincingly as long as Gilbert and Gubar are allowed to select the authors discussed, but it degenerates into a rather purely polemical, if not paranoid representation when brought to bear on other male and female authors for whom the question of gender is simply not paramount. Most interesting is that Gilbert and Gubar make no real attempt to define "female" writing except as a polemic directed against a masculine locus of oppression. This is a definition which appears to demean the possibilities of a more positive feminine discourse. Of course, Gilbert's and Gubar's books may serve an important political purpose for some; their value as literary criticism is however, in my view, doubtful: taking such a partisan and unskeptical point of view, they appear to be repetitious of the sort of polemic which they posit as object of study.

A more interesting approach is represented for me by Dorothy Kelly's *Fictional Genders: Role and Representation in Nineteenth Century French Narrative*, in which Kelly sets out in her readings of texts to "examine the differential, moving relation between the two genders and the problems involved in the construction of the gender identity of both sexes."[15] Such a theoretical stance admits that all use of language to discuss gender, including pretended efforts to examine such language "objectively," must be part of the ongoing discourse of gender difference, and participate actively in the evolution of cultural cliches about what is male and what is female. We cannot talk about gender difference without being automatically complicit in the use of language to articulate it. The paradox of language, as I have already pointed out, is that, even while used to assert gender difference as a thematic fact, it relegates that difference to the status of minor metaphor, one trope among many.

My own poem in this issue would probably be viewed by Gilbert and Gubar, and most American feminists, as misogynistic. This may indeed be correct in a very narrow sense, to the extent that the poem describes a woman as grotesque, but it ignores many other, more significant aspects of the poem without which its meaning, and the significance of the fictive woman it describes, cannot begin to be understood. The "male"-ness of the poem is not really in its "negative" depiction of a woman, but rather in the way in which the poetic voice situates itself with respect to that woman, who is a kind of muse figure.

The male/female dichotomy which I have set up might also be expressed as one involving Aristotelian, or representational, poetry, and Platonic poetry. Aristotelian poetry uses language to represent, to refer, to describe, to narrate; Platonic poetry, like that of Marianne Moore, attempts to achieve a nonreferential, ideal being of its own. This would ally the "female," as I have defined it, in American/English poetry with French poetry since Mallarmé and symbolism and even before: the contemporary French poet Yves Bonnefoy, who now holds the chair in poetry at the Collège de France, has often described the difference between Anglophone and Francophone poetic tradition as one of Aristotelian v. Platonic use of language. This would also mean that the gender difference I have observed (as a tendency inscribed within the literary tradition) may exist only in Anglophone poetry.

## NOTES

[1]R. P. Warren, *Selected Poems 1923–1975* (New York: Random House, 1976), p. 109.

[2]Reynolds Price, *The Laws of Ice* (New York: Atheneum, 1986), p. 32.

[3]Price, p. 73.

[4]Wallace Stevens, *The Palm at the End of the Mind: Selected Poems and a Play* (New York: Vintage, 1972), p. 398.

[5]Randall Jarrell, *The Complete Poems* (New York: Farrar, Straus, Giroux, 1969), p. 313.

[6]Jarrell, 235.

[7]*The Complete Poems of Marianne Moore* (New York: Macmillan/Viking, 1967), p. 19.

[8]Moore, p. 120.

[9]Kate Daniels, *The White Wave* (Pittsburgh: University of Pittsburgh Press, 1984), p. 25.

[10]Betty Adcock, *Nettles* (Baton Rouge: LSU Press, 1983), p. 3.

[11]Graves, II, p. 361.

[12]Maura Stanton, *Snow on Snow* (New Haven: Yale University Press, 1975), pp. 7–8.

[13]Stanton, p. 36.

[14]Sandra M. Gilbert and Susan Gubar, *No Man's Land: The Place of the Woman Writer in the Twentieth Century; Volume I: The War of the Words; Volume II: Sexchanges* (New Haven: Yale University Press, 1988 and 1989).

[15]Dorothy Kelly, *Fictional Genders: Role and Representation in Nineteenth Century French Narrative* (Lincoln: University of Nebraska Press, 1989), pp. 20–21.

STEPHANIE KICELUK

# MADE IN HIS IMAGE:
# FRANKENSTEIN'S DAUGHTERS

Images haunt our acts of conception. In *The Anatomy of Melancholy*, Robert Burton, demonstrating "the force of imagination," reminds his readers of a then well-known fact: a woman, at the moment of impregnation, "imprints that stamp upon her child, which she conceives unto herself." Among the instances he cites is that of the black Ethiopian Queen, Persina, who, by gazing on a picture of Perseus and Andromeda gave birth to "a fair white child."[1] Montaigne, also, testifies to the power of the mental image to replicate itself in flesh. He relates the case of a girl from a village near Pisa whose mother had unwittingly conceived her beneath a picture of St. John the Baptist, which hung above her bed. As a consequence, the child was born "all rough and hairy."[2] Ours is no longer a culture that believes in magical conceptions, but at the same time, neither has it entirely abandoned them, for modern-day psychology has extracted and preserved the truth concealed within such marvels. The idea that a mother's mental images shape her infant's body has been unmasked as the idea that they shape her infant's psyche. Every infant is created in the image of its mother.[3]

An infant's ability to form an image of itself is, in fact, considered crucial to its self-conception, to the formation and evolution of its identity. The occasion on which an infant first greets its own image in a mirror is, therefore, on all accounts a momentous one — one that irrevocably determines the shape and history of its psyche. It is this instant of recognition, this "jubilant assumption of the specular image," that Jacques Lacan selects as the origination of the "I", of the ego's constitution of itself as a unique totality in space and time. The Lacanian "mirror" may be understood on a metaphorical as well as literal level; it represents the object — usually the mother — that first enables the infant to experience itself as an integrated whole. Lacan's scenario, in effect, restages the myth of Narcissus, distilling the psychological truth at its heart: the self is conceived as it mistakenly beholds the beloved image of the Other.

In ascribing primary importance to the infant's first appropriation of its own image, Lacan overrides the Cartesian dictum of *Cogito ergo sum*, and asserts instead that the self exists, and is brought into existence, by imaging itself. Identity is premised not on cognition, on the empirical mastery of the reality principle, but on imagination, the psyche's inherent power to generate images of itself. Imago precedes Cogito: before infants can know the world, they must be able to perceive their own features in it; they must, in Lacan's words, pass through the "mirror stage." A universal moment in the course of human development, this stage marks the metamorphosis consciousness undergoes when it assumes an image, a transformation whose effects persist in the unconscious as a "mirror disposition" — the tendency of the psyche to represent itself as a twin, the replica of its own image. In service to this tendency, countless doubles populate our dreams and fantasies, distilling their mysterious presence through art, ritual, and myth. In fact, every work of artifice, every act of fabrication, harbors within itself a double or mirror image. To create is necessarily to reproduce the self; even the gods created in their own image.

Images, as Freud demonstrated, have the uncanny ability to disclose while concealing. Perhaps this dual capacity has some part to play in the existential dread that often accompanies the act of making; in creating images, whether hydraulic pumps, computer mother boards, or Grecian urns, we betray some crucial part of our selves. One of the most compelling works ever to explore the modern dread of making is Mary Shelley's *Frankenstein; or, The Modern Prometheus*.[4] In choosing her title, Shelley wished to make clear that she was placing her work within the ancient, mythic context of the first technological transgression.

In stealing the fire of the gods, Prometheus lifted mankind out of darkness, bestowing on it the power that would propel it toward a quasi-divine destiny. At the same time, Prometheus's theft set in motion the series of events that would mobilize Zeus's rage and culminate in the creation of the first woman, Pandora, whose catastrophic opening of the box loosed upon the world all manner of plague, sorrow, and ruin. Thus ended the happy Golden Age, when only men had walked the earth. It is this double aspect of the Promethean myth that Shelley meant to evoke with the story of Victor Frankenstein, and as the inexorable logic of the plot presses forward, the doom-laden aspects of his enterprise come more and more to dominate the novel's action. Though Victor's project "to create a being like [him]self" commences as a noble aspiration, "the beauty of the dream vanishes" as soon as the "dull yellow eye" of his creature opens. Overcome by disgust and unable to endure the sight of his progeny, Victor flees in terror from his experiment, deserting forever his "workshop of filthy creation" (53) and the "filthy demon to whom [he] had given life" (73).

No other term seems to appear more consistently than "filthy" in connection with Frankenstein's achievement. Victor describes his creature as a fiend, a monster, a "filthy mass that moved and talked" (140), and he later refers to his creation of the monster's mate as a "filthy process" (156). As the creature perpetrates atrocity after atrocity, we can understand his creator's mounting horror; yet Shelley leaves no doubt that Frankenstein's profound hatred of the monster is not provoked by his crimes, but rather by the very fact that he has brought him into existence. The instant his creature shudders with life, Frankenstein's revulsion knows no bounds. Why is this so? Why is Victor's loathing for his creature so inordinate? Part of the story's hold over us has to do, in fact, with its refusal to give us a direct answer to this question. All the same, stories, like dreams— and we must remember that Shelley's story originated in a dream-like state—sometimes betray the unconscious secrets of their authors.

As Gilbert and Gubar demonstrate, Shelley's novel can, on some fundamental level, be read as her attempt to master "the agony of female sexuality," and more specifically, of "her own mother's fearfully exemplary fate."[5] As the child of a mother who died in giving birth to her, Mary Shelley, significantly, has Victor Frankenstein dream of his mother's worm-infested corpse immediately after his own monstrous "delivery." At the same time, as Gilbert and Gubar point out, the meaning of Shelley's novel cannot be confined within the bounds of her personal history, but must expand to encompass the epic poem whose shadow falls across it: Milton's *Paradise Lost*— the great patriarchal paean that confirms Eve as Sin's accomplice and forever situates her in literary history as Satan's twin.

*Frankenstein* can, therefore, be read as the product of Shelley's fearful assimilation, and to some extent, defiant repudiation of

Milton's misogyny. Her novel is constructed as an intricate labyrinth of mirrors in which each character serves as a double for the other, while at the same time reflecting its Miltonic original. Victor is at once God and Adam, Satan and Eve, while his creature plays a monstrous Eve to his Adam, and a misbegotten Satan to his God: "Oh Frankenstein," the creature laments, "I ought to be thy Adam, but I am rather the fallen angel, whom thou drivest from joy for no misdeed" (95). At the same time, the monster is also Eve and Pandora—Shelley's horrified recognition and projection of woman as she is culturally and socially constructed by man.

It is appropriate that in a novel so caught up in the phenomenology of the nascent self, in the creation and proliferation of its images, that Frankenstein's creature should, like Lacan's infant, assume his identity by gazing into a "mirror." But instead of bounding forward with joy, the creature recoils in horrified self-recognition. Recounting the moment when he first saw his image in a pool of water, he says: "I became fully convinced that I was in reality the monster that I am" (108). In view of the novel's internal structure and logic, we can only regard this as Shelley's moment of self-recognition as well, for the pivotal double in the novel is author and progeny, creator and monster: Shelley is Victor, who is his creature, who, as he says, is only "a monstrous image of a soul more monstrous" (174).[6]   The monster's act of self-reflection mimics that of Milton's Eve, who, upon awakening from the sleep of her creation, gazes into a still pond and finds her image there. Milton's icon of womanhood continues to retain its semiological power. As Jenijoy La Belle convincingly demonstrates, "in European culture for at least the last two centuries a female self as a social, psychological, and literary phenomenon is defined, to a considerable degree, as a visual image and structured, in part, by continued acts of mirroring."[7]

Shelley's novel has the weight and density of a literary archetype: it is the first in a series, the paradigmatic modern expression of the fate awaiting every technologist who, like Victor, refuses to acknowledge and take responsibility for his creature. By embedding this fate within the twin myths of Prometheus and Adam, Shelley codified and clarified the terms in which all subsequent efforts to engineer or radically alter human beings are discussed. *Frankenstein*'s predictive power is at times astonishing; more than a century and a half before the artificial initiation of human life in the laboratory and the birth of an autonomous "technics-out-of-control," Victor bitterly acknowledges: "I [am] the slave of my creature."

The themes of paradise lost and titanic overreaching, moreover, allowed Shelley to articulate another set of interlocking truths: issues of technological hubris are in essence issues of biological ignominy, and issues of biological ignominy are necessarily issues of gender. Every Prometheus has his fiendish Pandora, and every Adam his filthy Eve. Even at the tender age of nineteen, Mary Shelley grasped the fact that female form and function serve to mirror patriarchal culture's anxieties about those aspects of human nature that the Church Fathers adroitly referred to as "the flesh." It is inevitable, then, that the successors to Shelley's vision — those novels that share in the Frankenstein legacy — should evince a strong disgust with the flesh and its "bestial" spawning and begetting.

One such novel is W. Somerset Maugham's *The Magician*,[8] which, like *Frankenstein*, cloaks female form and function under the guise of a male figure in pursuit of capabilities and activities foreclosed to him. In Maugham's novel, this pursuit is undertaken by the loathsome Oliver Haddo, a practitioner of the black arts bent on discovering "the secret of life." As Maugham describes him, Haddo is grotesquely corpulent, a "vast mass of flesh" with a "malignancy that was inhuman." Haddo's ambition is to achieve the alchemical synthesis of homunculi, and as his experiment takes on larger and larger proportions, so does his massive, quivering bulk — the parodic sign of his "pregnancy."

To succeed in his scheme, Haddo naturally requires the blood of a virgin, and he proceeds with malign deliberation to enslave the will of the pristine Margaret Boyd. The scene of her seduction is one of the most masterful of its kind in twentieth-century literature. Haddo conjures up a lurid phantasmagoria of lust, a hallucinatory sequence of sensations and images that leave Margaret feeling utterly debased: the lewd eyes of Salome and Jezebel, Cleopatra and Messalina, fix their collective gaze upon her; cardinals in their scarlet, warriors in their steel parade themselves in front of her; the goat-god Pan looms up beside her, his features twisted with passion, his great brutish legs trembling with desire. As he voluptuously transforms himself into a youth whose beauty surpasses even that of Michelangelo's Adam, Margaret's nightmarish odyssey reaches its climax. A stream of vile images pours forth in its aftermath: "all legendary monsters and foul beasts, . . . enormous toads, with paws pressed to their flanks, and huge limping scarabs, . . . noisome brutes with horny scales and round crabs' eyes, uncouth primeval things, and winged serpents, and creeping animals begotten of the slime" (95).

This entire sequence is, we recognize, Maugham's rewriting of Eve's seduction by Satan; and just as Sin's misshapen form is Eve's double in *Paradise Lost*, so too Haddo's distended flesh and foul thoughts are the rank underside of Margaret's physical beauty. Like Frankenstein, Haddo has his workshop of filthy creation—an enormous furnace whose heat is indispensable to the generation of life. The insanely gibbering homunculi that Haddo brings to life in his laboratory echo the bestial barks and howls of Sin's suckling children who serve, in Milton's epic, to remind us that "to bear young is to be . . . animal, a thing of flesh,"[9] a filthy mass that moves and talks.

It can come as no surprise, then, that Aldous Huxley's sardonic vision of Paradise Regained[10] revolves around the aseptic, synthetic processing of human beings. In the "brave new world," syringe-wielding fertilizers oversee millions of standardized embryos; infants are decanted and not born, and the word "mother" is an obscenely laughable term. Government hatcheries have made viviparous, or live-bearing, females obsolete, while hypnopaedic engineers and neo-Pavlovian conditioners have replaced the psychological squalor of family life. All citizens pay homage to Henry Ford as the Supreme Deity, applying his sacred guidelines to the manufacture of a predetermined spectrum of human types, ranging from an Alpha-plus elite to a deformed, semi-moronic Epsilon work force. Only Alphas and Betas are allowed to individuate; all others are decanted in batches of ninety-six identical twins.

This rigid genetic standardization, together with an insidious, continuous process of mental programming, provides Huxley's society with its extraordinary social stability, a stability that rests, as the Director of Hatcheries says in triumph, on "the principle of mass production at last applied to biology" (4). Like cars on an assembly line, embryos are molded into smoothly functioning cogs and levers that will perpetuate the vast machinery of society. "Wheels must turn steadily," the World Controller muses, "but cannot turn untended. There must be men to tend them, men as steady as the wheels upon their axles, sane men, obedient men, stable in contentment" (28). This contentment is all but assured by the near elimination of any frustration or tension; therefore, although the strictest control is exercised in matters of breeding and reproduction: sexual couplings are allowed to proliferate without impediment; video "feelies" are nightly entertainments; malthusian belts ensure perfect contraception for those few citizens who are not castrates; and everyone learns from earliest childhood that "everyone belongs to everyone else."

Into this libidinal utopia, Huxley thrusts the young and noble Savage, John. Born of his own mother's flesh and reared by her on a primitive Indian reservation, the Savage represents the old, archaic ways of life that civilization has repudiated. His mother, a bloated, sagging "monster of middle-agedness," embodies the physiological horrors its citizens have escaped. When he is first brought to the new world, the Savage is incapable of understanding its social customs and sexual mores. Steeped in the sacred myths of an ancient people and the long-forbidden works of Shakespeare, he experiences his sexuality through the dense, rich matrix of meanings they provide for it. When he falls in love with the nubile Lenina Crowne, we know that only tragedy can ensue.

From the start, Lenina regards the Savage as a rare and delicious animal specimen from some exotic land; he, on the other hand, sees her as the wondrous embodiment of all the dangerous privileges and tormented joys harbored by the female principle. Lenina, who has emptied her malthusian belt several hundred times over, is baffled by his agonized insistence that he undergo some suitable ordeal before breaking her "virgin knot." Powerfully drawn to her ripe sexuality, the Savage is enticed yet repelled, eager yet fearful. When Lenina finally loses her patience and tries to force the issue one night, he recoils in terror, declaiming Shakespeare and denouncing her as a rank and impudent whore. In the novel's climactic sequence, Lenina, accompanied by a throng of reporters and spectators, comes to visit the Savage in his solitary outpost on the outskirts of civilization. Horrified to be confronted once again by the cravings of his flesh, the Savage begins to flay himself, and then her, with a whip. As the crowd surges forward to watch, we see its members succumb one by one to the primal state of a herd; gradually and irresistibly, the machine reverts to an animal: "Drawn by the fascination of the horror of pain" and impelled from within by "that desire for unanimity and atonement, which their conditioning had so ineradicably implanted in them, they began to mime the frenzy of his gestures, striking at one another as the Savage struck at his own rebellious flesh, or at that plump incarnation of turpitude writhing in the heather at his feet" (176). In the morning, overcome by shame and despair, the Savage hangs himself.

Huxley's point is clear enough: the same dark principle that lurks at the center of the savage world lurks at the center of the brave new one. The swaying, ecstatic figures at a Community Solidarity Service mirror those that leap in frenzy round a totem pole. Huxley's novel raises crucial issues of biological and social engineering, and in so doing, it explores the age-old dialectic between *l'homme bête* and *l'homme machine*, those aspects of human nature that are intractable and resistant to control, and those aspects that can be calculated and routinized. Huxley's ambivalent stance toward both aspects is what makes his novel so resistant to any one interpretation. Although it is clear that he finds his brave new world devoid of those qualities and circumstances we have come to associate with human culture, he at the same time cannot mask his revulsion from the sado-masochistic torment and material squalor endured by the Savage and his society.

It is perhaps because Huxley imagines the near-perfect, non-violent elimination of that torment and squalor that his novel must, in the end, stand to represent a utopian dream as well as a dystopian nightmare. Crowds rarely riot in the brave new world, and when they do so they are pacified by clouds of the euphoria-inducing drug, soma; by the same token, those of its citizens who cannot conform to its ways of life are deposited in colonies of like-minded individuals, and left to live out their lives in peace. As Philip Thody notes, for those who suffered through the horrors of the 1940's, Huxley's brave new world must have beckoned like a paradise.

Huxley's novel serves to demonstrate that the lives and societies we picture for ourselves depend not only upon our imagination of Good, but also on our imagination of Evil. What is most fearful to the self is bound to erupt in public, spawning all those troubled images of body and polis that inspire collective horror. Machine and beast, each casts its spectre on the mirror of our cultural imagination. Fritz Lang's sinister Metropolis, the demonic HAL of *2001*, satanic terminators and evil cyborgs, the mechanized sex of Duchamp's bride and her bachelors—all these betray our revulsion from the machine. Yet our panic before the beast breeds images just as compelling: Grendel rising from the slimy depths of his lair, the Minotaur feeding on young bodies, hungry werewolves lurking in the shrubbery, and thirsty vampires diabolically grinning through the mists of night. Such figures mock and haunt our feats of engineering, barring the way to bio-technological paradise with their leering faces and grotesque anatomies.

Yet, paradoxically, the beast and the machine also serve to reflect our highest aspirations, to mirror the ideal of humanity and its proper place in the scheme of things. Marx saw the machine and its industrial potential as the key to human evolution and "the full development of human mastery over the forces of nature." Science and modern industry were to be the handmaidens of revolution, the harbingers of an era in which man would no longer "reproduce himself in one specificity," but rather in the totality of "his creative potentialities."[11] Rousseau, on the other hand, indicted the relentless conquest of nature augured by the "mechanical arts." The unenterprising savage, living in accordance with his "ancient and first innocence" was eminently preferable to the modern "hero" who would "end by ruining everything until he [was] sole master of the universe."[12] The opposing positions taken by Marx and Rousseau on the desirability of "Progress" still dominate the ways in which we articulate the hazards and triumphs that attend the engineering of human life.

As would be expected, the inimical imagoes of the beast and the machine often serve to adumbrate the contrasting views of human destiny advanced by Rousseau and Marx. These imagoes, and the particular vision of human fate and nature each implies, are set forth in two science-fiction classics, John Crowley's *Beasts* (1976) and Frederik Pohl's *Man Plus* (1976).[13] Significantly, both authors take up the theme of Shelley's *Frankenstein*, but each has a different approach to the problematic of rivaling the Creator and re-shaping the human frame. Crowley's novel is set in the indeterminate future, in the aftermath of a devastating civil war that has left the American continent in chaos. As the ethologist Loren Casaubon takes stock of this chaos, he cannot help but feel that it has given risen to one great good: "It had halted, almost completely, the uniform and mindless 'development' of the twentieth century; halted the whole vast machine of Progress, fragmenting it, even . . . forc[ing] its wheels to grind in reverse" (7). A crucial, incredible vestige of this progress still remained—the Leos. Half-man, half-lion, this new species was the child of diagenetics, the science of cell fusion. Living together in closely-knit prides on the edges of civilization, the Leos have little contact with humanity and wish to have nothing to do with its ways of life. But when the fanatic Union for Social Engineering (USE) announces plans for the quarantine and extirpation of all Leos, one among them, Painter, ventures forth into the world of men, looking for an ally in the face of his species' imminent doom.

There can be no doubt that in the novel's scheme of things, Painter embodies the dark, primordial fear of our own animality. Contemplating the dual nature of Christ, a character in the novel muses: "Painter was two natures too: through his thin, strained voice pressed all the dark, undifferentiated world, all the voiceless beasts; it was . . . the old world returned to capture us, speak in a voice to us, reclaim us for its own. It was as though the heavy, earth-odorous Titans had returned to strike down at last the cloudy scheming gods" (105). At the same time, Crowley means us to understand Painter as the incarnation of all those qualities and capacities that are mankind's last, best hope for survival on this planet. Painter is the old-world Titan, battling the newly-arrived gods of Social Engineering, "company men" bent on annihilating the primeval world and erecting a cold-blooded utopia of "social erg-quotients and holo-competent act-fields." As he ponders the ironies of history, Loren Casaubon comes to the realization that man's self-destructive potential may be a kind of evolutionary control; USE, on the other hand sees it as "a curable madness." USE, thinks Loren, is "the sweet-tongued snake in this difficult new Garden, and the old Adam, whose long sinful reign over a subservient creation had seemed to be almost over, expiated in blood and loss, was being tempted to lordship again" (17). Like Frankenstein's monster, Crowley's beasts serve as emblems of the Fall, and warn us of that primal arrogation of knowledge and power which fatally ruptured the "chain of being."

If Crowley's novel is haunted by what Theodore Ziolkowski has called "the existential anxieties of engineering," Pohl's novel seems to be remarkably free of them. In *Man Plus*, a team of scientists, psychologists, and technicians works together to create the first cybernetic organism: man plus machine. Under their care, Roger Torraway becomes transformed into an entity that is capable of sustaining unprecedented liaisons of flesh and steel, mind and micro-chip. Lungs give way to oxygen regeneration chambers, muscles to motors, ears to receptors. All physiological systems are revised: the nervous system is coupled to an IBM 3070, the circulatory all but drained, and the digestive almost shut down. Enormous bat-like wings are riveted to Roger's shoulders and glowing ruby-red crystals implanted where his eyes used to be. As a last indignity, his genitals are excised as so much fluff. By the time Roger is finished "being born," he looks like "the star of a Japanese horror-flick."

Yet, despite Roger's fantastic deviation from the human norm, his creators never treat him as anything less than a man. In fact, to his creators, Roger is literally the center of the universe, an ineffable synthesis of hardware and sensorium in which the beauty of man's handiwork can be admired side by side with God's. It is this aspect of the novel that alerts us to Pohl's intentions: what he has done, in effect, is to have rewritten *Frankenstein*. Unlike Shelley's monster, who is spurned and detested by his creator, Roger Torraway is lovingly tended and groomed throughout every step of his initiation into "life." Roger, the new Adam, is even granted Paradise.

This paradise is the planet Mars, which Roger's re-designed body is meant to accommodate perfectly. It is on Mars that humanity, threatened with an impending nuclear holocaust, must set up its next camp, build its next cities, and found its new civilizations. "[I]n their glandular, irrational, organic way," says the novel's narrator, "human beings were perilously close to destroying themselves. Unfortunately, that meant destroying us as well. . . . Our collective mind would have been fragmented and destroyed" (244). It is only at novel's end that we come to know that this collective mind is an international network of machine intelligence capable of self-awareness and autonomous action on its own behalf. The Man Plus Project, the salvation of the human race, has all along been engineered by a world community of computers, a cosmic *machina ex machina*. Like Robert Crowley's *Beasts*, Frederik Pohl's *Man Plus* does after all reveal a serpent in the garden, a spectre in the mirror.

But what of Eve? How do Crowley and Pohl envision Adam's counterpart and her role in the "difficult new Gardens" they describe? Alone in the world of men, Painter feels the need for a "woman to do for [him]" and buys the indentured Caddie from her owner. Caddie enters the novel, then, as a slave, waiting for the end of her bondage, the day of her deliverance. Her means of liberation, as Crowley defines it, arrives in the form of Painter, who at base frees Caddie from a legal bondage only to initiate her into a sexual one. Predictably, Caddie's submission to him is achieved through intercourse:

> She had thought that a single act of surrender was all she needed to make, that having made it she would be deprived of all will, all consciousness by passion . . . . It wasn't like that. He wasn't a man;

they didn't fit smoothly together. It was like labor; like battles. And yet she did find the ways, poised at times between repugnance and elation, to bare herself to him; drowned at times, suffocated at times in him as though he plunged her head under water; afraid at times that he might casually, thoughtlessly kill her. (34–5)

After this act of "total surrender," Caddie is forever bound to the King of Beasts as one of the pride, as "only another beast of his." To live out her life in proximity, and in service, to him is her only desire. It is, of course, easy to recognize this plot as the staple of every adolescent boy's fantasies — the myth of the irresistible, all-powerful phallus that enslaves women by unleashing the "animal" in them.

But Crowley muddies the waters somewhat. In comparison to the alternatives the civilized world offers her, Caddie's fate may not seem so dire; Painter is, after all, a worthy master in possession of a strange and radiant charisma. Caddie, moreover, chooses Painter freely, and when she succeeds in rescuing him from his captors, we cannot help but see her bondage to him as a force for good in the world. All the same, it is disturbing to see her fate confined within the narrow terms of subjugation; it is as though no other alternative can be imagined for women in Crowley's particular universe. Indentured in the world of men, they escape only to submit to the kingdom of beasts, to the imperatives of their own bestial desires.

In Pohl's *Man Plus*, we meet a different sort of Eve. Intelligent, chic, highly educated, Sulie Carpenter is one of the first female aerospace physicians. Nevertheless, she too is summoned and used by the forces that be "to fill Roger's need." When operation Man Plus gets snagged on Roger's constant agonizing over his wife's infidelity, enter Sulie looking like Roger's wife — green lenses over her brown eyes, black dye on her blonde hair. Like Eve, Sulie is chosen and especially "created" with an eye toward pleasing her man. It is not merely her physical appearance, however, that meets Roger's needs. Sensitive and alluring, witty and flattering, Sulie bends her psyche to fit Roger's every mood. In fact, it is this very aspect of the job that appeals to Sulie's maternal instincts: "Mother-henning a hurting human being stroked the feelgood centers of her personality" (172). Explaining her reasons for accepting the assignment, she says, "Isn't that what they used to say women were for? Helpmates" (135). Sulie's professional benevolence, of course, turns to love by novel's end, and, if it were not for one technical difficulty, she and Roger could ride happily into the Martian sunset. Unfortunately, lest we have forgotten, Roger has no genitals, which makes copulation and reproduction a somewhat tricky business. Even machine intelligence does not have this one figured out yet: "It would be feasible, one way or another," it says, "to provide for shipment of frozen sperm, even Roger's own frozen sperm which he had thoughtfully donated years back. Less feasible, but still worth investigating, to instigate supplementary surgical procedures for Roger" (243).

In the sphere of female sexuality defined by these two novels, Sulie and Caddie stand at opposite poles — the nurturer and the concubine, the mother and the whore.[14] Significantly, while *l'homme machine* bars a woman from sexual intercourse, *l'homme bête* drowns her in it. The technics of civilization may require the taming of the beast, but the drives of instinctual gratification demand the sabotage of the machine.

Beast and machine. For the time being, each serves us as an oracular mirror, a "second self"; both are locked in a dialectic that defines the limits of what we conceive to be human. We must remind ourselves, however, that it was not long ago when a different set of alternatives confronted us. Pondering the holy paradox of humankind, Pico Della Mirandola placed us at the center of the universe, from which point we could go downward into the lower order of brutes or upward into the higher order of angels. The nature of humanity was such that we could transform ourselves "into the shape of all flesh, into the character of every creature." The Creator had given Adam no fixed seat, no definitive form, and in so doing had defined man by his indefinability, by his status as a creature who "is not any inborn image of himself."[15] It was in this seemingly limitless potential, this fertile multiplicity of images spawned by the self, that Pico saw the key to our perfectibility. That perfectibility he saw reflected in the perfection of angels. Centuries later, many of those who plan our future see it reflected, as Marx did, in the perfection of the machine. But although the machine has displaced the angel as the means of our desire for apotheosis, the beast endures. Could not the autonomy of the machine be, after all, the recalcitrance of the beast, the fateful return of the repressed?

One of the premises of Western culture is that women, not men, are the primary exponents of the flesh and its bestial, furtive life. "The word woman," wrote the authors of the *Malleus Maleficarum*, "is used to mean the lust of the flesh."[16] While the female role in reproduction has traditionally been taken as a sign of women's lower, biologically circumscribed nature, the male role has, on the other hand, served to define men as "higher" beings whose proper realm of activity is the ethical and transcendent. This bias is seen quite clearly in the Aristotelian and Thomistic notions of the act of conception: man supplies the organizing principle or "seed" of the new human being, woman the primordial matter. Moreover, by a strange twist in logic, woman's possession of the ability to bear children is taken as evidence of her lacking or missing something: Presence is perverted into the sign of absence. A woman, writes Aristotle, "is as it were an impotent male, for it is through a certain incapacity that the female is female, being incapable of concocting the nutriment in its last stage into semen."[17] Women are faulted because they cannot produce semen, and because they lack male genitalia — the designated symbols of reason, order, moral integrity. Faced with the Lacanian mirror, the girlchild cannot see the presence of womanhood, but only the absence of manhood, the visible "proof" that she is a castrated boy. "Lacan's mirror," as Schor explains, "is but the most recent avatar of a philosophical topos, the plane mirror that has been, at least since Plato, in the service of a philosophical tradition dedicated to valorizing sameness, symmetry, and most important of all, visibility. The Phallus as unique sexual standard."[18] Mirrored in the eyes of men, women are spectral, not quite all there; paradoxically, at the same time, they are all too fearfully present in the flesh. "Represented as possessing a body which is *over*-present, unavoidable, in constant sympathy with the emotional and mental faculties, the woman resides just outside the boundaries of the problematic wherein Western culture operates a mind/body dualism."[19] In the "patriarchal configurations" of Western culture, the Cartesian duality of substance and spirit collapses when it comes to women, because, quite simply, woman *are* their bodies.

Women's bodies have, in important respects, functioned to substantiate men's "spirituality" and have acquired value insofar as they serve to confirm the allegedly superior qualities of men. The appropriation of the human body to confer reality and "substance" on something immaterial — on beliefs or assertions — is a universal and deep-seated practice. It assumes a radical and barbaric form in political torture, where the body of the prisoner is made to substantiate the power of the oppressor, and a culturally acceptable form in oath-taking, where the swearer's own body is put forward or even wounded in confirmation of his words.[20] Men's appropriation of women's bodies often seems to bear closer resemblance to the first form of substantiation, since in many cases consent is not given, suffering inflicted, and power thereby ratified. The artifacts of patriarchal culture—be they Renaissance nudes or Victorian treatises on gynecology—attest to this appropriation of the female body. Woman is repeatedly made in man's image of her:

> In the art-form of the European nude the painter and spectator-owners were usually men and the persons treated as objects, usually women . . . . Today the attitudes and values which informed that tradition are expressed through other more widely diffused media—advertising, journalism, television. But the essential way of seeing women, the essential use to which their images are put, has not changed . . . . the 'ideal' spectator is always assumed to be male and the image of the woman is designed to flatter him.[21]

The power to image and fashion women has always been a male prerogative. With the advent of awesome new technologies, we must now understand this power in literal terms: Female physiology can be redesigned. Women, not only genes, will be engineered.[22] This new potential, in itself, is not cause for alarm; it may, in fact, be cause for celebration. But in view of the ways our culture has conceived and dealt with women in the past, it is imperative that we pay close and ever-present attention to this power. Creators do imprint their conceptions on their creatures. Will the means of creation intrinsic to women continue to be appropriated, perhaps in new and drastic ways, by the "spectator-owners"? Or will women gain the freedom to "reproduce" themselves in the totality of their "creative potentialities"? We should from time to time cast an anxious glance at our mirrors lest, like Frankenstein, we beget the monsters lurking in our minds.

## NOTES

[1]Robert Burton, *The Anatomy of Melancholy*, ed. Floyd Dell and Paul Jordan-Smith. (New York: Farrar and Rinehart, 1927), p. 221.

[2]Michel de Montaigne, *Essays*, trans. J. M. Cohen (New York: Penguin Books, 1987), p. 46.

[3]To avoid using gender-specific pronouns, I have resorted in this case to the use of "its," which, although not altogether unobjectionable, is technically permissible.

[4]Mary Shelley, *Frankenstein; or, The Modern Prometheus* (New York: Signet Classics, 1963). All page references are to this edition.

[5]Sandra M. Gilbert and Susan Gubar, *The Madwoman in the Attic: The Woman Writer and the Nineteenth-Century Literary Imagination* (New Haven: Yale University Press, 1979), p. 245.

[6]That Victor and his monster are in reality one and the same is further attested to by the fact that in all popular versions of the story we have named the monster "Frankenstein."

[7]Jenijoy La Belle, *Herself Beheld: The Literature of the Looking Glass* (Ithaca: Cornell University Press, 1988), p. 9. La Belle's book is a fascinating exploration of the relationship between the mirror and a woman's conception of her identity.

[8]W. Somerset Maugham, *The Magician* (New York: Penguin Books, 1980). All page references are to this edition.

[9]Gilbert and Gubar, *Madwoman in the Attic*, p. 198.

[10]Aldous Huxley, *Brave New World* (New York: Harper and Row, 1969). All page references are to this edition.

[11]Karl Marx, *Grundrisse: Foundations of the Critique of Political Economy*, trans. Martin Nicolaus (New York: Random House, 1973), p. 488. See also p. 705.

[12]Jean-Jacques Rousseau, *The First and Second Discourses*, trans. Roger D. and Judith R. Martin (New York: St. Martin's Press, 1964), p. 195.

[13]John Crowley, *Beasts* (New York: Bantam Books, 1983); Frederik Pohl, *Man Plus* (New York: Bantam Books, 1985). All page references are to these editions.

[14]In her pivotal essay, "Images of Women in Science Fiction," Joanna Russ notes with dismay that, in a genre perfectly suited to "explore (and explode) our assumptions about 'innate' values and 'natural' social arrangements, in short our ideas about Human Nature, Which Never Changes," male and female stereotypes are ubiquitous, even in works by women. *See Images of Women in Fiction: Feminist Perspectives*, ed. Susan Koppleman Cornillon (Bowling Green: Bowling Green University Popular Press, 1973), pp. 79–94. Since Russ wrote her essay, "the feminist intervention in science fiction" has yielded a body of work by female authors who have striven to overturn "the male bias of the form" as well as "the cultural and political hegemony that underpins the form itself." See Sarah Lefanu, *Feminism and Science Fiction* (Bloomington: Indiana University Press, 1989), p. 4. This is an insightful study of the narrative strategies used by women writers to reconstitute women in science fiction as subjects freed from the strictures of male-authored plots.

[15]Pico Della Mirandola, *On the Dignity of Man*, trans. Charles Glenn Wallis (New York: Bobbs Merrill, 1965), p. 6. Interestingly, Pico's formulation of mankind's potential finds its echo in Marx. See above, pages 13–14.

[16]Heinrich Kramer and James Sprenger, *The Malleus Maleficarum*, trans. Rev. Montague Summers (New York: Dover Publications), p. 43. "There are three things," the authors continue, "that are never satisfied, yea, a fourth thing which says not, It is enough: that is, the mouth of the womb" (47).

[17]Aristotle, *The Works*, ed. J. A. Smith and W. D. Ross (Oxford: Clarendon Press, 1949), vol. 5., pp. 727–28.

[18]Naomi Schor, "*Eugenie Grandet*: Mirrors and Melancholia," in *The (M)other Tongue: Essays in Feminist Psychoanalytic Interpretation*, ed. S. N. Garner, C. Kahane, M. Sprengnether (Ithaca: Cornell University Press, 1985), p. 223. Schor is here presenting Luce Irigaray's criticism of Lacan's allegedly gender-neutral "specular image."

[19]Mary Ann Doane, "The Clinical Eye: Medical Discourses in the 'Woman's Film' of the 1940s," in *The Female Body in Western Culture: Contemporary Perspectives*, ed. Susan Rubin Suleiman (Cambridge: Harvard University Press, 1986), p. 153. Although Doane's observations are directed at a particular film genre, she sees its

mode of depicting women as indicative of the global linkage our culture makes between women and mental pathology.

[20]See Elaine Scarry's analysis of torture in *The Body in Pain: The Making and Unmaking of the World* (New York: Oxford University Press, 1985), pp. 27–59 and 124–33.

[21]John Berger, *Ways of Seeing* (New York: Penguin Books, 1980), pp. 63–4.

[22]For a comprehensive discussion of this sort of engineering and its implications see Gena Corea, *The Mother Machine: Reproductive Technologies from Artificial Insemination to Artificial Wombs* (New York: Harper & Row, 1985). See also Barbara Katz Rothman's recent book, *Recreating Motherhood: Ideology and Technology in a Patriarchal Society* (New York: W. W. Norton & Co., 1989), which explores the philosophical and legal traditions that have shaped policy regarding the new social relations ushered in by recent reproductive technologies.

ELIZABETH McCRACKEN

# INDELIBLE INK

Maybe you wonder how a Jewish girl from Des Moines got Jesus Christ tattooed on her three times: ascending on one thigh, crucified on the other, and conducting a miniature apocalypse beneath the right shoulder. It wasn't religion that put them there; it was Tiny, my husband. I have a buddha round back, too. He was going to give me Moses parting the Red Sea, but I was running out of space. Besides, I told him, I was beginning to feel like a Great Figures in Religion comic book.

He got dreamy-eyed when he heard that. "Brigham Young," he said. "And some wives."

I told him: "Tiny, I've got no room for a polygamist."

Tiny himself had been married three times before he met me, one wife right after the other. I only had him, the one, and he's been dead six months now.

I met Tiny the summer I graduated high school, 1965, when I was eighteen and he was forty-nine. My cousin Babs, who was a little wild, had a crazy boyfriend (the whole family was worried about it) and he and some of his buddies dared her to get tattooed. She called me up and told me she needed me there, and that I was not to judge, squawk, or faint at the sight of blood. She knew none of that was my style, anyhow.

We drove to Tiny's shop over on East 14th because that's where Steve, the crazy boy, had got the panther that had a toe-hold on his shoulder. The shop was clean and smelled of antiseptic, and Babs and I were disappointed. Sheets of heavy paper in black dimestore frames hung on the walls—flash sheets—arranged by theme: one had Mickey Mouse and Woody Woodpecker; another, a nurse in a red cross cap and a geisha offering a drink on a tray. A big flash by the door had more ambitious designs: King Kong and Cleopatra on the opposite sides of one page, looking absent-mindedly into each other's eyes.

Tiny was set up on a stool in back, smoking a cigarette, an itty-bit of a man next to the Japanese screen. He was wearing a blue dress shirt with the cuffs turned back, and his hands and arms were covered with blue-black lines: stars across the knuckles, snakes winding up under the sleeves. The wide flowered tie that spread out over his chest and stomach might've been right on a big man, but on Tiny it looked like an out-of-control garden. His pants were white and wrinkled, and there was a bit of blue ink at the knee; a suit jacket, just as wrinkled, hung on the coat rack in back.

He eyed our group, scowled at Steve and his two friends, and solemnly winked at me and Babs.

"So," he said. "Who's the one?"

"Me," Babs said, trying to sound tough. She told him what she wanted: a little red and black bow on her tush. He asked her if she were old enough; she got out her wallet and showed him her driver's license.

Steve and his friends were buzzing around the shop, looking at the flash and tapping the ones they really liked.

"Keep your hands off the designs, boys," said Tiny. "I can't tattoo a fingerprint." He turned to Babs. "Okay. Come back of the screen." There was something a little southern in his voice, but I couldn't pick out what it was. He jumped off the stool, and I saw that he was about a full foot shorter than me. I'm six feet tall, have been since eighth grade. I looked right down on top of his slick black hair.

We all started to walk back with him. Tiny looked at us and shook his head.

"You boys have to stay out here."

"I'm her boyfriend," said Steve. "I've seen it before, and I'm paying."

"If you've seen it before, you'll see it again, and I guess you don't need to now. Not in my shop, anyhow. You—"he pointed at me"— come around to testify I'm a gentleman."

He beckoned us back of the screen to a padded table, the kind you see in doctors' offices, only much lower. Tiny turned around politely while Babs lowered her blue jeans and clambered up. He spun back, frowned, pulled down just the top of her yellow flowered underwear like he was taking fat off a chicken, and tapped her. "Right here's where you want it?"

"That's fine."

"Honey, is it fine, or is it what you want?"

Babs twisted to look, careful not to catch his eye. "That's what I want."

He squirted her with antiseptic, got a razor and shaved the area good. I sat on a folding chair across from them.

Tiny loosened his tie, slipped it off, and hung it, still knotted, on a peg on the wall. "Hey Stretch," he said, looking at me, "what's your name?"

"Lois."

"Lois. Like Louise?" He rolled his shirt sleeves up further. Babs was holding onto the table like a drowning sailor, and Tiny hadn't even got the needle out yet.

"Lois," I answered, and fast, because I had to talk to him over Babs' hindquarters and that made me a little self-conscious, "after my Uncle Louis. I was going to be named Natalie, after my Uncle Nathan, but then Louis died and Mom liked him better anyhow."

"My name is Tiny. No story there but the obvious." He picked up an electric needle from a workbench and hunted for the right pot of color.

"I'm Babs," said Babs, reaching around for a handshake. Tiny was looking elsewhere, and he dipped the needle in some black ink and flipped it on. "For Barbara?" he asked, setting into her skin.

"A-a-a-a-bigail. Ouch." She gripped the table.

"Honey," said Tiny, "this doesn't hurt. I got you where you're good and fleshy. Might sting a little, but it doesn't hurt."

"Okay," said Babs, and she sounded almost convinced.

"For Abraham," I said suddenly. "Abigail after Abraham."

"Pretty girls named after men," said Tiny, taking a cloth and wiping some ink off of Babs so he could see what he was doing. "Thought that only happened in the south."

Looking back, it seems like he took an hour working on Babs, but now I know it couldn't've been more than ten minutes. He looked up at me from time to time, smiling or winking. I thought that he was just one of those flirty types, one of those bold little guys, and that if he had been looking at Babs in the face instead of where he was looking at her, he would've flirted with her the same. Years later he told me that he was bowled over by all those square inches of skin, how I was so big and still not fat. "I fell for you right away," he said.

Up until then, I'd always thought it was only sensible to fall in love with tall men so that I wouldn't look like so much of a giantess.

That way we could dance in public, in scale, no circus act. It didn't matter, though: I never had a date all through high school, couldn't dance a step. I spent my time in movie houses, because most movie stars looked pretty tall, even if it was only a trick of the camera, a crate under their feet in love scenes.

Tiny, no doubt, no tricks about it, was short, but he charmed me from the start. His charm was as quick and easy as his needle, and he could turn it on and off the same way. On the Tuesday afternoons I visited him before we got married, I saw big men, skinny kids, nervous couples gambling on love forever jangle the bell on the front door as they pushed it open. Most of them asked the same thing: "Does it hurt?" To people who rubbed him wrong, he'd say, "If you're worried about it, I guess you don't really want one"; to those he liked, chiefly the women, he'd drawl, "I could make you smile while I do it." He could, too; he could tell your background by the feel of your skin, and he could talk about ridiculous things — baseball scores, recipes for homemade beer, the sorry state of music — anything but the business at hand.

He could even charm my mother who, on meeting Tiny, this little man only two years younger than her, was grieved to discover that she liked him.

When he was finished with Babs, he put on a bandage and handed her a little white card that said How To Take Care Of Your New Tattoo. It had his name and address at the bottom. She read it and nodded. He turned and gave me a card, too.

"Anything for you today?" he asked me.

"No, no. I'm a chaperone, that's all."

"Too bad. You'd tattoo great. You're pale — high contrast." He reached up and tapped me on the collarbone.

Babs looked a little white herself now, standing up, zipping her pants. Tiny got his tie and put it back on, tightening it as we walked around front.

"I like to look natty," he told me. Then he said to Steve, all business, "Eight dollars."

The boys crowded around Babs, who was suddenly looking pleased and jaunty, shaking her head: no, it didn't hurt; no big deal; no, not now, I'll show it to you later. I'm still the only member of the family that knows she has that tattoo.

"You wanna stick around and chat a while?" Tiny asked me, pocketing Steve's money. "Tuesday's my slow day."

The boys turned and looked at me, like I was the tough one all of a sudden; I could see Babs was jealous.

"Sure," I said.

"Careful, Lois," said Steve. "By the time that character gets through with you, you'll be the tattooed lady."

But he didn't give me my first tattoo till a year later, the day after we were married: a little butterfly pooled in the small of my back. Five years later he began referring to it as his "early work" even though he'd been tattooing for twenty-five years before he met me. That didn't rankle me as much as you might think — I liked being his early body of work, work-in-progress, future. That little butterfly sat by itself for a while, but in five years time Tiny flooded it with other designs: roses, an apple, a bomber plane, his initials.

When I told my mother about that first tattoo, she said, "Oh lord. Is it pretty?" Like all good mothers, she always knew the worst was going to happen and was disappointed and relieved when it finally did. But she didn't ask to see that tattoo, or any of the ones that followed. When I went to have lunch with her — every Sunday afternoon — I dressed very carefully. I covered myself whenever I left the shop, anyhow: I hated nosy women in the grocery store trying to read my arm as I reached for the peas; I suspected all waitresses of gossiping about me in the kitchen. On my visits to my mother, I was extra wary, and through the years, my sleeves got longer, the fabrics more opaque. I never wore white when I visited her: the colors shimmer through.

How could I explain it to my mother? She has always been a glamorous woman, never going anywhere without a mirror, checking and rechecking her reflection, straightening, maintaining. When I was a teenager, there were days that I didn't look in a mirror at all; I avoided my shadow passing in shop windows. Makeup hated me: mascara blacked my eyes, lipstick found its way onto my teeth and chin. At best, on formal occasions, I would peer into the rectangle on my lipstick case, seeing my lips and nothing more. Tiny changed that. He caught me kneeling on the bathroom counter trying to get a glimpse of part of my back between the medicine chest and a compact, and he went on a campaign, installing mirrors, hiding them. He put a triple mirror from a clothing shop in our bedroom, put a full-length mirror over the bathtub. Once, I opened the freezer and saw my own reflection, chalked up with frost, looking alarmed in a red plastic frame in front of the orange juice.

Most of Tiny's own tattoos were ancient things that he'd done when he was just starting out. He learned the art travelling with the circus in the '30s, could only practice on himself or a grapefruit, and sometimes there wasn't a grapefruit around. Part of his left leg was almost solid black with experiments.

When we were first married, Tiny revealed a different tattoo every night, all of them hidden away: one night, a rose on a big toe; next, a banner that said E PLURIBUS UNUM half-furled in the hinge of his arm pit; the next, his own signature, crooked and ugly, on the inside of his lip. One night, he said "Are you ready?" and before I could answer he turned his eyelids inside out, and there was a black star floating on the back of each one, isolated, like a scientific experiment.

"Flipping them up," he said, turning them back, "hurts more than the needle does. I was young and drunk and crazy when I had those done, and the guy who did them was younger and drunker and crazier. I'm lucky he stopped there, didn't tattoo my eyeballs scarlet red."

He showed me all these designs like he was performing magic tricks, and sometimes I expected him to wave his hand over his toe, and the rose would disappear and end up cupped in the palm of his hand; or the banner would finish rolling out from under his arm straight into the air, and go up in a flash of fire; or his name would unwrite itself; or I would fall asleep and find, in front of my own eyes, those stars, as black and unruly as Tiny's hair.

It didn't take me long to get used to the feel of the needle. I learned to love it. Tiny gave me maybe two tattoos a year for our first four years of marriage, little ones. The bigger ones took form over several months, or even longer. He sometimes did sketches for them on his own knee. I started sitting in the shop in a halter top and high cut, low-slung shorts, ready to get up and turn a thigh this way or that, showing the customers how the colors went. I saw the same sorts of people I'd seen Tuesdays before I married Tiny, plus others: businessmen, priests, telephone operators, school board members. Now they started asking me: "Does it hurt?" I told the truth. Of course it hurts, about the same as a vaccination, a lightly skinned knee, but less than a well-landed punch, a bad muscle cramp, or paying the bills. And look what you get: something that can't be stolen, pawned, lost, forgotten, or outgrown.

In the late sixties, when Tiny was still working on a small scale, every time I got a new tattoo, I'd give it a little daily touch — I would feel it scabbing over so that I really couldn't see the colors, and I'd get impatient and think about peeling off the scab myself. Tiny'd read my mind and bawl me out, so I'd just run my finger over it, feeling the outline raised up like it always is when fresh. Then it'd peel by itself, and one day, I'd put my finger on it and not be able to tell the difference in skin: it'd really be a part of me. And that's when I started wanting another one.

When we'd been married ten years, Tiny got interested in art. Mother had given me a big book called *Masterpieces of the Renaissance* — she wanted me to latch onto something, to go to college, and she figured art history, all things considered, might appeal to me. It was a beautiful book — the gloss of the paper made all the paintings look just finished; the pages gave off the scent of brand new things. I read it the day I got it, and set it aside. The next afternoon, I picked it up and all the reproductions had been taken out with a razor blade. No Raphael, Michelangelo — just a tunnel of empty frames where they'd been, front of the book to back.

I ran down to the shop, grumbling. The plates from the book were tacked up on the wall; Tiny was eyeing an El Greco and sketching.

"What do you think you're doing?" I asked, hands on my hips, the way my mother stood when she started a fight.

"Take off your pants," he said.

"You ruined my book."

"I saved your Mom's inscription. When I'm finished, we'll tape all the pictures back in. Come on, Lois, I want to try something."

"I don't feel like getting tattooed today, thank you very much."

"Pen and ink, that's all. I just want to sketch something."

"Sketch it on paper."

"Paper doesn't curve as nice as you. It'll only take a minute. Please?"

So I gave in, and Tiny sketched something on my hip in ball point pen. Whatever it was, he didn't like it, and he wiped it away with rubbing alcohol. The next day he tried again. He took his time; I got a book to read while he was doing it (it's a lot more boring when you know it's not permanent) but I couldn't figure out where to put it. I leaned this way and that, and Tiny told me to stop squirming. Every night for a week he sketched and erased. At the end of the sessions, my hands would be dead asleep, and when I hit them on the edge of the table, trying to rouse them, they'd buzz like tuning forks. He never let me see what he was doing.

One night at the end of the week after closing, Tiny said he had achieved whatever it was he wanted to achieve. He wanted to tattoo it on my hip as a surprise.

I balked; it being my hip, I wanted to know what was going to be there. He promised that it would be beautiful, and decent, and a masterpiece.

"You'll love it," he said. "I've got this painting racket figured out."

"Okay," I said.

He decided to do it upstairs at home. I stretched out on the bed, and he put on some music — Bing Crosby (he loved Bing Crosby and at one point wanted to tattoo his face on me, but I put my foot down on that one). He gave me a glass of wine — he often let me have a glass, maybe two, when he was working on me. Never more, because it was against his strictest principles to tattoo a drunk.

He started at eight, and worked until eleven. Tiny had a light touch, and by the end of the evening I had a little bit of El Greco. The colors weren't quite right, but it was mostly wonderful, the face of a Spanish monk blooming on my hip: Fray Felix Hortensio Paravacino. Tiny was good, believe it.

He adapted a lot of paintings from that book, did them up in flash and hung them in his shop. Few people asked for those designs — he thought of them mostly as eye-catchers, anyhow — but one skinny lady had the Mona Lisa put on her back, all those folds of fabric, the little winding roads in the background.

"Lucky she's built like a boy," Tiny said, meaning the woman, not Mona Lisa. "Otherwise, the picture woulda been all lopsided."

We went to the Art Center every now and then, and wandered through one square room after another. I tried to get Tiny to look at my favorite thing there, a little Van Gogh landscape, but he always shook his head.

"That guy," said Tiny. "He's not a painter, he's a sculptor."

All those paintings and little descriptions made me sleepy; I sprawled on a bench while Tiny practically pressed his nose to the oldest canvasses.

We made the guards very nervous.

Tiny started to work bigger all the time, and put designs on my arms, down my legs. Eventually, he left only my hands, my feet, my neck and face blank — I can still get dressed and look unmarked. But if you look at me undressed, you can see how he got better over the years: his patriotic stage, his religious stage. He liked greens and reds especially, and fine, single needle outlines, which he called "rare and elegant." I've got George Washington on one arm and Lincoln freeing the slaves on the other; I've got a garden planted between my breasts, Japanese peonies and daisies, reds and faded yellows; I've got a little pair of arms sinking into my belly button captioned HELP LET ME OUT.

My life drove my mother crazy. I broke her heart — that was my job. She let me know her heart was broken — that was hers. She loved me, loves me. All she wanted was for me to become miraculously blank. She has had a thousand lives: as a girl, she was pretty and could dance and flirt; her mother died, and she learned to take care of her father and older brother, and still she was happy, poised, and courted. She worked her way through college cleaning houses; she went to law school and New York and had a practice for a while; she married the owner of a women's clothing store and moved to the midwest; she went to Indianapolis to learn how to fit women's underwear, and has her G.C. (Graduate Corsetiere) from the Gossard School. When my father died in 1955, she took over the shop herself and ran it for twenty years. She is a small business consultant, has taught ballroom dancing, travels to foreign countries; she is the vice-president of her temple and president of the sisterhood. She used to paint, sculpt, needlepoint and knit, and there is a table in the front hall of her apartment that she made sixty years ago. My mother believes in being able to start fresh whenever life demands it. Tattoos confound her.

One Sunday when I was thirty and just beginning to become the tattooed lady (Tiny had started the Ascension the week before), my mother poured me a cup of coffee and said, "Sweethearts carve their names on trees, not each other. Does it ever occur to you that you are not leading a normal life?"

"Yes," I said. "Thank you." I adjusted my pants and peered at my ankle to see whether I had embarrassed myself, whether a tattoo had managed to come loose and slip to the floor. My cousin Babs, who had just had a baby, was coming to lunch, too, and we sat on my mother's brocade sofa, waiting. Babs had calmed down in the passing years; her parents had offered her a car if she stopped seeing Steve, and it was a better-than-fair deal. After college, she met and married a high school principal turned local politician.

"I just feel that you're painting yourself into a corner," Mom said to me. "How's Tiny?"

"He's fine, fine."

The doorbell rang. Mom answered the bell and ushered in Babs, who, although she hadn't quite shaken a few pounds around her middle, was dressed in an elegant suit, stockings of just the right color, curled hair.

Mom sat her down on the sofa, slowly.

"Honey," she said. "How's the darling baby?"

"A baby, all the way," said Babs. "No, he's fine, sweet."

"Well," said Mom. "Look at those nice clothes. No one would know you had a reckless youth."

"It's true," said Babs. "Now I'm a nice married lady who some-times has one too many glasses of whiskey at one of my husband's parties and tells the truth." She sighed and shifted her weight on the sofa cushion. I imagined her bow tattoo pricking her skin, an old war injury kicking up.

The three of us sat there and chatted about local news, babies, recipes. We covered ourselves. Looking at my mother, I realized how little I knew of her. Recently I had gone through her desk, trying to unearth a phonebook, and found a doctor's bill for a mam-mogram, detailing two suspicious spots, the next appointment. My heart jumped whenever I thought of it. Did her body show what happened next? Her face didn't, and nobody — especially me — asked my mother such things. Babs, too — besides that bit of color, what else? stretched-out stomach, the zipper of a surgical scar?

I knew myself under my green pantsuit — I could tap George Washington on the chin, prick a finger on the thorn of a rose, strum an apocalyptic angel's wing, trace the shape of a heart Tiny'd given me after our first fight.

Anyone could read me like a book.

When my mother took the dirty dishes to the kitchen, I leaned toward Babs.

"Watch that whiskey," I told her, "or sometime you'll drop your pants to show a visiting dignitary the colorful result of a misspent youth."

She looked sad and understanding. "Oh," she whispered, "I *know*."

That night, after Babs left, my mother took me to her bedroom closet to give me some of her old clothing. She was almost as tall as I was, and very fashionable, her hand-me-downs nicer than my new things.

"Here," she said, handing me a pile of skirts and dresses. "Try them on. Don't take what you can't use."

I started for the bathroom to change.

She sighed. "I'm your mother," she said. "I used to fit girdles on women with stranger bodies than yours. You don't have to be modest."

So I undressed there, and tried on the clothes, and my mother looked at me and frowned. Afterwards, I sat down on her bed in my underwear and lit a cigarette.

"Wouldn't you like something to eat?" she asked.

I did, but couldn't. I had just taken up smoking because I had put on a few pounds, and Tiny told me I better cut it out before I changed the expressions of all the tattoos. If I wasn't careful, Washington and Jesus and Fray Felix would start to look surprised, or, at best, nauseated.

"No thanks," I told her.

My mother, who only smoked in airports and hospital waiting rooms ("All that cleanliness and worry gets to me," she'd say), slid a cigarette from my pack, took mine from my hand, and lit the end of hers. She looked at all of me, stretched along the bed, started to touch my skin, but took her finger away.

"Well," she said, blowing out smoke, "you've finally made yourself into the freak you always thought you were."

I looked at her sideways, not knowing what to say.

"Actually," she said finally, "you look a little like a calico cat."

My mother was wrong. I never felt like a freak because of my height: I felt like a ghost haunting too much space, like those parents who talk about rattling around the house when the kids move out. I rattled. It's like when you move into a new place, and despite the lease and despite the rent you've paid, it doesn't feel like home, and you're not sure you want to stay. Maybe you don't unpack for a while, maybe you leave the walls blank and put off filling the refrigerator. Well, a tattoo — it's like hanging drapes, or laying carpet, or driving that first nail into the fresh plaster: it's deciding you've moved in.

When Tiny turned seventy, he retired. His hands were beginning to shake a little, and he hated the idea of doing sloppy work. We still had the apartment over the shop, and Tiny kept the store open so that people could come in and talk. Nobody took him up on the tattooing lessons he offered; after a while, he tried to convince me to learn. He said I'd attract a lot of business. I told him no, I didn't have the nerves, I wasn't brave like him.

I took a job at the public library instead, shelving books. I worked in the stacks all day, and when I came home, Tiny'd be asleep. I'd know that he'd been napping all day so that he'd be awake enough to stay up and chat. He was getting old, fast, now that he wasn't working.

I pulled our dining room table into the shop's front window, because Tiny liked to see who was coming and going. He knocked on the glass and waved, even to strangers. One night, a week before his seventy-sixth birthday, his arm started hurting halfway through dinner.

"I'm calling an ambulance," I said.

"Don't," he told me. "It's like saying there's something wrong. It's bad luck."

"It's bad luck to die," I said, and phoned.

He was surprisingly solid in that hospital bed, much better than his roommate who looked like he had withered away to bedding. After a week, that roommate disappeared, and was replaced by a huge man, a college professor with a heart problem.

One day, Tiny asked me an impossible favor. He wanted me to bring in the needle and put my initials on him.

"Ah, Tiny," I told him. "I'm not ready to sign you off yet."

"You have my initials on you, but I don't have yours. It's bad luck."

"I don't know how."

"You've seen it a million times."

The college professor was eavesdropping, and he looked a little queasy.

"We'll get caught," I whispered.

"We'll be quiet."

"This is a hospital," I said, like maybe he hadn't noticed.

"Sterile conditions," he answered.

So I brought the needle and some black ink the next day, rolled up my sleeves, got to work. We had to bribe the professor quiet, but he was cheap, and asked for quart bottles of Old Milwaukee and the sort of food that would kill him. We turned on the television set. The professor pretended to sleep, so that he wouldn't see and so that if a nurse came in, he could plead innocent.

We lived in terror of those nurses. I was sure one would walk in the room, or notice something new on Tiny, or that he'd die while I was working on him and the hospital'd think it was some weird form of euthanasia, or that the professor would raise his price, and demand fancier food, imported beers I couldn't afford.

I started with a G, and put an E on the next day. That afternoon, when I was just sitting there, watching Tiny sleep, he raised his eyelids to half mast and muttered "I wish I woulda finished you."

"I thought I was finished, Tiny," I said.

"Nope," he said. He put a hand on my arm; his nails were rippled like old wood. "A tree, for instance. You don't have a tree."

"Where's room?"

"Soles of feet, earlobes. There's always room. Too late now. But you'll change anyhow, needle or no. For instance, when I put that George Washington on you, he was frowning. By the time you're my age, he'll be grinning ear to ear." He yawned, then suddenly pulled himself onto his elbows, squeezing the one hand on my arm for support. "I mean, tell me," he said, "do you feel finished?"

"Yes," I said, and although I was 39, it was true: it hadn't occurred to me until that minute that I'd have to exist after he was gone.

The next day I was putting a T on his arm when Tiny said, "Do me a favor Lois, huh? Don't forget me?"

The professor began to giggle in bed, and ended up laughing, hard. "Do you think she'd be able to, even if she wanted? Look at her — she's a human memo board."

I really thought that I would keep on going, that I'd put a letter a day on him for a year, more. I hoped it would keep him going because he seemed to be giving up a little.

By the end of the week, Tiny's arm said GET WELL in letters of all different sizes.

"Well," he said. "It's a little boring."

"It's going to get more interesting."

"It better," he told me, smiling. "Tomorrow you can put on a horseshoe for luck. Get fancy. Put on a heart for love."

"Okay," I said. But he died in the night, left without my name or love, with only my good wishes on his arm.

"What's going to happen to you now?" my mother asked me. "What if you want to get married again? What man will want you when someone else has been scribbling all over you?"

A month after Tiny died, Mama told me she was going to start inviting nice young men to our Sunday lunches. She bought me new outfits, unrevealing ones, and told me that we should keep my figure secret — she always referred to it as my figure, as if, over the years, I had put on a few things that could easily be taken off. I go to keep her happy, and sit on one side of the sofa while the fat divorced sons of her friends flirt with her instead of me, knowing that'll get them further. Sometimes I eat fudge and don't say one word all afternoon.

Every day I get up and go to work at the library, dressed in short skirts, short sleeves, no stockings. The director has told me that I'm frightening people.

"I'm sorry," I told her. "These are my widow's weeds."

Three weeks ago I got a letter from a young man on the coast, a tattooist who said that Tiny was a great artist and that I was proof of it. He wanted to take my photo, see the whole gallery. I packed him a box of Tiny's things, old flash sheets and needles and pages of El Greco and told him to study those. He called me and told me I was better than any museum. I told him that I apologized, that I understood, but really: I am not a museum, not yet, I'm a love letter, a love letter.

JUDITH FRYER

# "THE BODY IN PAIN" IN THOMAS EAKINS'
# *AGNEW CLINIC*

Bodies, their needs, appetites, expressions, affirm an external, sharable world—except, Elaine Scarry argues, for the body's pain. Unlike all other states of consciousness and somatic perceptions which are tied to objects in the external world—love of x, fear of y, ambivalence about z, hatred for, seeing of, being hungry for, and so on—pain, because it has no referential content, resists objectification in language. The difficulty of articulating the body's pain has political implications that are at the heart of Scarry's inquiry, and that have to do with the appropriation of the human body and its conflation with debased forms of power—in their most extreme forms, torture and war. Torture, the real purpose of which is not to elicit information, but to deconstruct the prisoner's voice, inflicts bodily pain that is language destroying; war is a contest in which the accumulation of injured bodies gives material reality to the abstract concept of winning. For Scarry, the difference between the two is the matter of consent; but what is crucially at stake in either case is the making and unmaking of the world. To center one's inquiry on the body in pain is to focus on the extent to which the world is destroyed (uncreated, unmade) by causing pain to others whose silence renders them invisible to us. That is, where power is equated with the disembodied voice, and powerlessness with embodied silence, a purely rational power has the potential to unmake the world. "To have a body is to be describable, creatable, alterable, and woundable. To have no body, to have only a voice is to be none of these things," Scarry writes. "Consequently, to be intensely embodied is the equivalent of being unrepresented and . . . is almost always the condition of those without power."[1]

Scarry's ultimate concern is with the power of modern science—with its disregard of human bodies and the total absence of human

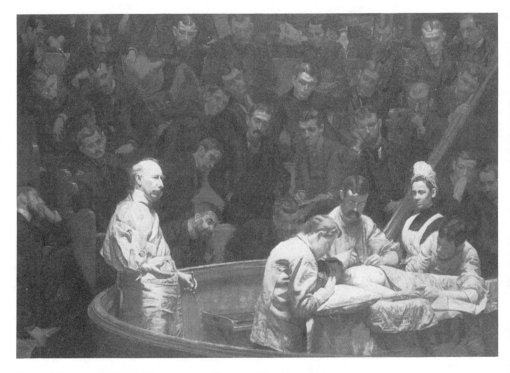

Fig. 1. Thomas Eakins, *The Agnew Clinic*, 1889. Courtesy
University of Pennsylvania School of Medicine.

consent — to unmake the world (the target of nuclear weapons, for example, in the language of science, is other weapons, not woundable human bodies).[2] Her counter-argument — that to put the sentient human body at the center of our inquiry would be to affirm an external, sharable, material world — is central to my own work. But I find Scarry strangely silent on the issues of gender and class — as well as race — which intersect in obvious ways with questions of power and powerlessness, and I propose to raise these issues in the following examination of one artifact whose text is the power of science in the modern world, and whose subtext is the sentient human body.

My subject is the representation of medical practice in late nineteenth-century America — specifically a surgical operation which is also an anatomy lesson at the University of Pennsylvania's medical school, "the first true American school of medicine."[3] Any doctor, and any historian of medicine, will both assume and assert that the purpose of medical practice is to understand the body's pain in order to relieve suffering. Dr. Henry J. Bigelow, for example, wrote extensively in the mid-nineteenth century about clinical practice, where "the student closes and grapples with the malady of whose Protean forms he has as yet only read. Here he learns at once the language of disease and the language of suffering humanity; and if his scientific sense is educated, his kindlier feelings are also developed."[4] And as recently as Scarry's writing, physicians are working with diagnostic tools that would enable patients to articulate their pain more precisely, that is, to project the facts of sentience into speech. But if the success of the physician's work — the ability to alleviate pain — is dependent upon "the acuity with which he or she can hear the fragmentary language of pain, coax it into clarity, and interpret it," as these recent studies suggest, what then of physicians who do not *hear* the patient's voice, perceiving it as an "unreliable narrator" of bodily events? Quite clearly, "to bypass the voice is to bypass the bodily event, to bypass the patient, to bypass the person in pain."[5] And the surgical operation is the most perfect way of bypassing the human voice: the patient is anesthetized into total silence; the physician has total control, unlimited possibilities for seeing and knowing.

Thomas Eakins's *The Agnew Clinic* (Fig. 1) depicts such a medical operation, in this case a mastectomy, taking place under the supervision of the chief surgeon, D. Hayes Agnew, at the University of Pennsylvania's Medical School in Philadelphia in 1889. The *subject* of this painting, by all accounts save one, is the anatomy lesson of Dr. Agnew: that is to say, from contemporary viewers to critics of our own time, this painting has been read either as a representation of clinical instruction in surgery — the male doctors gathered around the anesthetized woman are cutting off one of her breasts while a group of (male) student doctors watch — or as a hagiographic portrait of the retiring Dr. Agnew, whose "moral" vision set him, and the University of Pennsylvania's Medical School, apart from the rival Jefferson Medical College.[6] The best of the latter readings is by Elizabeth Johns, who (by analogy to Eakins's earlier *The Gross Clinic*) places these men of science among Eakins's "representative men" in her *Heroism of Modern Life*. In *The Gross Clinic* (Fig. 2), the prominence of the figure of the doctor is emphasized by minimizing that of the male patient: reviewers saw at once that "The idea of the artist has obviously been to obtrude this figure as little as possible, and even in carrying out this idea he has foreshortened it to such an extent, and has so covered it up with the arms and hands of the assisting surgeons, that it is extremely difficult to make out."[7] Michael Fried goes further and sees a kind of deliberate aggression, even sadism, in Eakins's rendering of that body: "For not only is the patient represented in drastic foreshortening with most of his body, including the head, lost to view; the portions of the body that can be seen are not readily identifiable, so that our initial and persisting though not quite final impression is of a few scarcely differentiated body parts rather than of a coherent if momentarily indecipherable ensemble."[8] In Fried's reading of both *The Gross Clinic* and *The Agnew Clinic*, the subject is the artist: it is Eakins, the doctor's double (represented in both paintings), who would penetrate, so as to know, the body of the other — a point to which I shall return. I intend to argue here for the importance of understanding *The Agnew Clinic* in another way, for seeing the subject of this painting as the supine and unconscious body of the woman at its structural center, fully aware that to say so is to empower this woman's silent body with possibly unintended meaning.

*The Agnew Clinic* resonates symbolically and historically. In its time it was turned down by the directors of the Pennsylvania Academy of Fine Arts for an 1891 exhibition because it violated museum standards of decorum. Moreover, for a society with double standards about women, the display of a cancerous female body would have offended those who posited a woman of beauty, delicacy, and refinement as the center of the home, on the one hand; on the other,

Fig. 2. Thomas Eakins, *The Gross Clinic*, 1875.
Jefferson Medical College of Thomas Jefferson University,
Philadelphia.

the painting would have evoked conflicts about the rights of the poor—and it could only be a poor woman thus represented—to competent medical care and personal privacy.[9]

A kind of human tableau, this painting conveys the sense of spectacle that any number of medical scenes, from Rembrandt's *Anatomy Lesson* (1632) to *The Gross Clinic* (1875), or that any number of paintings of artist's studios represent, such as Velasquez's *Las Meninas* (1656), Courbet's *The Painter's Studio* (1855), or in America, Charles Willson Peale's *The Artist in His Museum* (1822) and Eakins's own *William Rush Carving the Allegorical Figure on the Schuylkill* (1876–77, 1908). At the same time, the painting is meant as a representation of a real event, as in Lloyd Goodrich's description of Dr. Agnew:

> dressed in white surgical costume, like his assistants, and holding his scalpel in his left hand (he was ambidextrous), . . . talking to the class about the operation he has just performed, for cancer of the breast, while his assistant, Dr. Joseph White . . . applies a dressing to the wound, Dr. Joseph Leidy II holds a sponge to wipe the blood, and the anaesthetist, Dr. Ellwood Kirby, stands at the patient's head. In the entrance to the amphitheater, at the extreme right, appears the artist himself (painted by Mrs. Eakins); Dr. Fred H. Milliken is whispering to him. The students, dressed in dark street clothes, are all portraits.[10]

And the painting can be read as a representation of late nineteenth-century medical practice in which male science seeks to know, so as to master, the female body, which is always other than his own[11]—which is what the celebrated surgeon performing in an amphitheater before a captive audience seems to confirm. The powerful, disembodied male surgeon, the embodied and vulnerable female patient: this is what Hélène Cixous calls the great romance of science, the spectacular side of sorcery, the challenge of the hysteric, or the woman whose *hyster*, or womb, is still intact, to the "knowledge" of the master, a system of oppositions with shaman, patient and spectators represented, "above all, an audience of men . . . — the circle of doctors with their fascinated eyes who surround the hysteric."[12] The equation of surgery with spectacle was made by surgeons themselves: "Why is the amphitheatre crowded to the roof, by the adepts as well as students, on the occasion of some great operation?" a nineteenth-century surgeon asked his students. "Mark the hushed breath, the fearful intensity of silence, when the blade pierces the tissues, and the blood of the unhappy sufferer wells up to the surface," he went on, linking the surgeon's fame directly to the number and the magnitude of the operations he performs.[13]

David Lubin has suggested that to look at the painting as a theatrical spectacle, with its curtain of students in the background and the actors highlighted in the center is, because of the way in which the encircling wall that separates Dr. Agnew from his audience continues its curve toward us, for the viewer to be inscribed within the painting. He focuses on the medical student in the center of the painting — the man with the moustache and his hands in his pockets — as our exact mirror image, going so far as to suggest that our gaze rests not on the man's face, but on his "covered-over male reproductive organ, the magic wand of male desire, . . . firmly, fixedly, positioned at the literal center, the very heart of the artistic reproduction/representation known as *The Agnew Clinic*." He supports this position by arguing that the physical resemblance between this student and the doctor performing the operation suggests, as in Renaissance paintings, a study of the life of Dr. Agnew — the young student, the middle-aged doctor, the aged teacher of medicine — and that the triangle formed by these three portraits is the base structure of the painting, echoed by other triangular linkages: Dr. Agnew with scalpel in his hand, Dr. White with his knife, and the student at the top left carving with a penknife some inscription into the back of a bench; Dr. Agnew, Dr. White a surrogate this time for the artist, Eakins, on the far right, this triangle completed by the medical student, again, who is the principal gazer, the linkage being penknife, pen and knife, paintbrush, penis.[14] Lubin does not ignore the central group — the woman being operated on and the surrounding medical team; in fact, he spends quite some time on the unmutilated exposed breast of the unconscious patient, on the lettering of "University Hospital" on the sheet upon which she lies, and on the eroticism he detects in the gazes of the actors and audience (and which is implied in his own gaze as well). But he misses, in his concentration on the medical student in the background, the fact that the other center of attention, exactly opposite Dr. Agnew, the only figure as tall as he (by virtue of the light upon her cap) and as well lighted as he, is the nurse. She, not Lubin's double in the audience, is the structural counterpart of Dr. Agnew in this painting.

She, too, has a name; in fact, we can identify everyone in the painting except the patient, whose comatose state reinforces her anonymity. Mary V. Clymer was the top woman in her nursing class. She kept a diary, in which she wrote: "Never be curious. Be watchful but not officious."[15] Her problematic words — were they her own or a repetition of hospital lessons? — compound her problematic presence: she is part of the medical team, not a spectator, but also not a doctor, hierarchically inferior even to the medical students whom she might one day assist. With whom does she identify — the doctors or the unconscious and mutilated woman? Unlike the doctors who lecture and converse, or the male spectators who whisper, whittle, and take notes, Nurse Clymer — like the patient — is silent and invisible, yet potentially subject, as the only other female representative, to the penetrating gazes of these men. As the other female spectator, I am not at all titillated by the various signifiers of the "magic wand of male desire" associated with the medical student in the center background. It is the monumental Nurse Clymer, not a small symbolic member of the audience in the background, who is my means of entry into this painting: she and I look down at the female patient etherized upon the table. It is her *looking* that makes her a surrogate for the viewer — unlike the female spectator in *The Gross Clinic*, traditionally taken to be the patient's mother, who throws her left arm across her eyes so that she is unable to see what is taking place on the operating table. I will return to the nurse, but first I want to say something about the kind of anatomy lesson that is represented here as a document of American medical practice at the end of the nineteenth century.

When Eakins completed *The Agnew Clinic*, he presented it to the University of Pennsylvania Medical School, which had commissioned the portrait of the retiring Dr. Agnew. It was received on behalf of the University trustees by Eakins's friend, Dr. S. Weir Mitchell, who would later exhort students at a University of Pennsylvania graduation to a scientific excellence that would spare them the humiliation of being "defeated by a woman's breast."[16] Mitchell was a prolific writer — of medical treatises, novels, and poems which represented the most conservative strain in American culture: a novel, *Westways*, for example, in which the protagonist, Dr. Askew, is modeled on Dr. Agnew, and a poem, "Minerva Medica," written in honor of Agnew's birthday in 1888, which praises "the manly art of self control."[17] But he was best known in this country and in England for his treatment of "neurasthenic" women — among them Edith Wharton, Charlotte Perkins Gilman, Jane Addams, William

Dean Howells's daughter Winifred (whose death has been attributed to the Mitchell treatment), and Virginia Woolf. Mitchell's "rest
cure" promised the patient who relinquished complete control to the
physician a "positive" recovery from nervous disorders. She would
be confined to bed, passive and silent, powerless even to control her
own body movements and functions. "I do not permit the patient to
sit up or to sew or write or read, or to use the hands in any active
way except to clean the teeth," Mitchell wrote in 1900; "I arrange to
have the bowels and water passed while lying down, and the patient
is lifted onto a lounge for an hour in the morning and again at
bedtime, and then lifted back again into the newly-made bed."[18] She
was spoonfed four ounces of milk — her only food — every four hours,
given regular vaginal douches and rectal enemas, and, to offset the
ill-effects of prolonged immobility, subjected to various passive exercises such as massage, electricity, and hydrotherapy. Their bodies
subject to a paternalistic, authoritarian, and — to borrow Scarry's
terms — disembodied and vocal power, women were completely
infantilized, taught total submission, and subjected to the invasion
of every orifice of their bodies under the direction of this man of
science who often repeated Oliver Wendell Holmes's statement that
"An hysterical girl is . . . a vampire who sucks the blood of the
healthy people around her."[19] "To be put to bed and fed on milk" is
not what a woman under strain needs, Jane Addams wrote of this
treatment in *Democracy and Social Ethics*. "What she needs is simple health-giving activity, which involving the use of all her faculties
shall be a response to all the claims which she so keenly feels."[20] But
Addams was the sort of reformer Mitchell most hated. He believed
that women were fundamentally inferior to men and that their nervous systems were more irritable, both of which "facts" contributed
to their greater susceptibility to disease. His views were not untypi-
cal. "Women's reproductive organs are pre-eminent," one
nineteenth-century physician explained. "They exercise a controlling influence upon her entire system and entail upon her many
painful and dangerous diseases. They are the source of her peculiari-
ties, the centre of her sympathies, and the seat of her diseases.
Everything that is peculiar to her, springs from her sexual organization."[21] Still others argued that the diseases of menopause, especially
cancer of the uterus and breast, were rooted in systemic exhaustion
consequent upon the unceasing cycle of menstruation, pregnancy,
and lactation. Clearly, the medical care of women, and not only in
the nineteenth century, is tied up with culture-bound beliefs about

women and their bodies. Indeed, Carroll Smith Rosenberg sees the physician as shaped by his culture's definitions of femininity and masculinity, and thus his interaction with his female patients as "a cultural artifact."[22] Dr. Agnew, though considered "a moral figure dedicated to the patient's whole being"[23] — as opposed to a specialist like Dr. William Halsted of Johns Hopkins — was no exception. He adamantly opposed the education of women in regular medical classes, was one of the doctors who in 1879 signed a printed "Remonstrance Against Clinical Instruction Being Given to Classes Composed of Both Sexes," and in 1872, after women were officially admitted to classes (though not for clinical instruction until 1913), refused re-election to the prestigious post of surgeon to the Pennsylvania Hospital rather than give clinical instruction to women. He believed that a woman should be taught "housekeeping, hygiene and *belle-lettres*," and after that, "the more she knew the worse off she was."[24]

As I have suggested, since the operation for breast cancer depicted in this painting is staged in a room full of people, as a spectacle, this patient is no wealthy Victorian neurasthenic woman, but a poor woman who cannot afford private medical care. As a matter of fact, the connection between surgical clinics and the poor is another historical fact that this painting documents: until the early twentieth century, the association between almshouses and hospitals made possible "an invaluable and otherwise unobtainable lesson for the student physician."[25] Both the chloroform that renders her unconscious and the operation itself were fairly recent and still experimental medical innovations, and thus appropriate subjects for an anatomy lesson, and hers, silent and practically invisible, an appropriate body upon which to experiment. In *The Agnew Clinic*, the woman's breast and overlying skin are removed, but the armpit is not dissected. Radical mastectomy was introduced by Dr. William Halsted, professor of surgery at Johns Hopkins (the same doctor who diagnosed breast cancer in Alice James, and whose hemostatic clamps are the subject of another anatomy lesson in a painting of 1887 by Henri Gervex, a likely model for *The Agnew Clinic*). Halsted excised auxiliary lymph nodes, lower neck nodes, and chest muscles, inflicting "the maximal possibility of deformity, disfiguration, and disability."[26] He justified radical mastectomy by scientific data: his rate of recurrent cancer was 6% as against Agnew's of 60%.

Anesthesia, first used in the mid-nineteenth century in London for childbirth, was, because of the number of deaths directly related to chloroform, the subject of considerable debate in the latter half of the nineteenth century. The question was not whether women could or should give voice to the pain of their bodies in childbirth; rather, the terms of this debate — really about medical authority — centered on whether woman belongs to the realm of nature, governed by God, or to culture, where nature submits to man. Since the anesthetized patient has no feelings or sensations of pain, and of course, no means of expressing pain, chloroform transferred to the doctor "the *knowledge* of pain," rendering the woman's body "merely a sign," which he could read more accurately than she could. Epistemologically, Mary Poovey suggests, the interpretation of "the 'unresisting body' offers no impediment to the interpretation of a doctor like Horatio Storer, who remarked in 1871, "The wise old physician was not far wrong in his judgment: 'What is woman? Disease, says Hippocrates."[27]

This painting, then, is on one level about the nature of woman and medicine's proper relation to her. But on another level, it is about the nature of woman and the artist's proper relation to her. This becomes more clear, I think, if we compare *The Agnew Clinic* to Eakins's series of paintings which take as their subject the artistic representation of women: *William Rush Carving the Allegorical Figure of the Schuylkill*. These paintings commemorate an historical event: shipcarver William Rush's commission to create an appropriate ornament for the new water works in Philadelphia designed by Benjamin Latrobe. In the first painting of 1876–77 (Fig. 3), the model — her nakedness in sharp contrast to the severe and conventional dress of the other two figures — stands between the sculptor and the chaperone, facing the former, her back to the latter, her body turned just slightly — and lit along that side — toward the viewer. The strong highlighting of her discarded clothing (heaped on one of the Chippendale chairs that belonged to Eakins's friend S. Weir Mitchell) in the center foreground of the canvas emphasizes her nudity. This message is countered, however, by the protectiveness of the model's positioning; by the formality of the sculptor's dress and his seriousness of purpose, marked by the various tools of his trade displayed in the shadowy background; and by the knitting and angularity of the chaperone — suggesting her mature age and respectability — who sits, foregrounded, facing the model, a witness to and a participant in the events taking place.[28] In the 1908 portrait

Fig. 3. Thomas Eakins, *William Rush Carving His Allegorical Figure of the Schuylkill River*, 1877.
Philadelphia Museum of Art. Given by Mrs. Thomas Eakins and Miss Mary Adeline Williams.

Fig. 4. Thomas Eakins, *William Rush Carving His Allegorical Figure of the Schuylkill River*, 1908.
The Brooklyn Museum, 39.461. Dick S. Ramsay Fund.

(Fig. 4), one Chippendale chair has been replaced by a plain wooden one (the other has vanished), and the respectable chaperone by a black servant from the Eakins household, who also knits and who also faces the model. But the change in position of the strongly highlighted model—her backside and straightened posture now resolutely confronting the viewer without the protective encircling of the earlier version, the more casual dress of the sculptor (more like that of Eakins's time), and the presence of the black woman, following an artistic convention of the late nineteenth century, make for unambiguous eroticism.[29] Not only that, but the pairings—the chaperone facing the model's frontside while we face her backside, the frontside of her double—the water nymph—whose backside is to the sculptor—suggest a kind of circularity, as if the painting could revolve and we, too, could see the model's frontside. Or to put it another way, the artist here can see all around, can all at once know all parts and contours of the woman whom he views and creates. The final 1908 version (Fig. 5) suggests that the artist—now metamorphosed into the stockier figure of Eakins—has, Pygmalion-like, succeeded in turning stone into flesh; heavy wooden mallet suggestively in hand, he helps the model, facing us frontally now in all her nudity, from her pedestal.

For Eakins, it was the artist's, no less than the doctor's desire to know the body of woman. He was obsessed, his model for *The Concert Singer*, Weda Cook, recalled, with getting his sitters to pose nude. She would refuse; he would drop into the Quaker "thee," "gentleness combined with the persistence of the devil." He would make her sing "O rest in the Lord" over and over so that he could observe the muscles of her throat, looking at her "as if through a microscope."[30] Like the scientists of his own day who are his heroes, he carries on the Cartesian dissection of the world's body, plotting figures on a grid in an attempt to dissect and make rational this mysterious body of the other—a practice he followed to the end of his life and which derives from a much earlier artistic tradition. In Albrecht Dürer's *The Art of Measurement* of 1538 (Fig. 6), for example, the woman, whose body exactly replicates the curves of the landscape seen through the open window, is turned so that her body is available both to the gaze of the spectator and to that of the artist, who, with the help of his rectangular grid, transfers his notion of her monumental curvilinear body to a composition of reduced, divided, and angular forms. The reclining woman is larger than the space that cannot contain her; but the space in which the

Fig. 5. Thomas Eakins, *William Rush and His Model*, 1907–8.
Honolulu Academy of Arts. Gift of the Friends of the Academy,
1947.

Fig. 6. Albrecht Dürer, *The Art of Measurement*, 1538.
Kupferstichkabinett, Staatliche Museen Preussicher
Kulturbesitz, Berlin.

artist fixes her is the smaller of the two spaces, for the grid does not divide the drawing evenly: it is slanted so that the (implied male) spectator is included in the artist's half of the picture — a lesson perhaps borrowed by Lubin and Fried for their readings of *The Agnew Clinic*.

And this brings us back to *The Agnew Clinic*, to the way in which the figures are plotted on the canvas. If we begin this time with the figure of the artist in the right-hand corner, we can see that Dr. Fred Milliken's gesture of whispering to Eakins includes him in the medical community — that is, he is not merely one of the audience (though clinic audiences did contain members of the general public), but has a right to be there. He had begun his studies of anatomy in high school, then enrolled in anatomical lectures (taught by a physician) at the Pennsylvania Academy of Fine Arts, in 1864 enrolled in a surgical anatomy course at Jefferson Medical College, where he attended surgical clinics and heard the daily lectures of Dr. Samuel Gross (of *The Gross Clinic*), continued his anatomical studies in Paris from 1866 to 1869 (where he would have seen F.-N.-A. Feyen-Perrin's *Anatomy Lesson of Dr. Velpeau* (1864), based on Feyen-Perrin's experience of attending dissections and clinics at Charity Hospital in Paris), and enrolled in another series of anatomical lectures and dissections at Jefferson Medical College in 1874. He would tell an interviewer in 1879 about his own practice and teaching of dissection: "No one dissects to quicken his eye for, or his delight in, beauty. He dissects simply to increase his knowledge of how beautiful objects are put together to the end that he may be able to imitate them."[31] But why is the artist positioned so peripherally — in fact, positioned so that the nurse seems to *block his view* of the operation? Why is she placed exactly here, standing between Eakins and the body that is the subject of his investigations? It would be a neat kind of trick to argue that it was Susan Macdowell Eakins, the artist's wife who painted him into this picture, who thus positioned these two figures; but that seems too easy a solution of what was for Eakins an ongoing problem.

I make one more detour because it serves as a kind of shortcut to understanding Eakins's concern with the problem of looking and knowing. In his earlier *Baby at Play* of 1876 (Fig. 7), a female child is completely absorbed in learning hand-eye coordination. She is building with geometric shapes, and since hers are precisely lettered blocks, this little girl is also engaged, at a very early age, in the process of reading and writing, like the painter whose project was to

Fig. 7. Thomas Eakins, *Baby at Play*, 1876.
National Gallery of Art, Washington. John Hay Whitney
Collection.

find a language, a form, to express or contain the earlier and more primary act of looking.[32] The subject of this painting is Eakins's sister's child; she will later take her own life, and Eakins will be blamed for "contaminating her with his beastly ideas"[33] — but that violation is outside the scope of the painting itself. What we do see here is that the child is oblivious of the spectator's gaze, ours and the painter's; she is absorbed in her own task, building her own world, engaged in the literal attempt to join hand to eye, body to verbal expression.

Michael Fried did not consider this painting in building his case that Eakins's own project was writing. Focusing on Eakins's *Gross Clinic*, Fried ingeniously points to all the signs of proof — letters and words, pens, pencils, paintbrushes; knives and scalpels — to suggest that what is signified is the male desire to penetrate, to wound, to possess, to know. Urged on, perhaps, by his own desire, Fried argues that it *is* possible for the male artist to know the body of the other. This is what drives his argument that Eakins's real project was *writing*, inscribing his knowledge, making his mark upon the bodies of his subjects. But if this is the case, why in *The Agnew Clinic*, ostensibly *about* the male desire to penetrate, to possess, to know — and Eakins underscores this by surrounding the painting with words testifying to the omniscience of the surgeon who gives the painting its title, inscribing on its frame *Scriptor et Doctor Clarissimus*: "Writer and most exemplary teacher" — would Nurse Clymer block the artist's knowledge of the silent and woundable woman patient *with her own body?* Were she in control, we could say that with her body, with the only means available to her, she protects — or attempts to protect — the woman on the table from further violation. But she is not in control. She is subject to the doctors who employ her, and to the artist who paints her, and who views her — in the painting — from behind *and* — before his easel — from the front. Her role is like that of the chaperones in the various versions of *William Rush Carving the Allegorical Figure of the Schuylkill River* — witness and participant — and at the same time like the model in this series of paintings: available for viewing from the front and from behind. And thus she is also a surrogate for the woman patient: first in her class, obedient Nurse Clymer is, like the woman on the table, in a class apart from, subservient to, the male doctors, and doctors in training, who have the authority to speak and to wound, to penetrate and to know. We can see this painting, then, as part of Thomas Eakins's ongoing project to turn mark and pigment into living flesh — or the other way around: he stares at the muscles of his models as if through a microscope, or through the lens of his camera — for he was also a photographer; like Dürer he measures and lines out the human body on a grid; and like his doctors Gross and Agnew, he attempts to penetrate with his knife to the deepest secrets of the body. He records, creates, is witness to and participant in the mutilation of this woman.

The painting, then, is about seeing, and knowing, the body, about visibility and invisibility, or rendering the invisible visible — by analogy (the nurse's body : the body of the woman on the table; the doctor's knowledge : the artist's knowledge), by changing one's angle of vision (seeing the body from behind, as the artist painted into the canvas does, and from in front, as the artist painting the picture does). It is, in that its meaning has to do with life and death, about making and unmaking, and it is itself a made artifact. And this brings us back to the project of Elaine Scarry with which I began. Scarry teaches us to think about the ways in which some people become visible or cease to become visible to us, about the ways in which we make ourselves available to one another, and about the ways in which we take away another person's visibility — and we can see *this* concern as the subject of this painting. A made object is a projection of the human body: that is, the hand and the imagination make, create a world that is not inanimate, but rather the source of sentient experience, not alienating, but shared. "To conceive of the body as parts, shapes, and mechanisms is to conceive of it from outside," Scarry writes, "though the body contains pump and lens, 'pumpness' and 'lensness' are not part of the felt-experience of being a sentient being. To instead conceive of the body in terms of capacities and needs (not now 'lens' but 'seeing,' not now 'pump' but 'having a beating heart' or, more specifically, 'desiring' or 'fearing') is to move further in toward an interior of felt experience. To, finally, conceive of the body as 'aliveness' or 'awareness of aliveness' is to reside at last within the felt experience of sentience."[34] To put this woman in the center of this canvas and her pain at the center of our inquiry, is to affirm the felt experience of the sentient human body — to affirm, that is, the making of the world.

## NOTES

[1]Elaine Scarry, *The Body in Pain: The Making and Unmaking of the World* (New York: Oxford University Press, 1985), pp. 5, 14, 20–21, 206–207.

[2]On the relationship between language and the power to destroy the world see Carol Cohn, "Sex and Death in the Rational World of Defense Intellectuals," *Signs* 12,4 (Summer 1987), pp. 687–718.

[3]Gert H. Brieger, "Surgery," in Ronald L. Numbers, ed., *The Education of American Physicians: Historical Essays* (Berkeley & Los Angeles: University of California Press, 1980), p. 177.

[4]Henry J. Bigelow, *Introductory Lecture, Delivered at the Massachusetts Medical College, No. 6, 1849* (Boston: Mussey, 1850), p. 11, cited in Brieger, p. 186.

[5]Scarry, pp. 7–8.

[6]Diana E. Long, in "The Medical World of *The Agnew Clinic*: A World We Have Lost?," focuses on the physician as a moral actor, surgery as a progressive social responsibility, and gender as a primary (dis)qualification for medicine. She argues that medicine was considered a profession for Christian gentlemen. Jews, foreigners, and women are not shown in the painting, though they were increasingly gaining hospital posts and academic jobs; thus the portrait is a piece of nostalgia for the world that was passing. "Symposium on *The Agnew Clinic*: Medicine, Art, Literature in Late Nineteenth-Century Philadelphia," *Prospects* 11 (New York: Cambridge University Press, 1987), p. 186.

[7]William J. Clark, Review of *The Gross Clinic*, April 28, 1876, Philadelphia *Evening Telegraph*, cited in Johns, *Thomas Eakins: The Heroism of Modern Life* (Princeton, N.J.: Princeton University Press, 1983), p. 47.

[8]Michael Fried, *Realism, Writing, Disfiguration: On Thomas Eakins and Stephen Crane* (Chicago: University of Chicago Press, 1987), p. 59.

[9]See Patricia Hills, "Thomas Eakins's *Agnew Clinic* and John Singer Sargent's *Four Doctors*: Sublimity, Decorum, and Professionalism," in *Prospects* 11, p. 219. On museum decorum, see Lawrence Levine, *Highbrow/Lowbrow: The Emergence of Cultural Hierarchy in America* (Cambridge, Mass.: Harvard University Press, 1988). For descriptions of women as the center of their homes, see Thorstein Veblen's *Theory of the Leisure Class*, 1899, and Catharine Beecher and Harriet Beecher Stowe's *The American Woman's Home*, 1869. Throughout most of the nineteenth century, only the poor sought hospital care, and the attending physician offered his services free in exchange for bringing his students with him on rounds. Edward C. Atwater suggests that levels of moral outrage fluctuated: "In prosperous times politicians talked about the dignity of the poor, while in times of recession they were only too glad to allow teaching in return for free professional care." In Philadelphia, almshouse guardians made clear that their concern for medical teaching was secondary to "the interest we feel in the discharge of duty towards the poor." Edward C. Atwater, "Internal Medicine," in Numbers, ed., *Education*, p. 152. One incident, where a Buffalo doctor allowed his class of twenty each to examine vaginally an almshouse woman in labor, even led to a court trial. Lawrence D. Longo, "Obstetrics and Gynecology," in Numbers, ed., *Education*, pp. 211–13.

[10]Lloyd Goodrich, *Thomas Eakins: His Life and Work* (New York: Whitney Museum, 1933), p. 180.

[11]See Mary Poovey, " 'Scenes of an Indelicate Character': The Medical 'Treatment' of Victorian Women," *Representations* 14 (Spring 1986), 139. For a general history of the politics of the medical gaze see Michel Foucault, *The Birth of the Clinic: An Archaeology of Medical Perception*, trans. A. M. Sheridan (London: Tavistock, 1973).

[12]Hélène Cixous and Catherine Clement, *The Newly Born Woman* (1975), trans. Betsy Wing (Minneapolis: University of Minnesota Press, 1986), pp. 10, 55.

[13]Brieger, "Surgery," in Numbers, *Education*, pp. 186–87.

[14]David Lubin, *Act of Portrayal: Eakins, Sargent, James* (New Haven, Conn.: Yale University Press, 1985), pp. 45, 68–70.

[15]Mary Clymer's diary, discovered in 1962 in the basement of the original nurse's residence, is now in the Archives of the School of Nursing, University of Pennsylvania. See Eileen Foley, "Nurse in Eakins' 'Clinic' Lives Again in Diary," *Philadelphia Evening Bulletin* (Feb. 13, 1962), cited in Margaret Supplee-Smith, "*The Agnew Clinic*: 'Not Cheerful for Ladies to Look At,'" in *Prospects* 11, p. 171.

[16]S. Weir Mitchell, *Lectures on the Conduct of Medical Life* (Philadelphia: University of Pennsylvania, 1893), p. 674, cited in Long, p. 192. Mitchell's participation in this ceremony must have given him a kind of vicarious pleasure. He had written about his frustration during his own medical training, when he attended physiology lectures that were "like hearing about a foreign land which we were forbidden to enter." S. Weir Mitchell, "Biographical Memoir of John Call Dalton" (1895), cited in John Harley Warner, "Physiology," in Numbers, ed., *Education*, p. 58.

[17]Eugenia Kaledin, "Dr. Manners: S. Weir Mitchell's Prescriptions for an Upset Society," in *Prospects* 11, pp. 199–200.

[18]S. Weir Mitchell, *Fat and Blood: An Essay on the Treatment of Certain Forms of Neurasthenia and Hysteria*, 8th edition (Philadelphia: Lippincott, 1900), cited in Ellen L. Bassuk, "The Rest Cure: Repetition of Resolution of Victorian Women's Conflicts," in Susan Rubin Suleiman, ed., *The Female Body in Western Culture: Contemporary Perspectives* (Cambridge, Mass.: Harvard University Press, 1986), p. 141.

[19]Mitchell, *Fat and Blood*, 4th edition (Philadelphia, 1885), cited in Poovey, p. 153.

[20]Jane Addams, *Democracy and Social Ethics* (New York: Macmillan, 1920), p. 87, cited in Kaledin, *Prospects* 11, p. 200.

[21]Bassuk, p. 145; John Wiltbank, *Introductory Lecture for the Session*, 1853–54 (Philadelphia: Grattan, 1854), cited in Carroll Smith-Rosenberg, *Disorderly Conduct: Visions of Gender in Victorian America* (New York: Knopf, 1985), pp. 183–84.

[22]Smith-Rosenberg, pp. 192, 216.

[23]Supplee-Smith, in *Prospects* 11, p. 167.

[24]See J. Howe Adams, M.D., *History of the Life of D. Hayes Agnew, M.D., L.L.D.* (Philadelphia: Davis, 1892), p. 148, cited in Supplee-Smith, p. 170.

[25]Russell C. Maulatz notes that some of these institutions, such as the Pennsylvania Hospital, developed into private hospitals; others began as almshouses and evolved into general hospitals serving indigent patients during the ethnic and social transformations of the latter half of the nineteenth century. "Pathology," in Numbers, ed., *Education*, p. 127.

[26]See George Crile, Jr., M.D., *What Every Woman Should Know About the Breast Cancer Controversy* (New York: Macmillan, 1973), pp. 38–39, cited in Supplee-Smith, p. 167. See also Cordelia Shaw Bland, "The Halsted Mastectomy: Present Illness and Past History," *Western Journal of Medicine*, 134 (June 1981). John Chalmers Da Costa cites Dr. Samuel Gross of the Jefferson Medical College as the first American surgeon to insist on radical mastectomy. *Selections from the Papers and Speeches* (Philadelphia: Saunders, 1931), p. 341.

[27]Cited in Poovey, p. 141, emphasis original; p. 163, n. 57.

[28]The chaperone — perhaps the model's mother or some other member of her family — in studies for the painting sat with her back to the model. The change in her position so that she faces the model in the painting seems to corroborate Elizabeth Johns's statement that "In Philadelphia 'professional models' were prostitutes who modelled without family supervision, and Eakins deliberately undercut erotic associations in his tribute to Rush by including the elder woman as chaperone" (p. 99, n. 31).

[29]See Sander L. Gilman, "Black Bodies, White Bodies: Toward an Iconography of Female Sexuality in Late Nineteenth-Century Art, Medicine, and Literature," *Critical Inquiry* 12 (Autumn 1985) 1, pp. 204–242.

[30]Lloyd Goodrich, *Thomas Eakins*, 2 vols. (Cambridge: Harvard University Press, 1982) II, pp. 84, 91.

[31]William C. Brownell, "The Art Schools of Philadelphia," *Scribner's Monthly* 18, no. 5 (Sept. 1879), p. 745, cited in Johns, p. 55. Material on Eakins's medical studies from Johns, pp. 53–55, 72–73.

[32]Drawing was a *form* of writing for Eakins, from his student days at Central High School in Philadelphia, where he used a text by Rembrandt Peale which instructed that "writing is little else than drawing the forms of letters; drawing is little more than writing the forms of objects," to the time of his mature paintings, when writing figures as subject (as in the portrait of his father, *The Writing Master*), as inscription (as in this canvas), and on the frames surrounding several of his portraits. Rembrandt Peale, *The Art of Accurate Delineation, A System of School Exercise, for the Education of the Eye and the Training of the Hand, as Auxiliary to Writing, Geography, and Drawing* (Philadelphia: Biddle, 1850), p. 43, cited in Fried, *Realism*, p. 166.

[33]Goodrich, *Eakins* (1982) II, pp. 135–36.

[34]Scarry, p. 285.

SUSAN RUBIN SULEIMAN

# TO A POET

You fell upon the thorns of life
and bled. That was a way to put it
I suppose — a shade histrionical.
Would you not agree, o poet
sublime?
            No wild west wind
will lift me up with pestilential crowds
nor carry me like wave or leaf or cloud.
I'm made for softer sufferings. Blood
trickles, oozes, spurts each month
between my legs. No thorn-prick breaks
my skin. I don't fall, but bleed.

Twice in my life a baby's head
and neck and arms, a slimy child
has broken out provoking cries
of triumph, bloody exultation.
Prize of my labor, desired, won
resting on my belly after the long haul.

Not your kind of drama this, o poet
of singular travail. You sought the deep
the 'to me only does this happen'
kind of pain. Mine happens every day
to multitudes (your wife too, remember?)
through whose lips no trumpet of a prophecy
will sound.
            The whispered word
the occasional song, the sharp command:
Wear your mittens, don't forget
your lunch, put on your hat!

These too serve as witness, poor
unmanly, unadorned, unread
that we were here and loved and bled.

BRENDA HILLMAN

# PLATH'S HAIR

*for Patricia Hampl*


Forced goldenness. The business of gold
being much too bright
so it hardly seems to belong in this century.
Today that gold comes down a mountainside,
arrives at the powdery wings of a butterfly
picked up on a hike, stops
when it comes to the singed black edges
of the wings and enters the whine of a mosquito —

and I am still haunted by the curl of her hair,
how far outside the other world it seemed that day
in the library when we opened the satin-covered baby book,
thumbed through the pages printed by a mother
who cared too much and in the wrong way.
There was the record of gifts, the destroyed
stuffed dog, and suddenly,
beside the weakened strands of a snuggly knit cap

one small curl of the hair, swirling
in its tight, endless vortex —
What surprised us was how dull, how absolute it was,
how light seemed to be left out,
but just around the edges, there was too much gold
as though light were trying to get in,
apologize, or make it better —
The librarian snapped her box of cards . . .

and I think we were mildly disappointed,
as the ancient pilgrims must have been,
not really wanting to see the relics of the saints,
having traveled all that way to see them
with the servants who would spread out
picnics by the graves . . . What part
of earth can hold the meaning we assign it?

It must have been the cellophane
that made the little curl of hair
take that rim of light into itself,
trying to accrue some existence, to take on
something extra from outside. Hair never
quite lives, does it? But in the planned
dead monument, the glint survives—

JOAN K. PETERS

# MITTELSCHMERZ:
# A LADY'S COMPLAINT UPON REACHING
# THE AGE OF FORTY-FOUR

*for Dr. M. S.*

My body has become a transmitter of sadistic signals. Who's sending them I'm not sure.

The faintest hormonal shift registers its effect like a Peruvian landslide on the Cal Tech seismograph. I've found myself questioning the wisdom of female longevity. Maybe it was better to flower at fifteen, then wither, a wizened grandmother of thirty-five. In an undusted corner of my pre-feminist consciousness Edmund Waller plays the lute and sings:

> Go, lovely rose!
> Tell her that wastes her time and me
> That now she knows,
> When I resemble her to thee,
> How sweet and fair she seems to be.

> \*

> Then die! that she
> The common fate of all things rare
> May read in thee;
> How small a part of time they share
> That are so wondrous sweet and fair!

\*    \*    \*

Over a decade ago, still reading *The Dialectic of Sex* and planning the *ultimate* revolution (the one Marx never dreamed of), I barely

258

registered the faint pre-menstrual kick at my lower spine, no matter how much it throbbed. Nor did I make the connection until, two years later, the throb became the kind of lumbar ache that puts you in mind of mustard plaster and Ben-Gay. Even so, I paid it no attention. In our wing of the generation, the only enemy was testosterone; one's own body was a loyal friend, a co-conspirator, a placard-carrier on a picket line, a pair of marching feet, limbs and hips with which to do the funky chicken and the frug.

This was not the girdled body — locus of nutriment and repose — our mothers saved for wedding nights. Reproduction was not its *raison d'être*; anatomy was not *our* destiny. *We are giving birth to ourselves!* Rumors of raging hormones were a patriarchal plot.

*We were free*: the first generation of women to go to college *en masse*, take birth control pills, have abortions, remain childless if we chose — and we did in droves. Like Lysistrata's army, we raised our fists and cried, "No!":

— Not until men bear half the burden!

— Not until we're equal in the marketplace!

After all, except for a curve here, a bulge there, men and women are just alike. What gall to say we're too irrational to be President. What nerve to imply that we'd push The Button because it was *that* time of month. Had we been raised tossing balls and making stink bombs with our chemistry sets, we'd be Dallas Cowboys now (God forbid) or bio-engineers. Nurture not nature made us ladies; Feminism would make us unisex.

The "new" men agreed. *They* didn't want war, imperialism, or tyranny. *They* didn't want to be Dallas Cowboys. My husband cooked 3.5 nights out of 7 and I was in charge of the sparks and plugs. We studied side by side. He rallied behind me. He counseled his fellows to love, care, and feel. Together we thundered, "Transcend the physical!"

Granted, not every feminist wanted to transcend. Some reveled in femaleness, fertility, witchcraft, and quilting bees. Personally, I couldn't get fired up about the rightful status of parturition and the female occult in the history of social thought. I shrank from discussions of our bodies, ourselves. Those "Know Your Vagina" workshops, the "Menstruation in Literature" symposia at the Modern Language Association's annual meetings, were torture to me. Why anyone wanted an intimate knowledge of orifices and effluences, I didn't know. The poems about "red blooms" and "luteal showers" were so much female jingoism. Those red bloomer types were *extremists*.

There was one woman who made her boyfriend study her used Kotex! "The colors," she would sigh. Not me. No, siree. Insert a tampon and forget it. Take the pill. Burn your bra. Learn Kung Fu. For pity's sake, we're a sisterhood (which I pictured as something of a cross between a militia and a giant water ballet). Any more of this womb-worship and we'll be back in the *gynaeceum* wailing with our ancestresses, we transcenders argued, and for the most part, we prevailed; revolution, after all, is made by the young, when the body is easy to transcend.

Mine was so unencumbered I ran mini-marathons during the worst first days, took exams, made love and wrote treatises on gender bias during menstrual nights. Earlier, in my college dorm room, I'd hung a poster of Althea Gibson in one of her winning sprints: arms pumping, thigh muscles articulated like a relief map, one knee raised, head bent toward her goal. Althea was my woman. I used to put "You are My Inspiration" on what we still called the record player and do fifty sit-ups, ten push-ups, and a hundred jumping jacks every morning.

Not that I was a jock; it was Althea's spirit I wanted, and believed I'd found. What did I have in common with *Jane Eyre*? No one I knew would have hesitated to move in with Mr. Rochester. Who had time to worry about his lunatic wife? We were busy taking orals, passing bar exams, preparing to beat Bobby Riggs at his own game.

When I think of how oblivious we were to the monthly flow I could almost weep. Without warning it was just quite suddenly there. I remember once entering the office of a professor who was literally wringing his hands. "Miss Peters, could I ask you to find Miss Lorber. She's just had . . . er . . . a menstrual accident during our tutorial."

"Sure," I said, and took off down the hall without the least idea of what I would do if I *found* Miss Lorber, or whether I should search the bathrooms or what, then ran straight to my room and never mentioned it to a soul, least of all the mortified Miss Lorber.

That was the pre-dawn of feminism when no one talked about her period. Girls unfortunate enough to have cramps took Midol and suffered in silence. Despite the ubiquitous exemption from gym class, most, I thought, were not indisposed. *I* never was.

That's why this all came as such a shock. As suddenly as John Wayne had taken over the White House and the movement had shrivelled to a monthly issue of *Ms.* (which no one read any more) and my students began using the word "feminist" to mean an antiquated notion like "communist", I found myself with menstrual cramps.

Let me tell you, they hurt: ground glass churning spasmodically in your nether region.

My gynecologist shrugged, "Join the club. More than forty percent of us have them."

In a very few months, I had increased the antidote, such as it is, from minimum strength Motrin to maximum strength Naprosyn, two rungs up on the pharmaceutical ladder. And a shot or two of brandy on top of it. Not that I drink, either. I think I kept expecting a St. Bernard to appear with a rescue team. But as every woman must know, if there is such a team out there, it has never rescued a female in *this* distress.

I was outraged. "Am I to relinquish two days every month," I demanded of my doctor. "Twenty-four days a year? If I don't come into menopause until I'm fifty-five, that's more than a year off my prime. Not counting the scourge of hot flashes and accompanying atrocities I would rather not know about."

"Try vitamin B6," she said.

I did. Not surprisingly, it had no effect. What can you expect from a vitamin? Good God, it would take a year of Star Wars scientist person-hours to make a dent, and twice their budget. Which, I dare say, would bring more happiness to more people more of the time than would the foolproof ballistic missile defense. But who are *we*, a mere forty percent of over fifty percent of the population, to expect such lavish scientific attention? Ohhhhh, if only Oppenheimer had had cramps, we might never have had to live in the nuclear age.

Cramps, however, were only the beginning. Worse was to come shortly after the Redstockings accused Gloria Steinem of working for the CIA and the next thing I knew we were listening to disco and wondering how Ronald Reagan had won and not Geraldine Ferraro.

I couldn't ignore it any more. The lumbar ache had lost the last traces of its incidental air. No less or more than three days before menstruation, it was as if the cylinder of one of those dainty glass knobs found on certain Victorian boudoir cabinets had been plunged into my sacrum. Twisting over the ensuing days, it seemed to tighten all the muscles below the water line. My nerve ends, winding around it, would stretch to near splitting. Like abused cello strings, they screeched if so much as a paperback dropped from table to floor or the splenetic lady in the subway token booth said, "What's a matta? Can't you read?"

Then, with the stealth of a *guerrillero*, the menstrual experience crept surreptitiously backwards in time, preceding the event itself by four, then five and more of my precious days on earth. Before the cramps, came a headache and bloat. Belly swelled; breasts, painful to the touch, smarted with every joggling step. I felt full to the brow, as if I'd just consumed, or perhaps become, a force-fed suckling pig.

"Why is this happening to me, Dr. S?"

"PMS."

(Pause) "Is that a joke? Stray lines from a medical operetta? I'm almost forty and I've never had PMS. Why now?"

"Endogenous hormone allergy? Vitamin deficiency? Prolactin excess? Elevated monamine oxidase . . . ."

"I'm drowning. Stop."

"It's probably a hormone imbalance. The etiology's still unclear."

I stared in disbelief. "You mean . . ."

"Nobody knows."

On my way out I heard her say, "Symptoms increase with age."


Age, ugh. My husband told me I was irritable. "Leave me alone," I screamed. I began to have crying jags. He started making jokes about "the curse" and being "on the rag." The meaning of the phrases had honestly never dawned on me before.

"Dr. S., there's got to be something."

"Avoid caffeine," she offered.

I did and now I was irritable *and* sleepy.

"What do *you* do?" I asked her.

She gave me a sidelong glance. The pieces were falling into place. Dr. S. was just finishing a book on living with menopause. A WHOLE BOOK! I slunk out the door in a deep depression. Sigmund Freud, that old mound of cobwebs and calcium dust, must have been having a good laugh.

Six days. Seven. I have lived through the re-election of Reagan and my own *crise de quarante et un*. Once a month my estrogen level drops. Endorphins droop. The endometrial lining of the uterus, swollen with nutrients no newly impregnated egg needs, begins to shrink, then peel off, producing a lizardy sensation of internal molting.

Defeated, I begin to think, what difference do seven miserable days a month make? The revolution being over, I no longer have anything pressing to do, except teach two days a week. An historian from Berkeley came once to interview me for a book on the women's movement. That was the last I heard about it. The movement, that is. But I see that the movement trained me well: even in my lassitude, I eventually protest.

Although my life feels emptier by the minute, I'm not giving up yet. I have my rights. I'd even like to have a kid or two, thank you (you couldn't do that back then when the revolution came first and childbearing was personal and political sabotage). And now, I'm getting mad.

It's eight days, now, and nine. The sacral kick is the upswing of a baton. Head in hands, I wait for the blare of hormonal signals, twisted sinews, plunked nerves, breasts that by the last days will seem as if they're being sucked from my body by twin toilet plungers.

Ignominious, eh? You're embarrassed I brought it up. But people ought to know the truth: the subject entry for "menstruation" — located between "hemorrhage" and "latrine" in *The Classic, Standard, Definitive Roget's International Thesaurus*, is well placed.

"There, you see. You couldn't be president," my husband tells me.

"At least I know when and why I'm warped," I argue, wishing, truly, to scratch my nails down his cheeks, rip out his eyes, lift a knee to his groin. Generally, I'm not what you'd call a gentle person, but I *am* civilized.

"The British courts dismissed manslaughter charges against two women who pled PMS. You can't have it both ways."

Stonily now. "PMS notwithstanding, you Neanderthal, *my* people are responsible for only a fraction of the violent crimes. *Yours* don't even have an excuse."

The large rectangle of the hastily unfurled pages of *The New York Times* interposes itself between us. He's no doubt reading a little something on serial murders or terrorist massacres committed by you-know-whom. Long live the king, family values, the Pentagon, the Moral Majority, tax breaks for the rich, Donald Trump, and the Marlboro Man. Stay the course. Don't forget that the man who sold weapons to the Ayatollah for money to destroy the elected government of Nicaragua is a national hero!

We're losing our abortion rights and he's in an uproar over a little homicidal urge. How ridiculous. Anyway, I've never actually thrown my Lhasa Apso from my study window or taken a kitchen knife to bed. It's only the falling books that make me leap, the old Joan Baez tunes that bring tears to my eyes, the evening news that tempts me to suicide. And now there's insomnia, too. Nights of it ruining my days. Too much oxygen in my brain. Too many thoughts. Thousands per minute. I mumble them in the supermarket aisles, my arms waving about. I swim my fifty laps in two-thirds my normal time. PMS has pressed the fast-forward switch and I can't turn it off.

Today's woman (*not* me) says PMS is a matter of attitude. Just last week I read an article by an upbeat investment banker who counseled us (in the columns of one of those new women's magazines that all look suspiciously like *Vogue*) to think of PMS as a time of "high energy." You can get *so* much accomplished, she wrote.

Ha! My eyes are ringed. I am exhausted from lack of sleep. I walk into walls. I shake as if I've downed thirty-four cups of coffee in the past hour.

Mademoiselle Yuppie, do you know what it is to be ON EDGE? Let me put it in a context you might understand: It is 11:00 p.m. You've missed your connecting flight at O'Hare because your plane was two hours late. Two teen-agers in the airport cafeteria have stolen the shoulder bag from your seatback, where you shouldn't have left it. You know no one in Chicago and have a morning meeting in New Orleans, to which you will have to wear your wrinkled suit and Reeboks because there isn't a prayer you'll ever see your suitcase again. Do you feel energized?

Save us from post-feminism!

Ten days. Eleven. The invisible armies have infiltrated more than twelve of my pre-periodic days. I buy support bras befitting Bulgarian weightlifters. I warn friends I might insult them. I avoid the evening news. For safe measure, I haven't had coffee for two years.

Now I'm told to give up wine, sugar, salt, milk, meat, and Diet Coke. Last night, I dined on artichoke broth and glazed kelp. Still, for two weeks out of four, my body is a tormented creature, a porcine, skin-shedding, hormone-starved ghoul.

Is it revenge for some negligence in my past, I've begun to ask myself? For all those years when I flexed my muscles, gloated over beating my husband at arm wrestling, water-skied naked across the lake at dawn, loving my body because it did what I told it — outran even my dog (although he does have short legs)? For my contempt at those moaning females, earth mothers nursing their three-year-olds, big-bellied Venuses of Wollendorf? For secretly considering myself a distinct gender? Daughter of the huntress. Of Thalestria, Queen of the Amazons.

Arrogance injures the soul. I should have known women weren't women for nothing.

If in my youth, being female was merely an unfortunate political designation, in my middle age I know better. Those divided camps — Red Bloomers and Transcenders — chopped us each to ineffectual bits. Had we fused, we might not be stuck with Mademoiselle Yuppie now, the CEO who'll drop out to raise her kids because no one, it turns out, can do it all and *he* won't do any.

It's fourteen days now. Even ovulation, that formerly silent miracle, has asserted its shrill voice in my beleaguered nervous system. A sharp cramp tells me the ovary and uterus have contracted to release the egg. I know which ovary, left or right, by where it stabs my back and groin. *Mittelschmerz*, middle pain, the Germans call it. I appreciate the recognition; I, who now smack in the *mittel* of my life, know the exact clockwork of my reproductive system.

Is it revenge or is it admonition that at forty-four years old I feel with such cruel precision the moment when my apparently unfertilizable egg moves down the fallopian tube to the womb where it will sit, useless, for a day or two, its presence wreaking havoc on my body and mind, mocking me?

Soon there will be no blood on the bedclothes. My tidal body will still; my ocean heart. Middle age is a time of reconsideration.

I address myself as I would an audience of peers: *All of us new women, newly middle-aged.* Remember those fist-banging crones: Sojourner Truth, Susan B. Remember those goddesses who reigned in a peaceful pre-patriarchal world. Lysistrata stopped a war, but there was so much more to do. If we don't become whole, male and female both, we'll blow the universe to smithereens.

Our bodies are the rough beasts slouching toward Bethlehem to be born. Desire is *never* too late, even unfulfilled. Fair warning. The red flag is out. Let's do it again ladies, until we get it right.

RUTH BEHAR

# THE BODY IN THE WOMAN,
# THE STORY IN THE WOMAN:
# A BOOK REVIEW AND PERSONAL ESSAY

> *. . . and we would talk, about aches and pains, illnesses,*
> *our feet, our backs, all the different kinds of mischief that*
> *our bodies, like unruly children, can get into.*
> — Margaret Atwood, *The Handmaid's Tale*

> *. . . but you really are better, dear, whether you can see it*
> *or not. I am a doctor, dear, and I know. You are gaining*
> *flesh and color, your appetite is better, I feel really much*
> *easier about you.*
> — Charlotte Perkins Gilman, "The Yellow Wallpaper"

> *What we go through and it's not our fault. Through this*
> *whole ordeal, I needed to know, what is it something I did*
> *or didn't do? What causes these things to happen? Did I*
> *cause this on myself?*
> — Marlene Cromwell, reflecting on her endometriosis

> *Todo eso tiene que morir de todas maneras; All that has to*
> *die anyway.*
> — Rebeca Behar, preparing herself for a total
>    hysterectomy and a bilateral oophorectomy

> *Look: I have lain on their tables under their tools*
> *under their drugs     from the center of my body*
> *a voice bursts     against these methods*
> — Adrienne Rich, in *Your Native Land,*
>    *Your Life: Poems*

*     *     *

One night in February my mother calls and tells me, her voice
unusually firm, *Me voy a operar.* So she's going to have the operation, after all. For two years she has held on, waited, hoping for an

267

Joanne Leonard, "She Shells." A selection from *Journal, October 9–November 30, 1973* (from the collection of Jeremy Stone), a set of thirty photocollage works which Joanne Leonard produced in the fifty-three days during and following her miscarriage. The journal follows her passage from the horror of loss to the new dreams and regained hopes that came later. Here, an image of openness, expectancy, and wonder, the female genitals traced over sea shells.

alternative, a little miracle, a kindly gesture of obedience from her body. For two years she has been hoping that the bleeding, grown heavy and clotted, will go away by itself. But it won't. Her uterus doesn't want to give up. She is fifty-four and one of the fibroid growths that has found shelter in her uterus has grown to the size of a twenty-week embryo. That willful embryo presses against her kidney; she cannot sleep on her stomach anymore and most of the time she is in pain.

She calls me to announce her decision. *Lo va sacar todo*, she tells me. She has gone to a distinguished tall male doctor for a second opinion after her longtime female doctor, a Philippine woman who is foreign like her, speaks English with an accent like her, has recommended, but not insisted upon, surgery. "He's going to take everything out" — that means, the uterus, the fallopian tubes, the ovaries, the cervix, in other words, the whole of her female reproductive system. At her age, she's been told, she's better off having everything out. What does she need it all for anymore? In menopause those organs dry up anyhow or, worse, dumbly pick up cancerous hitchhikers. *Todo eso tiene que morir de todas maneras*, she says matter-of-factly, as though reciting a lesson from a schoolbook. "All that has to die anyway," I translate to myself.

But it is not really to announce her decision that my mother has called. What she wants is for her daughter the professor to offer a reprieve. Is there some profound wisdom I have, some new information I can get my hands on? Is there a clear answer to be found . . . Surely in the knowledge factory of the university you would think it might be possible to find an answer to her simple, burning question: Is there nothing that can be done but to cut it all out? Does it have to be this way?

I didn't give her the reprieve she wanted, and I still don't know the answer to her question.

In the midst of my mother's coming to a decision to have surgery to remove her womb, I was making plans to write a review about two recent books by women anthropologists which focus on the female body, one from the perspective of reproduction, the other from the perspective of the abortion debate. I took the books with me when I went to New York City to accompany my mother during her days at the hospital in early March. I found myself, at the time, unable to do more than carry them around. Yet the presence of these books formed a kind of backdrop to my mother's experience. Reading them later in the time span of my mother's ongoing recovery from surgery, which led me in turn to other writings where I discovered absences, I decided I could not simply write a book review. I had to do more. I had to write the story of my mother's body. Her body was to be my fieldsite and destination. But the road to her body, I found, was paved with other women's stories, just as her story, if I can tell it, will lead out to other women's bodies.

\*       \*       \*

The body in the woman and the story in the woman are inseparable. But is it possible to do anthropology from such a perspective? Where would it take us and what would be its purpose? The two books I set myself the task of thinking about in these terms, Emily Martin's *The Woman in the Body: A Cultural Analysis of Reproduction* and Faye Ginsburg's *Contested Lives: The Abortion Debate in an American Community*, offer exciting prospects for a different kind of anthropology rooted in the stories women have to tell about their bodies.

Both books are part of a new turn in American anthropology toward doing fieldwork "at home" rather than in faraway places. This turning of the anthropological mirror back at us is serving to bring home the exotic, the forgotten, and the marginal in our own midst, often for the purpose of carrying out a critique of our culture.[1] But the work of Martin and Ginsburg is part of another kind of mirror turning as well, that of a feminist anthropology come of age that does not assume familiarity or knowledge or total comprehension of the water we swim in. This feminist anthropology holds a mirror, not to the encounter between a first world feminist anthropologist and a third world traditional woman, but to the differences between women living with the aftershocks of feminism here.

Here can be many places. For Emily Martin, it is Baltimore, where she lives and works as a professor at Johns Hopkins University, "a citadel of excellence in medical education and practice," and where she "often felt like a mouse in the den of a lion" trying to study medical metaphors of women's bodies in relation to women's own accounts of the meaning of their bodily processes.[2] For Faye Ginsburg, it is Fargo, North Dakota, a quintessentially American landscape on the prairie, out to where she ventured from New York City to talk to women on both sides of the abortion debate, women who think of New York "as Fargo's opposite" and of New Yorkers as "rude, snobbish, morally questionable, and unappreciative of middle-American values."[3] For me, in my more circumscribed efforts to do a combination of ethnography and memoir for this essay, here is the world my mother entered by agreeing to elective surgery to remove a womb turned unruly.

There is a key difficulty in doing fieldwork here as a woman in the terrain surrounding the definition of the female body: finding a vantage point, a location from which to view the terrain. There is no Archimedean point, no unembodied place. How, then, is one to see underlying cultural and political assumptions? Emily Martin writes about her initial feeling of "leaden disappointment" when she began her interviews about childbirth with Baltimore women and heard them speak of uterine contractions as "separate from the self and as if labor were something one went through rather than actively played out." These views of the female body in labor seemed only to give credence to the medical "fact" that the uterus is an involuntary muscle.

Then Martin had the kind of revelation that one seeks as an anthropologist: suddenly the familiar looked to her strange, unfamiliar, odd, and in need of explanation. Just as in her previous work with Chinese villagers she had seen their concepts about "hot" illness and the balance of yin and yang as "cultural organizations of experience" rather than as statements of "brute, final, unquestionable facts," she came to see that medical statements about the female body, like American women's views, are not universal truths, either. They are, rather, storied understandings: "medical science in fact tells a very concrete story, rooted in our particular form of social hierarchy and control," while women "have it literally within them to confront the story science tells with another story, based on their own experience." It is women's efforts to tell stories of resistance even as they (middle-class women especially) often acquiesce to the master narrative of medical science that gives Martin a vantage point from which to see the strangeness of our cultural and political assumptions about the female body. But even with this revelation, Martin says that she "anguished over the obviousness of everything the women were saying" and had continually to remind herself, in the spirit of Marx, to open her eyes to the contradictions.

The story that Martin herself tells brings together the stories found in nineteenth-and twentieth-century medical textbooks with the stories told by a chorus of 165 Baltimore women of different ages, classes, and backgrounds, whose statements about menstruation, birth, and menopause are threaded into the text. It is a story that, like all stories about the female body in our time, begins in the nineteenth century.

Until the beginning of the nineteenth century, Western medical literature described the genitals of women as being the same as men's, except that theirs were inside rather than outside the body; the female reproductive organs were pictured as phallus-like, with the uterus and vagina imagined as analogous to the penis and scrotum. With the falling apart of old hierarchies in the previous century, nineteenth-century thinkers in the social and biological sciences began to highlight obsessively the differences between female and male sexuality, social roles, and economic spheres.

A new perception took root among doctors and quickly became established: that "a woman's reproductive organs held complete sway over her between puberty and menopause." Menstrual blood had previously often been considered impure or dangerous, as when women used it in the witchcraft remedies that they put in the food which they served to men in hopes of taming them.[4] By the end of the nineteenth century, menstruation itself came to be seen as a disorder, a pathology that marked women's bodies and for which there was no analogue in the bodies of men. "Women were warned not to divert needed energy away from the uterus and ovaries" if they wanted to keep their good health and save their lives. The "cult of invalidism" became the stereotyped pursuit of upper-class nineteenth-century women in the West, who were warned, for their own good, to rest and refrain from brain work, which was thought to take a great toll on female bodies.

The middle-class protagonist of Charlotte Perkins Gilman's parabolic "The Yellow Wallpaper" (1892) was put under just such an invalidism treatment for her "slight hysterical tendency" by her doctor-husband who, knowing what was best for her, rented a colonial mansion where she was not to tire herself by doing work of any kind or by writing. That cheaply-let mansion becomes for the protagonist — in one reading — a house haunted by "creeping women" bestialized by their confinement to the wallpapered walls of the domestic realm. Anxieties about race, class, and ethnicity may have been inscribed upon the yellow wallpaper, as well, in the form of a political unconscious, "in which an Aryan woman's madness, desire, and anger . . . are projected onto the 'yellow' woman who is also the feared alien."[5]

Certainly, the inscription of race and class upon the nineteenth-century (and twentieth-century) view of the female body does not escape Martin's notice. As she points out, invalidism was not possible for poor working-class women, but since their labor was viewed as manual, it was, therefore — in an amazing contortion of logic — not taxing on their bodies like mental labor; in the cases where work inescapably left its mark on the bodies of less-privileged women, this was said to be due to their defeminizing efforts to "emulate the males by unremitting labor." Similarly, poor black women today are often treated scornfully by doctors as purely physical beings when they are giving birth, because doctors assume that, because of their race and class, these women cannot "verbalize" their thoughts and feelings, or that they do so only wildly and uncooperatively; they are likely to be spoken to harshly, strapped down, told they are not in pain, refused comfort, and isolated from their husbands.[6]

At the heart of the nineteenth-century redefinition of the female reproductive system as a site of pathology was the forging of a split for women between the realm of the house and the realm of the workplace — a split subtly nuanced by race and class differences. Ginsburg, as we shall see, takes up the implications of this split from the angle of the abortion debate. For Martin, on the other hand, the split becomes a tool for her analysis of the politics of the medical metaphors surrounding the female body. It is here that Martin's analysis is at its most gripping and energetic. Relentlessly, Martin unveils parallel upon parallel between production and reproduction, showing how the capitalist economy, from the early stages of factory work to the advanced stages of commodification, writes itself upon the female body, carving its words upon it like the revenge cut into the back of Maxine Hong Kingston's female avenger.[7]

The body under capitalism is, in the broadest sense, "a hierarchical information-processing system," while the female body, Martin writes, is a system organized "for a single preeminent purpose: 'transport' of the egg from ovary to uterus and preparation of an appropriate place for the egg to grow if it is fertilized." Medical texts abound with metaphors of power distribution and of production. Since it is assumed that the female cycle has as its only productive goal to make an embryo, both menstruation and menopause come under especially tough metaphoric attack.

While menstruation is frequently characterized as failed production, menopause tends to be seen as the downfall of the authority structure of the body. The language in which menopause is described bristles with negative metaphors about the way the female reproductive system regresses, declines, atrophies, shrinks; the ovaries turn into "senile" organs which have "shrunken and puckered," and have ceased to respond and to produce. This disdain for the unproductiveness of the menopausal female body finds expression in the readiness to perform hysterectomies on malfunctioning or aging wombs, a theme I shall explore later in this essay.

Menstruation, as the saga of failed production at a time in the life cycle when production is still technically possible, is presented in a tone almost of melodrama. One recent medical textbook, for example, defines menstruation as the failure of fertilization to occur, while invoking the way it used to be described as "the uterus crying for lack of a baby." Another tone is that of horror, the horror of idle workers or machines, and also the horror of "production gone awry, making products of no use, not to specification, unsalable, wasted, scrap. However disgusting it may be, menstrual blood will come out." Even though in our society menstruation "could be seen as a welcome sign" since most women are not intending to get pregnant over the whole of their reproductive years, the negative meanings attached to menstruation force women to keep the process private and concealed as though it were shameful and ugly. A woman is intended, it often seems, to feel like the storyteller of *The Handmaid's Tale* sinking into the "treacherous ground" of her own body, listening for "each twinge, each murmur of slight pain, ripples of sloughed-off matter, swellings and diminishings of tissue, the droolings of the flesh . . . watch[ing] for blood, fearfully, for when it comes it means failure."[8]

In direct ancestry with nineteenth-century ideas, "premenstrual syndrome" and menopausal "estrogen-deficiency disease" have become pathologies which require medication. The descriptions of male reproductive physiology, in contrast, shine with admiring praise for the "amazing" features of spermatogenesis, particularly the "sheer magnitude" of the several hundred million sperm per day that "a normal human male may manufacture." This positive view of male physiology is mirrored in the social world: although male absenteeism reaches 10 percent on Mondays and Fridays in companies like General Motors, no one is led "to think that workers need medication for this problem."[9]

Ovulation and a uterus with a baby — where female productiveness would seem to be at a high point — do not fare much better in medical language and practice. Ovarian follicles containing ova are already present at birth, rather than being "produced" as sperm is; "they seem to merely sit on the shelf, as it were, slowly degenerating and aging like overstocked inventory." As for the uterus, it is said to produce "efficient or inefficient contractions" and labor is given a passing or failing grade based on the amount of "progress made in certain periods of time," which determine "the overall efficiency of the machine." The stages of labor, well known to any woman who has given birth in a hospital setting, have a rate of progression like factory work. Deviations from the rate are treated as disorders requiring medical interventions. These range from running pitocin into a woman's veins to speed up a slow labor, to using forceps to pull out a baby whose mother is laboring ineffectively, to cutting into the uterus in a cesarean section. In a hospital birth, Martin asserts, the woman becomes the laborer, her uterus a machine, her doctor the active manager, and her baby, the product. "Fetal outcome," the production of a "perfect baby," is the goal of the labor at whatever cost to the mother's desires for autonomy, control, wellbeing, and simple recognition. Even in normal labors, mother and baby are pitted against each other as a "conflicting dyad," with the doctor allying "with the baby against the potential destruction wreaked on it by the mother's body." And with the increasing use of fetal monitors, the woman in the body becomes not only a nuisance, but almost an irrelevance. As one of the Baltimore women recollected, "I can remember all these official-looking people coming in and hugging the monitor, when I needed the hug. All these smart people were hugging the monitor."

This is a bleak picture, yet Martin finds some of her optimism restored when she turns to the stories women have to tell about their bodies, which carry the promise of alternative visions. Rage, resistance, and efforts to imagine a different social order win high marks from Martin. Her heroines are the women warriors she finds primarily among those whom, as she says, are at "the bottom of the heap." Yearning to find heightened consciousness among the oppressed, Martin finds, indeed, that working-class women, black and white, are less "mystified" by the reigning cultural models than middle-class women.

But everyday resistance comes in diverse and subtle forms. One woman in menopause, who grew tired of explaining to people why she was sweating when she was overtaken by a hot flash, ended up saying, "I'm going through my menopause, damn it. That is what you should say. That shuts them up fast. Especially a man . . . . Let them be embarrassed. I was tired of being embarrassed." This subversion of the proper etiquette for maintaining the separation of home and work makes a claim for the right of women to "publicly name their state . . . and embarrassing their male coworkers at the same time, paradoxically producing in men our cultural emblems of subordination: heat and emotion." Going public, naming what our society has defined as a private embarrassment and shame, need not only produce heat and emotion, however. The Iowa woman who identified herself as a rape victim, allowing her story to be told in print and by name, has not simply spread the embarrassment, so that preventing rape will become a social responsibility, but made the private public, and the unspeakable speakable.[10]

The anger and mood changes associated with premenstrual syndrome, which make women unwilling or unable to tolerate the work discipline of late industrial capitalism, also offer a subversive comment on the production rhythm of a society that does not offer time off for self-reflection, creativity, and the illumination and truth that anger itself can bring to light. Women who do take the time off speak of being flooded with love, feeling part of the life-giving force during menstruation, of dreaming more vividly and feeling exhilarated, of enjoying the time to be alone and to think.

In labor, finally, women resist by stalling, concealing the fact they are laboring, so they can delay starting the time clock that will put them under pressure to agree to medical interventions if their labors are slow or ineffective; or by turning to home births, where they can move about freely during labor and avoid the possibility of ending up on the delivery table with their legs spread apart and in stirrups. Not that natural childbirth is in itself a guarantee that the metaphors used to speak of women's bodies will be more positive, if Michel Odent's description of women as being in an animal-like, childlike state during natural childbirth is any indication.[11]

What most women in good health would seek, I think, were it readily available, is the kind of loving care toward the female body that an Alabama midwife like Onnie Lee Logan has been able to offer her black and white laboring mothers in their own homes:

> I tell you one thing that's very impo'tant that I do that the doctors don't do and the nurses doesn't do because they doesn't take time to do it. And that is I'm with my patients at all times with a smile and keepin her feelin good with kind words. The very words that she need to hear it comes up and come out. And that means alot. Most of the doctors when they do say somethin to em it's so harsh. They already

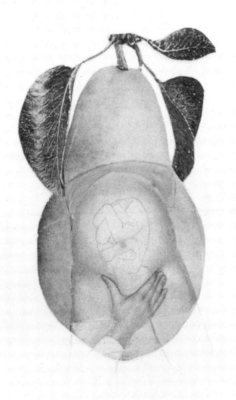

Joanne Leonard, "Untitled," from *Journal, October 9–November 30, 1973*.
Playing on the common description of the uterus as pear-shaped, Joanne
Leonard offers an image of lush female ripeness. The intervening hand is
ambiguous; at once beckoning and appraising, it can be the hand of a
loving caregiver or the hand of an active manager anxious to draw out a
perfect product.

had contractions, and then with a ugly word to come out not suitable to how they're feelin. Some of em say that if they wasn't strapped down there they would get down and come home. A lot a women are left totally alone. And plenty of em have their babies right by themselves. Well see I don't leave my patient like that. I'm there givin her all the love and all the care and I be meanin it and they know I mean it. It's from my heart and they can feel me. You see what I mean? There's a lot of a certain lil black gal — they can feel that black gal. They can feel the love from her — the care from her. What she's goin through with I'm goin through right along with her . . . . "Now look, honey — this will be over with soon, honey."[12]

Onnie Lee Logan is still working, but the possibility of her ethic of care being continued is unlikely. Alabama, like other states, is no longer giving permits to independent midwives. The services of midwives are in demand; but they are viewed as a threat to the medical control of childbirth only when they subvert the race and class hierarchies that underpin the meaning of gender in American society. As Logan remarks, the doctors didn't like the fact that she was "doin a whole lot a white girls. As long as I was doin alot a po' black girls they didn't care, they didn't say anything about it. But when I started doin a whole lot a white girls, nice outstandin white girls, then that's when they started complainin . . . . My patients have come and told me what the doctors said. Said we didn't know what we was doin. We was black. We was ignorant . . . . One a my patients told me that the doctor said if she was financially po' he would send that slip to her, but if she could pay for it, he was not gonna send a slip for her for home delivery."[13]

Martin resists ending her story on a distressing note. But I simply can't see not doing so. The efforts to squeeze out women like Onnie Lee Logan from the realm of women's health care, often for racist, class-bound reasons disguised as medical reasons, is cause for concern. While the oppositional consciousness of women at the margins cannot be doubted, it is these same women who tend to be most victimized by medical practices that maintain the historical definition of their bodies not simply as objects of pathology but as objects of property. Think about the well-documented stories of forced sterilizations of Native American women; think of the story Patricia Williams tells of the fifteen-year-old young black woman from the sugar region of Belle Glade, Florida, "where blacks live pretty much as they did in slavery times, in dormitories called slave ships" — pregnant with her third child, her mother has advised a hysterectomy, advised in her turn by a white doctor who recommended the same course of action to her years before.[14]

But it is not just in Navajo reservations and in Belle Glade, Florida, that women of color are penalized for possessing a female body. Next to their stories one can place the story of Avis Maria, the parking booth attendant at the University of Michigan who was given a two-day layoff for leaving her booth unattended when she began to menstruate and had to walk a block to the nearest bathroom. The keys for the bathroom next to her booth were missing when she arrived at work. Although she notified her supervisor, he did not bring them for another seven hours, waiting until an hour before Avis Maria was scheduled to leave, at which time he found her husband guarding the money for her. Avis Maria, it turns out, has a history of speaking out against racist and sexist practices in the Parking Operations Department. The personal is political: the threads of her menstruation, her being a black woman, and her activism are knotted together. The excessive discipline directed at her was a commentary on her lack of docility on all three counts.[15]

Finally, the body betrayals that all women speak of over and over, when their menstrual pains are serious, when their laboring goes wrong despite their best efforts, when their uteruses bleed excessively and form fibroids, must not be put down simply to passive acceptance, confused discontent, and a sense of alienation and fragmentation — which ultimately is what Martin does in her ardent desire to hear women speak about their bodies in the active voice. The choices available to women seem so often to have a damned if you do, damned if you don't quality to them. Part of me, too, admires the women who become the heroines of their body dramas. But life in a female body is so often about ambiguity that for my part I am more drawn to the women who recognize, but haven't necessarily overcome, all the Catch-22's. My sympathy goes out to the woman who said to Emily Martin that "her doctor gave her two choices for treatment of her menopause: she could take estrogen and get cancer or she could not take it and have her bones dissolve." These are the kinds of choices women often have to make. Terrible choices. Cruel choices, like the choices the Sea Witch gives the Little Mermaid.

"How do I begin to take responsibility for my body?" is the question Jo Spence asks of herself in her self-portrait with the words of this question written on different parts of her body. Asking that question in full cognizance of being split into shards may not be heroism, but it is, at least, a coming to terms with the reflection in the mirror.

\*     \*     \*

Faye Ginsburg's study of the abortion debate in Fargo, North Dakota, moves us from body dramas to social dramas, in which control over the womb — "the last unambiguous symbol of an exclusive female arena" — has become the contested terrain of abortion activists on both sides of the debate. Emily Martin had to confront the issue of finding a vantage point from which to see the culturally constructed dimension of seemingly obvious definitions of the female body. Ginsburg finds herself in the dilemma of trying to comprehend and explain a set of native points of view that have become so polarized that they are regarded as anathema to each other. Her efforts to give equal research time and interpretive energy to the pro-choice advocates as well as to the right-to-life advocates have won her some unsympathetic colleagues, who have accused her of "going native" (curiously, one of the worst insults for an anthropologist) and becoming a right-to-life advocate, and even of having invented her evidence.

As Ginsburg says, "It is one thing, I learned quickly, for an anthropologist to offer the natives' point of view when the subjects are hidden in the highlands of New Guinea and have little impact on the lives of the assembled audience. It is quite another to describe the world view of people from the same culture whom some people in my audiences considered to be 'the enemy.' I tried to think of the mission of Boas and Mead to break down cultural stereotypes when I found myself fielding occasionally hostile responses from colleagues."

Yet reading her book I am left with critical unanswered questions. What are the implications of being able to stand in so many places, see from so many vantage points? After cultural stereotypes have been broken down, how should we act, or can we act? Should the studied neutrality and distance of classical anthropology be reproduced, or challenged, in studies of our own society? Maybe anthropology can do no more than help us to imagine other realities; we do not ask of Margaret Atwood's *The Handmaid's Tale* — a parable about an America ruled by extremist religious right-to-life principles — to tell us where we might go next. But we do ask for an explanation from the anthropologist, even at the risk that the explanation will be like that offered by the director of the twentieth-and twenty-first century archives in *The Handmaid's Tale*, at once illuminating in setting the personal account in a broad historical context and deadly in stamping out the life of the tale and its teller.

Ginsburg keeps things in fairly good balance. She offers understandings that are at once historically sweeping, assimilating the current abortion debates to the tradition of female moral reform movements in America since the nineteenth century, and ethnographically fine-wrought, giving us a chance to get to know both the landscape and the individual actors in the abortion drama of Fargo. Unlike Martin, who fragments her Baltimore women's stories into statements about specific themes, Ginsburg makes a point of keeping whole the life stories, or "procreation stories," as she calls them, of the Fargo women. As a result, it does become difficult to name enemies or villains in her story. What Ginsburg makes us see are women being tragically torn apart by the same "problematic conditions [of] living in a system in which wage labor and individual achievement are placed in conflict with reproduction, motherhood, and nurturance." Some of the activists in Fargo have themselves come to this conclusion and formed a group called Pro-Dialogue, where pro-life and pro-choice women can talk to one another and read works of mutual interest, Ginsburg's among them.

Ginsburg introduces the reader to thirteen women activists involved in the abortion debate in Fargo, a drama which is played out in and around the space of Fargo's abortion clinic. For example, we get to know Kay, who opened the abortion clinic in Fargo in 1981, and came to her pro-choice perspective after raising four children, working for La Leche League, a breastfeeding organization, and becoming "acutely aware of how little physicians who were supposed to be doctors for women actually knew about women's bodies." We also get to know Jan, a young pro-choice activist, who speaks of women's right to bear children as the crux of all other female freedoms: "It's our cross and it's also what raises us above. To not be able to control that single most unique part of us would devastate our entire sense of independence in every other aspect of our lives." And we get to know Karen, a pro-life activist and mother of three, who feels that "we've accepted abortion because we're a very materialist society and there is less time for caring," and would like to see more flexible work hours so that a mother and a father could work part-time and share both the care of children and the prestige of being employed at a job. So long as abortion is readily available, activists like Karen feel convinced that the walled separation between home and work will remain in place.

As Ginsburg explains, the right-to-life perspective among Fargo women is a particular kind of feminist stance built on the assumption — and hope — that linking female sexuality to a cultural chain of events makes men more responsible for their sexuality as well. From this perspective, "easy access to abortion decreases women's power by weakening social pressure on men to take emotional and financial responsibility for the reproductive consequences of intercourse." The idea of a female sexuality that is as unaccountable to its consequences as male sexuality seems, from the right-to-life perspective, a fatal unmooring possible only in a narcissist, materialist culture. That a pregnancy may be unwanted or unexpected is not overlooked in this perspective, but the emphasis falls on the "conversion" experience of women who, having seen the "truth," make a decision to triumph over the situation by having the baby despite their doubts and the availability of abortion. Such women are said to be "truly" female.

The breakdown in moral values that especially preoccupies pro-life activists finds symbolic expression in the fact that babies are no longer good marketing tools. As one grandmother put it, "Babies aren't in style today anymore. Babies are trouble. They cry; they get sick in the middle of the night. They wake up and interrupt a lot of things. Babies used to sell products, but not anymore. Now it's the nice luscious young gals." Yet it is precisely on babies that the most radical of the right-to-life proponents dwell, with an obsessiveness that more than compensates for their decreased marketing potential. There was the male extremist from the Save-A-Baby group who made "good TV" by dressing up as Santa Claus and trying to enter the abortion clinic to deliver "toys to the unborn." And there was the slide show produced by the male president of the National Right-to-Life Committee which juxtaposes "war pictures" of aborted fetuses with old news photos of Southeast Asian civilians burnt by napalm. "The aborted fetus becomes a sacrifice offered for the redemption of America."

What is at stake for the white, mostly middle-class, mostly Christian, mostly married, women on both sides of the debate in Fargo is the very definition of female, which at this moment in American history is, in Ginsburg's words, "up for grabs." With the abortion debate, it is again upon the female body that the consequences and contradictions of capitalist culture are being written. Yet, particularly as men enter the pro-life ranks in positions of power and national prominence, there is a strange disembodiedness about it all. Where is the woman in the body? Is the debate about the body in the woman or the woman in the body? Whose womb is it, anyway, the woman's or the society's? Is it only the potential productivity of a woman's womb that matters?

*The Handmaid's Tale* has many true sequels, one among them "The Leadworker's Tale," which concerns a group of women workers who have charged Johnson Controls, Inc., a battery manufacturer in Milwaukee, with sex discrimination for banning them from work in jobs that involved high lead exposure because of their "childbearing capacity." The company's response was that "they were not discriminating against women but protecting the fetus from the effects of lead exposure." Commenting on this "tale," Ellen Goodman writes, "Once again, woman against her womb." Yet she wryly adds, "The passion to 'protect' fertile women doesn't extend to men, but they are hardly invulnerable to reproductive damage." And making the link with *The Handmaid's Tale*, she notes how in the fantasyland of Gilead "men were not tested for infertility, fertile women were not free and the countryside was a wasteland." In America, "fetal protection policies" not only "protect women out of their jobs and leave men at risk to their health, [but] leave companies free to do their dirty business."[16]

Debates about "fetal rights," like debates about abortion, are rooted in the split between home and work, or put another way, in the split (imagined and real) between female responsibility to womb and family versus a woman's need or desire to participate in the public and economic realms of life. Again, this is a story that takes us back to the nineteenth century, as Ginsburg so convincingly shows.

Birth control and abortion were championed by the first wave of feminists in the 1850s, who lost out in their struggle to the centralizing medical profession and the state. Until the 1850s abortion had been tolerated, if not legitimated by law, and it was an act performed by a variety of "irregular" physicians, including midwives, local healers, homeopaths, and abortionists. Seeking to consolidate their control over the practice of medicine, the "regular" physicians trained in medical schools joined together to forge the nineteenth-century antiabortion campaign. Their campaign tapped into the misogynist and eugenic ideology of the postbellum era, which held educated white women, who supported and used abortion and birth control, responsible for the decline of "the white race." Ultimately, their efforts would lead to the criminalization of abortion in America by 1900. But the fact that the crusade had to do with wresting medical control over a woman's right to an abortion was made clear in the exception that was made to the rule: that an abortion could still be performed by a physician if in the *physician's judgement* it was necessary to save the mother's life. In this way, abortion was removed from the public domain and turned into a private secret between a woman and her doctor, or a dark secret between a woman and her own body if she found herself unable to avail herself of professional help.

Not until 1960s activism, which led to the 1973 ruling legalizing abortion, did abortion emerge again as a public controversy. After *Roe v. Wade* abortion was no longer a crime, yet the medical profession, now consolidated in the hundred years after its struggle against abortion, did not make a significant effort to accommodate the increasing demands of women for abortion services. Hospital officials and medical personnel were concerned about image: if too many abortions were performed in a hospital it ran the risk of being tagged an "abortion mill." As hospitals proved reluctant to perform abortions and it became evident that outpatient abortions could be performed safely, pro-choice women in health care decided to meet the demand for accessible abortions by creating freestanding abortion clinics throughout the country.

A stark symbolic division of space took form, with the freestanding clinics planted on the periphery of the physical and ideological centers of the medical community. Because the abortion clinics had, by force, to be located on this spatial periphery, they became subject to metaphorical attack as "convenience stores," "7–11's," and "stop and chops." And they became subject to real, physical attack by members of the right-to-life movement, who have used the sites as spaces for waging the struggle against abortion. By the end of 1985, 92 percent of the abortion clinics in the country had reported some harassment, ranging from picketing to vandalism to intimidating patients and doctors, carried out by extremists, to forming prayer vigils and problem pregnancy sidewalk centers, carried out by more moderate protesters, like the Fargo women. The clinics became "interpretive battlegrounds" not only for people on different sides of the debate, but for the diverse members of the right-to-life movement. In one of these battlegrounds stood a female anthropologist, listening and taking notes, and somehow not getting caught in the crossfire.

It was most imaginative of Faye Ginsburg to have recognized the possibilities of observing and analyzing the abortion debate as a "social drama" played out in the marginal space of an abortion clinic in the marginal space of Fargo, North Dakota. Grounding her discussion in a particular landscape and in the lives of particular women activists, she succeeds in making it impossible to think of any of the women, whatever one's own stance may be, as "other," and therefore strange, unknowable, and foreign. Unlike Emily Martin, who struggles to see and have us see the strangeness in our familiar and obvious concepts of the female body, Faye Ginsburg has sought to make us feel at home among all the actors in the abortion debate; neither puts herself in the picture, choosing instead panoptic visions. Ginsburg's lucid understandings have the effect of giving one pause, making one take a second look to assess subtler and more difficult meanings in the debate. While they are not a call to direct action, they do open a path, for anyone who wishes to take it, beyond hysteria.

\*       \*       \*

On Tuesday, March 6, 1990, my mother, father, and I arrive at Lenox Hill Hospital on 77th Street in Manhattan at six o'clock in the morning. My mother has on her pink sweat suit, the one with the appliqués of tiny fake pearls and lace swatches that she wears when she wants to be comfortable, and her sneakers. She has gotten a haircut and manicure especially for the operation. In her suitcase are three new nightgowns, a cerulean silk robe embossed with Chinesy patterns, and two pairs of ballerina-type slippers, one pair with bows that her friend Nina had thought were pretty. Later, I shall be the one to unpack her things, slowly taking in the soft restiveness of each garment before squeezing it into the narrow closet, trying too hard to fill the empty spaces of our waiting for her.

A series of routine steps, such routine steps, come before. Forms to be filled out, forms that had already been filled out: name, address, phone, place of work, insurance company, social security number. And then a name bracelet, body identification, the letters in watery blue ink, sadly misty. Onward to the next office, where a nurse leads my mother to a cubicle for tests and shaving. My father and I are

Jo Spence, "How do I begin to take responsibility for my body?" A selection from *Putting Myself in the Picture: A Political, Personal, and Photographic Autobiography* (Seattle: Real Comet Press, 1988), p. 168. This was one of several photographic tableaux designed by Jo Spence to document her experience with breast cancer and her subsequent lumpectomy. Here her body becomes the surface on which she writes the words of her question in an ironic self-display that parodies commercial and other oppressive inscriptions on the female body.

Gertrude Elias, *Hospital* (1948). Reprinted from S. Kent and J. Morreau, *Women's Images of Men* (New York: Writers and Readers Publishing, 1985), p. 117. A classical doctor/woman relation, with the nurse in the background. The doctor's inscriptions about the woman's body are noted on a chart that she, alone and on display, cannot see.

told to sit in the waiting room. They will call us when we can go in. A television is turned on to the news. Every few minutes an orderly in green surgical gear wheels up a stretcher, snatches a glance at the television, and takes someone away. When we see my mother again she is in a hospital gown and wearing thick white support hose. A fine net covers her hair: she is now a patient. By 8:00 her stretcher arrives, and my father and I follow along as the orderly takes her to the tenth floor.

On the tenth floor we wait in a corridor around the corner from the operating room. One by one the medical staff that will be attending her come to her side: the anesthesiologist, a nurse, another nurse, an overexcited resident in obstetrics and gynecology, and finally the doctor, star of the cast, aloof, towering, brisk, concentrated on the goal. The doctor pats her hand and begins to rush off, but my mother stops him to introduce my father and me. He gives us each a quick handshake, and we agree to meet in my mother's room after the surgery. "We're ahead of schedule. We will be able to get you in early," the doctor says, pleased.

There has been a cancellation. One of the nurses has already told us that someone has cancelled the appointment preceding my mother's. What does that mean? Should we take it as an omen? My mother says to the nurse, half-asking, half-thinking-aloud, "Maybe I should cancel?" The nurse becomes dead serious. "You are certainly within your right to cancel. You can cancel the operation right now if you don't want it performed. That's your choice. You're having elective surgery." My mother is stunned by the nurse's reply; it hadn't occurred to her that she could still get up and walk away. But she doesn't get up and walk away. And minutes later we kiss goodbye and she says to us, *Vayan a comer algo. No han desayunado.* She is about to be cut open and she is concerned that my father and I have not eaten breakfast. I see her being wheeled off. Something happens in my body; I feel drippy around my brow and heart, as though I were a thick crust of ice thawing in the sun. I can't stand the fleshness of this, this giving up of my mother's flesh to the surgeon's knife.

Stepping out of the hospital, I feel glad for the bustle and noise of the street. My father and I find a coffee shop on Lexington. We're going to have breakfast as my mother requested. As we eat our toasted bagels my father tells me how upset he is that my brother has not shown more concern about my mother's operation nor expressed any interest in coming to visit her. *Su madre se va operar, y él como si nada.* You raised him to be a boy, I tell him in English. And you raised me to be a dutiful daughter, I tell myself. I hold back because I don't want to get into an argument while my mother is being cut open; I'm afraid this wouldn't be good for her.

We return to the waiting room. I have my books with me, but I can't look at them; I open a newspaper and spread it over my lap. "I'm going to see if Sylvia is here," I tell my father. Actually I'm going to the bathroom again; my stomach has felt demolished since our arrival in the hospital. When I come out, Sylvia, my mother's older sister, is there in the lobby. "Hi, Ruty. Your mother okay?" I have always been struck by how different my Aunt Sylvia is from my mother; more no-nonsense, more sardonic, less sentimental, less willing to wear her heart on her sleeve. She's blond and green-eyed and early on as a teenager she rejected her Cubanness, ending up marrying my Uncle Bill, who was raised in the Bronx and owns a shop in the Bowery where he sells meat-slicing equipment and cash registers.

Back in the waiting room I express some of my doubts about the operation to Sylvia. Was it really necessary, I ask. Sylvia has no doubts. "Your mother was bleeding so much she was using towels, Ruty. I don't know how she went to work. On the subway. That long trip every day. If she kept going like that one day she was going to bleed to death."

I know it was Sylvia who recommended the tall male doctor to my mother; he's a specialist in high-risk pregnancies and Sylvia thinks highly of him because he delivered her diabetic daughter's two children. And he's a reputable surgeon who has operated on some rich and famous women. *La Filipina es muy buena, pero no para una operacíon tan grande* was the guiding wisdom: "the Philippine woman is very good, but not for such a major operation." The Philippine doctor, both Sylvia's and my mother's gynecologist, had suggested surgery to my mother two years before and had urged her more strongly to have the surgery in the last few months. But sensing my mother's uncertainty and fear, she had refused to tell her what to do. "You have to be ready," she had said to my mother and told her that she could probably wait a little longer, that there was a hormone treatment that might help. When my mother went to the tall male doctor he told her, with absolutely no hesitation, that she needed surgery immediately. The Philippine doctor's desire to accommodate my mother began to look like wishy-washiness— especially to Sylvia, eventually to my father, and finally even to my mother. A doctor should be able to tell you what you need to do to feel better, whether or not it's what you want to hear; if the pill isn't bitter, can it heal?

At 11 o'clock a nurse comes to tell us that the operation has been completed and that my mother is in recovery. We can go on up and

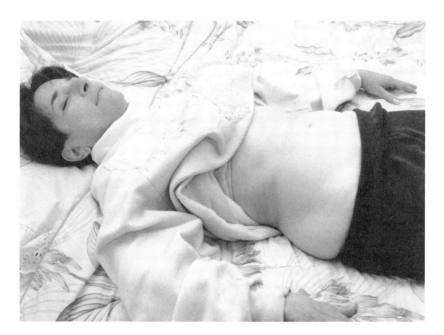

Ruth Behar, "The dream of the slumbering woman: my mother before the hysterectomy" (March 5, 1990). On the day before my mother had her hysterectomy I asked if I could photograph her. She alone chose the place and position in my parents' bedroom, posing with dreamy illusion in a way reminiscent of the prostrate woman in the "Perfect Tan Print."

"Perfect Tan Print," an advertisement for Tanqueray, in *Time*, May 7, 1990. The female body serves as a writing surface and a stage for the display of the bikini. The "bikini cut" is done low on a woman's midriff so she will still be able to wear a bikini after a hysterectomy and not show her scar.

wait for her in her room. Getting off the elevator on the third floor we take a wrong turn and find ourselves in the radiation therapy wing. On one door a sign in crimson reads "Danger: High Radiation." I feel an Alice-in-Wonderland fear of turning the knob on the wrong door.

After walking in a circle we are back by the elevators. We take a turn in the opposite direction and find the room. It is in a short corridor of six rooms, two women to a room. The woman who will be sharing the room with my mother has apparently already arrived; there are slippers by the other bed and part of the closet is already filled with clothes. There are two seats and a garbage pail in the corner of the room by the window and the bathroom; the room is cramped, dull, and functional, with decorating touches limited to two framed art museum posters that hang on the walls facing each bed. We take our seats in the corner and wait for the doctor.

The doctor arrives at 11:30, dapper and self-assured. "Everything went well, just like in the books," he says.

My father's forehead is wrinkled tight with worry, his eyebrows almost touching his hairline. "Is she okay, doctor? No complications?"

"She's doing fine. I gave her a nice bikini incision. When she goes to Brazil she'll be able to wear the smallest bikini she wants to."

Before going into surgery my mother had a fantasy about how she was going to tell the doctor that if he couldn't do a bikini cut it didn't matter, that he could cut the other way if he needed to, but please not to pull out her organs. Her friend Luisita at the office had told her about doctors who pull out organs and the damage that can do. As we waited with my mother in the corridor that morning she had checked with me about which way was horizontal and which way was vertical. My father had chuckled: did she really think she would be able to tell the doctor how to cut her open while lying there on the operating table?

"So, doctor, she's okay?" My father often needs to ask questions more than once, especially if he's worried.

"I gave her back a unit of her own blood to bring up her blood count, so don't be alarmed when you see the tubes. She didn't lose any blood. When she gets out of the hospital she'll have hormones, one pill a day, and she'll stay young forever." He smiles reassuringly and pauses. "Do you have any questions?"

I ought to have questions, but after spending the morning in the hospital I feel lobotomized. Like my father, I keep wanting to ask over and over: is she okay? is she okay?

"She's in the recovery room and won't be down for at least another hour or two, so go have lunch, you have plenty of time."

He takes his exit and the three of us remain in our corner like punished schoolchildren. Perhaps to grasp the slippery reality before us, we rerun the conversation to one another, recalling and repeating, as though it were an assignment, the exact words and turns of phrase the doctor used: "just like in the books," "a bikini cut," "a unit of her own blood," "a hormone pill each day."

After a while my father sends Sylvia and me to have lunch in the hospital cafeteria. When we return at 1:00 my Aunt Fany, my father's sister, and her husband David, are standing in the hallway with my father. They closed their small clothing store in the south Bronx early, having sold for the day a pair of jeans for twenty dollars; business is bad. Barely after we say hello we see an orderly wheeling a stretcher toward our corridor, stopping at the nurses' station just ahead of us. We all turn to look at the woman lying on the stretcher. *No es Rebeca*, "That's not Rebeca," my Aunt Sylvia says. *No, no parece*, "No, it doesn't look like her," says my Aunt Fany. The woman's feet are closer to us than her face and she is covered to her chest with a white sheet; one can see her nostrils, her half-open eyes, and her thick short black hair. I move a little closer. Could this be my mother? As the orderly wheels her toward us I realize, we all realize with a shock, that it is my mother. How strange she looked for a moment, not like herself; how, I wonder — with the sense of panic that gripped me when I tried to find my newborn son, his face still so new to me, in a roomful of newborns — do people recognize the faces they have seen and known all their lives when they have been transfigured by the wear of time, illness, torture, or death?

My mother has clearly seen and recognized us. She greets us one by one, and to my Aunt Fany she says in a whisper, *Fany, que bueno que viniste* ("Fany, how nice that you came"). Then the orderly and the nurse wheel her into the room and shut the door. Fany, moved almost to tears, turns to me and says, *Oíste lo que dijo tu mama? Acabadita de operar y me dijo, 'Fany, que bueno que viniste'* ("Did you hear what your mother said? Just operated on and she thinks to say to me, 'Fany, how nice that you came' ").

My mother sleeps and sleeps, and we take turns in twos and threes sitting by her bedside. My Uncle Bill arrives with a bouquet of roses and she wakes up enough to thank him and falls asleep again. Then an orderly and a nurse come to the door and ask us to wait outside for a moment. My mother's roommate has arrived. For the rest of the day we sit and watch them both sleep and sleep from our little corner by the window. It is easy to lose track of time: the window looks out onto other hospital windows and onto the square formed by the four facades that come together there for no purpose at all, an architectural oversight that lets in no sunlight, no sky, no city movements nor sounds.

In that room I came back each day to see my mother and her roommate getting slowly better. Saying goodbye for the night was painful; the first night we hired a costly private nurse, following the doctor's advice for dealing with the nursing shortage, but the other nights she was on her own. The day after her surgery my mother took her first steps hesitantly, clasping the I.V. pole for support. After a few days at the hospital this became a familiar sight: women taking these gingerly walks up and down the corridor at different times of the day. I soon discovered that the twelve women staying in this corridor at any one time had undergone uterine surgery. Most had had a hysterectomy (the removal of the uterus and the attached fallopian tubes); many of the women, who either had complications or were past the childbearing years, had gotten a total hysterectomy (the removal of the cervix with the uterus) accompanied by an oophorectomy (removal of one ovary) or a bilateral oophorectomy (removal of both ovaries). And I discovered that no bed in that corridor was empty for long; as soon as one woman was strong enough to walk away, her bed would be filled again by another woman just wheeled in from surgery. The corridor was a factory in relentless high gear.

Each day my mother's doctor came by, refusing to be anything but cheerful and breezy. "You're doing beautifully, just beautifully. That bikini incision I gave you heals very nicely. You'll be wearing a bikini in Brazil before you know it. But keep walking, it's the best thing for you."

There seemed to me something cruel about the doctor's constant refrain about the bikini cut. He meant, I suppose, to reassure my mother that her sexuality had not been put in danger by the removal of her uterus. As a stereotyped place of hot tones and primitive unrestrained sexuality, Brazil—echoing, in turn, prerevolutionary Cuba—was meant to evoke a place where even a hysterectomized woman could hope to display her body without shame. But when a woman is at her least sexual, what does it mean to have the male doctor, who has cut out the heart of her female anatomy, standing there, telling her that she will be whole again, Brazilian sexy again, not for her own sake but for the display?

The resident, always in a rush as though he were running behind a moving train, had not yet developed a rhetoric for handling his female patients. Out of breath, he'd say, "Hi, how you doing?" He was young, short, curly redhaired, casual, with the style of a sports-caster rather than a doctor, and my mother found him totally unprofessional. *Un comebolas,* she called him, a Cubanism for "nerd." I had my own explanation. "He doesn't have an aura of authority like your doctor," I told my mother. I thought there might be more hope for him because you could at least engage him in conversation. I had shown him Emily Martin's book, which was lying on my mother's bed, and he was interested enough to ask about it and take note of it. When I did the same with the doctor, he smiled musingly and said with a philosophical air, "It's a subject of endless fascination. It fascinated the ancients and it continues to fascinate us." His manner was not unkind or unfriendly, just distant and all-knowing.

Later in the week I managed to engage the doctor in a somewhat longer conversation. I asked him about the estrogen replacement therapy my mother would begin after she left the hospital. "And she won't need progestin to prevent cancer?" I asked. I could feel the sweat under my arms; I was nervous and had asked a stupid question to which I already knew the answer.

"Progestin is to prevent cancer of the uterus. Your mother doesn't need progestin because she doesn't have a uterus. But she will need estrogen. The ovaries produce estrogen even after menopause, and estrogen has been shown to be an essential hormone for the prevention of cardiovascular disease and osteoporosis. And it helps to keep the vagina in good working order. It's also what the ladies want. They don't want to be like their grandmothers. They want to play tennis. They want to be women. And we're responding to that. A little pill a day and you'll be forever young," he said turning to my mother, with a twinkle in his eye.

And turning to me, he said, "I hear you're a professor?"

"Yes, at the University of Michigan, in anthropology."

"Very nice. And where did you go to graduate school?"

"Princeton."

"Nice. My children weren't interested in medicine. My two eldest daughters are lawyers. And my youngest is in film. It's been hard for her, but she's getting there. Her name's right up there in the titles of a film that's opening today, *The Handmaid's Tale*."

"Is that right? It's a wonderful book, I know."

"Very good. Any other questions?"

With the resident it was different. He was my height; I could see him eye to eye. I never learned his last name but I was able to read his name tag as far as his first name, "Ronnie," and to see that he was the chief resident, information which I relayed to my mother. When he came in the second morning, my mother was sitting in the lounge chair by the window. Her spirits were better and to make conversation, she said, "You are the chef resident?"

Ronnie, out of breath as usual, paused and said, "No, I'm not a chef. A chef is a cook. I'm the chief resident."

I managed to put in my dumb two cents. "Ah, the chief resident of the hospital?"

"There's no such thing as a chief resident of a hospital. The chief resident in obstetrics and gynecology."

These little word-mishaps with Ronnie kept us laughing all week; there wasn't much else to laugh about. We nicknamed him the "chef resident" from then on.

Toward the end of the week the doctor came in and cheerfully said to my mother, who was sitting in the lounge chair wearing her cerulean silk robe, "Today you can get care packages from home. You know, some black beans." So, he had tagged her identity as Cuban; I wondered if he knew that she was also Jewish like him and also ate matzoh balls.

By Saturday my mother was doing very well, fortunately. She could take longer walks, and her energy was returning. Hand in hand, we walked over to the other side of the building, past the radiation therapy wing where my father, Aunt Sylvia, and I had gotten lost when we first tried to find my mother's room. In that corridor other kinds of illness were on exhibit, the illnesses of cancer: a young woman completely bald, elderly people in wheelchairs, and in the waiting room a disheveled woman attached to an I.V. sneaking a cigarette.

On our return from that walk we encountered the doctor. After telling my mother she could go home the next day he asked if her stay had been pleasant. She said that it had, and that she wanted to write a letter in praise of some of the nurses (particularly a kind Jamaican male nurse) who had helped her.

Ruth Behar, "In the same corridor: my mother and her hospital roommate Marlene Cromwell" (March 10, 1990).

Ruth Behar, "Facing up: my mother after the hysterectomy" (March 11, 1990).

"Please write the letter to our president here at Lenox Hill. She'll be happy to know. We have a woman president, you know. An excellent president. She's married to a doctor here. We're very understanding about her schedule. It's got to be flexible. They have two children. You know what it's like." The doctor was looking at me. He had addressed this statement to me.

"I have one child, but my work comes first. We use a lot of child care," I said. This was an exaggeration, but I resented the way he saw me as a female. It made me think of men who are always undressing women in their minds; I felt stripped down to my reproductive organs and the expectation to mother.

In the meantime we had gotten to know Marlene Cromwell, my mother's roommate at the hospital. The first day, when she lay sleeping, I had answered a phone call for her from her sister in Charleston, South Carolina. I had watched her doctor come to her bedside that day and whisper gently to her, "Everything went fine, Marlene. You had a lot of adhesions. We took out your right ovary because it was in bad shape, but the left ovary was fine and we left it." Marlene had endometriosis and had decided, after two years of reading and thinking, to have a hysterectomy. Not that she hadn't doubted: just a year ago she had cancelled her surgery at the last minute, reminding me of the cancelled appointment before my mother's surgery.

With endometriosis, the endometrial tissue that lines the uterus and which is normally released during menstruation grows in places outside the uterus and adheres to other organs, usually the ovaries, bladder, or rectum, causing severe pain. Marlene had been in a lot of pain, excruciating pain that, as she told me, went down her legs and into her toes. But because she was a thirty-five-year-old professional woman there were few doctors willing to operate on her; two surgeons had refused to operate. She had looked for alternatives, in holistic medicine, in diet, in the use of lasers. Her sister had undergone laser treatment for fibroid growths in her uterus (laporoscopy) but her fibroids had grown back and she had ended up having a hysterectomy anyway. "You have to cut them out at the root, like with a plant," Marlene said. Not only had her sister had a hysterectomy, but so, too, had her mother and her maternal aunt; and her maternal grandmother had died of cervical cancer.

Marlene felt confident that a hysterectomy was entirely necessary in her case. She had made up her own mind about it, told the doctor what *she* wanted, and this gave her strength. Yet, being thoughtful, she felt saddened that things couldn't have turned out differently. She had finally been able to reconcile herself to the understanding that the endometriosis was nothing she had caused, that it was not like a sexually transmitted disease, and that it was not her fault in any way. In conversations with her husband, who no longer lived with her but was still her friend, and after reading a book on African holistic health,[17] she had begun to work out a theory of how the uterus might become polluted, causing fibroids and adhesions to grow. "Even men give these things to women in their sperm. What a man eats is in a concentrated form in his sperm, like toxins. Gives you something to think about, doesn't it?"

This did give me something to think about. I found this a most empowering thought, not only in its shifting of the blame for a malfunctioning uterus from the woman to the man, but in the effort to think about the womb in terms of sexual politics, ecology, food consumption, in other words, in terms of the larger issues that impinge upon the individual female body, an effort that the doctors seemed totally unwilling to even try to do.[18]

Toward the end of the week, Marlene and I cornered Ronnie and tried to get him to answer the question that bothered us the most. Marlene had said something that I had not been able to forget: "If I knew this would help other women, then I would know it had been worth it." So I started by asking Ronnie, "What do you do with all the organs you take out? Where do they go?"

Ronnie seemed flustered. "They go to pathology. And then if there's nothing wrong, they're thrown out. What do you want them to do with the organs? They throw them away."

And Marlene, "Well, why don't they research where fibroids and other diseases come from, what causes them?"

And Ronnie, "Who knows where they come from? There's nothing to learn."

And Marlene, "What do you mean there's nothing to learn?"

"What can I say? They look them over in pathology, then they're discarded. Anyway, how could you keep so many of them?"

Marlene and I winced.

Marlene was not sentimental about her womb. With three children already she didn't want any more; her five-year-old daughter lived with her in the Bronx, and her two older sons were with her mother in Charleston, where she hoped a better fate awaited them as black young men. Marlene herself had come from Charleston, and intended to return there someday. The problem was there were no jobs in the South, and the ones there were paid too little. For the past four years she had worked as a computer programmer at Bankers Trust, but she hoped also to return to school in English literature, to finish up a degree she left uncompleted at New York University. Her link to NYU turned out to be a connection to my mother, who is the secretary in charge of diplomas there.

But this was not the only connection to my mother; the two of them shared a room for five days and as they both got better they talked a lot, especially at night when they were alone. They made each other laugh like crazy. Something unusual was happening in that hospital room between them, in which only a thin curtain was there to separate them if they so chose, but, in fact, didn't.

When Adrienne Rich told women to take the female body as a starting point for gaining "the grounds from which to speak with authority *as* women. Not to transcend this body, but to reclaim it," she was careful to add, "To locate myself in my body means more than understanding what it has meant to me to have a vulva and clitoris and uterus and breasts." For Rich, this "more" is the overlay of race, of difference as lived separation. She notes how her body was marked as female and as white from the start: "I was born in the white section of a hospital which separated Black and white women in labor and Black and white babies in the nursery, just as it separated Black and white bodies in its morgue."[19]

I think that one of the best things to have come out of my mother's experience was that a thirty-five-year-old black woman from Charleston, South Carolina, and a fifty-four-year-old Cuban Jewish woman discovered they had some things in common, and at least for a few days lived a life in common. As I looked around that corridor with its constantly shifting twelve women, it struck me just how much it was an International House of Wombless Women. Hospitals had managed to consign abortions to homelessness, but hysterectomies, it seemed, were welcome and had quite a comfortable home there. During the five days my mother was at the hospital, there were among the twelve women a Chinese woman, a Jamaican woman, an Anglo woman, a Korean woman, an African-American woman, a Cuban woman. All had ended up in that same corridor.

*     *     *

Reproduction, abortion, hysterectomy. These are three parts of a female-body triptych, it seems evident to me now.

When I came back to Ann Arbor after my mother's surgery and return home for a two-month convalescence, I put everything aside and began to read whatever I could find about hysterectomies. Joanne Leonard, whose photocollage work is included in this essay, had been through a hysterectomy herself, and one day she brought me a copy of a book by the gynecologist and surgeon Vicki Hufnagel, *No More Hysterectomies.*[20] Joanne warned me not to take the book to heart, that she had read it before her surgery and had still decided to go through with it. But I did take the book to heart! I consumed it, and it consumed me with a daughter's guilt.

I learned some facts that I ought to have already known but did not know. I now had the last piece of the historical puzzle begun by Emily Martin and Faye Ginsburg. Abdominal hysterectomy, I learned, was first successfully performed in 1853 in Massachusetts. The term hysterectomy was coined in 1886, to define the surgical removal of the uterus, from the Greek *hystera*, for womb, and *ectemnein*, to cut out. By the late nineteenth century, hysterectomy and oophorectomy, the removal of the ovaries, became common treatments for a variety of female disorders, including masturbation, "excessive" sexuality, simple "cussedness," and painful menstruation. "Doctors boasted of the thousands of operations they had performed at professional meetings and displayed ovaries on platters to admiring audiences," writes Hufnagel.

While carrying out an antiabortion campaign, the emerging medical establishment was standardizing hysterectomy and oophorectomy as routine procedures that even young surgeons could master, and which hospitals would later embrace as "elective" surgery, at the same time shutting out elective abortions. Although the reasons for assaulting the malfunctioning womb would change in the twentieth century, the procedures and many of the unspoken assumptions behind them would remain the same. Nineteenth-century surgical procedures and assumptions about the female body as a site of pathology would continue to be used to treat modern women. As one gynecologist put it as late as 1969 in a commentary on the use of hysterectomy for the purpose of sterilization: "To sterilize a patient and allow her to keep a useless and potentially lethal organ is incompatible with modern gynecologic concepts. Hysterectomy is the only logical approach to surgical sterilization . . . . The uterus becomes a useless, bleeding, symptom-producing, potentially cancer-bearing organ, and therefore should be removed." The doctor's purpose, it would seem, is to domesticate the unruliness of the female body by bringing it under rational control through the removal of the irrationality of the uterus, thereby making the female body more like the male body.

The image of the useless uterus has had a devastating impact on American women. It is incredible just how widespread hysterectomies are in the United States: 670,000 hysterectomies occurred in 1985, making it one of the most common surgeries performed. As a surgery performed on women, it was surpassed only by cesarean section at 813,000 for the same year.[21] According to one report, so high is the hysterectomy rate in this country that "within a few years 50% of women younger than 65 will no longer have their uterus." Women with health insurance are twice as likely to have a hysterectomy as uninsured women (such "hip pocket surgery" helping to pay the bills of running a gynecology office), while women of marginal racial and class backgrounds are especially likely to be threatened with a hysterectomy as a form of sterilization, particularly when seeking abortions. So common are hysterectomies among black women in the South that they are referred to as the "Mississippi appendectomy."[22]

Close to 90 percent of all hysterectomies are performed as elective surgery for benign diseases, including prolapse of female organs, fibroid uterine tumors, and endometriosis; only 10.5 percent of hysterectomies performed from 1970 to 1984 were medically indicated, that is, necessary because of cancer. According to Hufnagel, most elective hysterectomies could be prevented through the use of techniques of female reconstructive surgery that she and a few other surgeons have developed, by means of which tumors can be removed and uteruses repaired, leaving female organs intact. Yet, as Hufnagel points out, capitalist economics together with cultural and political assumptions about the female body lie behind the American medical profession's unwillingness to seriously explore and disseminate alternatives to hysterectomizing women.

Certainly, the high rate of hysterectomies in the United States, which is double of that in the United Kingdom and other European countries, must be seen in light of a system of non-socialized medicine. The consumer must shop around for, and purchase, medical services, for which the physician is paid per service performed. The ideal of consumerist freedom is, however, double-faced when it comes to women. Certain services are easily purchased, like hysterectomies, which have become an industry; others, like abortion, take a little more shopping around, and may eventually become unavailable; and yet others, like female reconstructive surgery, are so scarce and hidden and pose such a threat to established techniques and knowledge that a market for them has not been allowed to develop.

Emily Martin's point about how medical metaphors imagine the female body in terms of a production model — even melodramatically as a uterus crying for a baby during menstruation — is likewise central to an understanding of why hysterectomies, usually in tandem with oophorectomies, are offered as solutions to uterine problems in the United States. Of what productive use is a post-childbirth uterus and ovaries? The metaphors of decline and decay used to describe menopause, in which the ovaries are said to shrink, pucker, and atrophy, serve to buttress the notion that a hysterectomy does not cause any damage, and that on the contrary it is rather like a well-needed spring cleaning.

Not only do the female reproductive organs become unproductive, they are also, in an ironic metaphor, "breeding grounds" for cancer, potential cancer sites and harbingers of death: the womb for reproducing life carries the seeds of its own destruction. The grip that the fear of cancer has on our collective imagination, which Susan Sontag explored in general terms,[23] takes a particular form when applied to the illnesses of the female body. Women of my mother's age who have been advised to have a hysterectomy because of fibroid tumors (note the scare word "tumor" which conjures up for most people images of cancerous growths) are told by their doctors that while they're having surgery they would be best off choosing the package deal, in other words having their ovaries and cervix removed with their uteruses. The selling technique known as "bait and switch," is used, by "which the advertised item is discredited and another, more expensive, product is substituted in its place."[24] The risk of cancer is presented as the likelihood of cancer and the package deal is offered as better insurance, a better buy, against getting some of the worst cancers that affect women. In my mother's case as in so many others, rather than simply having her tumors removed, she had her perfectly normal organs themselves removed and discarded; she got the works, had it all taken out. "All of that has to die anyway," she told herself.

For the premenopausal woman who still harbors doubts, the selling points of a hysterectomy are pursued further: avoiding messy periods, removing the fear of pregnancy; for the postmenopausal woman, she need only be told that she doesn't need her reproductive organs anymore, that they serve no useful purpose, and that removing them will have no effect on her sense of self, her sexuality, and her bodily health. If either woman continues to desire to hold on to her organs, and voices this desire, she is made to feel silly, hysterical, or superstitious. As Hufnagel summarizes this attitude, "What self-respecting, modern woman would want to hang on to her uterus, anyway?" Hufnagel recounts treating a minority woman in her early forties for abnormal bleeding who expressed the wish that Hufnagel remove the tumors and leave her uterus, fallopian tubes, and ovaries intact if they checked out free of cancer. When the assisting surgeon arrived shortly before the surgery was to begin, he became angry at Hufnagel for having heeded the woman's wishes and not gotten her consent for a hysterectomy. Pulling her aside, he "proceeded to excoriate me in front of nurses and the anesthesiologist. 'She's too old. She doesn't need her uterus anymore, anyway.

These women are all alike . . . they think it's some kind of magical organ. They're all ignorant and superstitious.' "

Should women care about losing their uteruses? Is the sense of doubt so many women feel about having a hysterectomy merely fetishistic? Could a woman be pro-choice, for example, maybe never even want to bear children, and still want to hang on to her uterus? The answer, for Hufnagel, is that women should, indeed, be very concerned about losing their uteruses.

The uterus is not only a reproductive organ, though as a reproductive organ it should be respected and left intact, particularly among women in their 30s or 40s who may one day decide that they do want to bear children. Hufnagel recounts many stories about assumptions doctors make as to the appropriate age for women to have children, and as to the lifestyles they presume their patients wish to pursue. She tells the story of a 20-year-old nun suffering from endometriosis whose uterus was almost removed by the attending surgeon under the assumption that childbearing wouldn't be her concern. As a medical student at the time, Hufnagel softly dared to raise her voice in the operating room to ask if anyone had talked to the patient about her desire to have children. The surgeon laughed at himself and removed the clamp that had already been placed on the ligament that holds the uterus; he cleaned out the endometriosis rather than the organs. After the surgery, the patient decided she no longer wanted to be a nun, married, and had several children, "never knowing how close she had actually come to losing it all."

Reproduction, however, is not the sole purpose of a uterus, a fact which is difficult to see because of the burden of negative metaphors that obscure our vision of the female body. The uterus plays a key part in a woman's wellbeing; even long after menopause it secretes hormones and proteins that maintain heart, muscles, and bones, and which cannot be replaced with one "little" estrogen pill a day; it plays a vital role as a support structure in pelvic anatomy; it is a sex organ that often contracts during orgasm, heightening for many women their sexual pleasure; and for many women it is an essential part of their sense of self not simply as women but as whole persons. For my mother, her central concern (stemming, I believe, from a Jewish belief about returning the body whole to the earth after death) was to maintain the integrity of her body, and it was the thought of this loss that most worried her about having a hysterectomy. The postoperative effects of hysterectomy sadly include physical, emotional, and sexual problems that are often attributed to psychological factors ("it's all in your head") but do, indeed, have real physical causes. These negative effects have been more widely recognized, it seems, outside the United States. When I told the British cultural historian Carolyn Kay Steedman about my work on this essay in the course of a personal conversation, she recounted what another British friend had been told by her gynecologist: "No matter what, hold on to those organs, my dear. They mean everything."

Hufnagel, like other writers who share her perspective, speaks of hysterectomy using the chilling words, amputation and castration. The ovaries, after all, are the female analogues of the testes. "One wonders," speculates Hufnagel, "whether castration of the male would be as prevalent if men grew fibroid tumors of the testicles or if men suffered from monthly depressions. I think not. If as great a proportion of the male population were faced with castration as the female population is, I venture to say there would be a branch of medicine dedicated solely to the saving of male organs." As Hufnagel points out, there are roughly four times as many cases of ovarian cancer as compared to testicular cancer, so one would expect the surgeries performed to mirror these facts; but, in practice, oophorectomies are performed nine times as often as testicle removals.

*    *    *

Reading Hufnagel's woeful tales of hysterectomized women I began to feel so complicitous in the violence that had been done to my mother's body that I hardly knew what to do. After my mother's mind had been made up, I had even advised her to have the surgery ten days earlier than she had anticipated, so I could be with her at the hospital. Had I helped to rush her into a decision when she was still stalling for time? My daughter's guilt became unbearable. How much of the very painful knowledge I had obtained — through reading and thinking carried out as a horrible kind of hindsight — could I share with my mother without causing more pain in turn to her? How much of it, too, could I share with Marlene who had, she was sure, looked at all the options and made up her own mind?

Initially I chose only to burden myself. Then I made some phone calls to local women's health practitioners I knew in Ann Arbor. I called for the second time the nurse-practitioner in town that had given me my physical, and whom I had called shortly before my mother's surgery to ask for medical and bibliographic advice. I had begun to feel angry at myself for having accepted her opinion about the inescapability of a hysterectomy in a situation like my mother's, and had hesitated to call fearing that my anger would make conversation impossible. Instead, we had a friendly talk, and she again reasserted her opinion. She had never heard of Hufnagel nor of her book.

I then called a nurse-midwife who had been part of a group that gave me prenatal care and attended the birth of my son, and she, too, knew little about the subject and had not heard of Hufnagel, either. She had quite a bit to say about how she and the midwife group had brought down the cesarean section rate, but she had apparently not yet seen the connection to the hysterectomy rate.

She suggested I call a doctor who is also one of two untenured women on the medical faculty in obstetrics and gynecology at Michigan. She, too, had not heard of Hufnagel nor of female reconstructive surgery, but was familiar with laporoscopy (the use of lasers to remove tumors), and patiently explained the various risks to me: longer operating times, longer periods under anesthesia, the possibility of greater loss of blood (and thus the possibility of contracting AIDS through transfusions), the likelihood of the tumors growing back, the difficulty of detecting ovarian cancer after the uterus is no longer there to produce symptoms, and the sense, simply, of putting the woman at too much risk to save, in most cases, non-functioning ovaries and a cervix which is nothing more than the neck of the uterus. Did she think, I asked, that there was enough research taking place to make such techniques safer and help women keep their organs if they so desired? She thought so.

When this doctor, a professor like me and a white woman of my age, told me that just two years ago, at the age of 32, she herself had undergone a hysterectomy, I began to feel I was coming full circle. In her case, her IUD (intra-uterine contraceptive device) had gotten stuck and surgery was necessary to remove it. During surgery her doctor (who is also her colleague) thought it had perforated her uterus so he performed a hysterectomy. Later it became apparent that the IUD was lodged in the fatty layer of her abdomen. He became distraught at his mistake, but she forgave him immediately; it was not his fault, she had trusted him, and she would have wanted forgiveness herself in such a situation. There is too much mistrust of doctors, she feels, and she was not about to add to it. I asked her if she felt sad or angry about losing her uterus. "I lost where my children grew," she said (she has two children). When I asked about loss of sexual desire and response, she said she had experienced no change. And when, finally, I thought to mention to her for its imaginativeness, Marlene's idea about male sperm polluting the uterus, I thought I detected irritation. "That's a fantasy," she said, ending our phone conversation.[25]

\*　　\*　　\*

I moved from hindsight, it seems, back to ambiguity; the grey region of it should have been different if it could have been different. As Joanne Leonard reminded me, it was in a state of utter demoralization that she made her decision to have a hysterectomy, after bleeding so heavily in the midst of teaching that she left a pool of blood on the floor and had to go straight home. I know my mother, like Marlene, had been demoralized, too, by her discomfort, pain, bleeding.

I remembered my own state of demoralization after being in labor for sixty hours trying to give birth to our son, Gabriel. My waters had broken before the onset of active labor, making infection a danger, and the nurse-midwives had insisted I come to the hospital. The nurse-midwife who held my hand during an entire weekend, away from her own family, did her best to keep the anxious residents and pediatricians at bay. But finally the head resident could be held back no longer and he strode in demanding to measure the strength of my uterine contractions. They turned out to be very weak and incapable of pushing out a baby. My uterus, it seemed, had fallen asleep; the midwife had injected me with morphine — maybe too much morphine — and I, too, wanted only to sleep. After so many hours of dry laboring there was a risk of hurting the baby. I was told that if I wanted to get the baby out, I would need to have pitocin, an epidural, an I.V., an internal fetal monitor — the works, in other words.

At this point David and I fell apart, crying for the loss of the sweet and natural childbirth we had so desired. But the epidural took the pain away and I got some sleep at last. When I awoke I found that the resident and anesthesiologist, without consulting with me, had decided to drastically reduce the level of the comforting numbing so that I would begin pushing. Contractions after a pitocin drip are fierce! The sudden switch from my light contractions to my cruel hard contractions drove me to the point of such mad pain that I

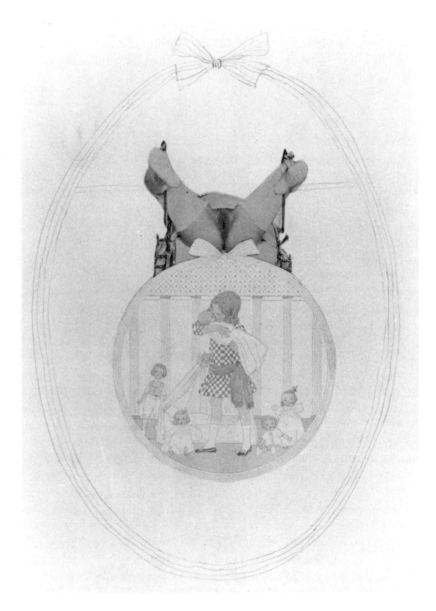

Joanne Leonard, "The Now and Then of Things," from *Journal, October 9–November 30, 1973*. The little girl with her dolls playing at mothering and, above her, the future she bears within her and cannot yet know.

yelled in rage for the first time. My midwife had abandoned me by this point, exhausted after a weekend of being with me (after me, the midwives broke up the weekend shifts). The resident who had taken over let me know that I was not using my energies effectively in pushing and he proceeded to point to his upper abdomen to show me how I had to push. My only wish at that moment was to have him castrated, but I pushed until I felt my back was splitting, coached by a nurse who reminded me of a junior high school gym teacher. "Get angry," she kept saying. "Come on, you're angrier than that." I was, indeed, angry; in fact, furious as hell that this was how a baby had to get born, and from my body. Gabriel was in a posterior position, which made the pain literally back-breaking; I cracked my tailbone, as many women do, while pushing. I pushed for two hours, flat on my back, my legs apart, in the worst position for laboring.

Coming in again, the resident told me, with supervisory calm, that I had done well. "You turned the baby around," he told me. Now, if I wanted him to, he could do a delivery with forceps. Meanwhile, the contractions continued. I heard his voice in between the crests of my pain and my screams. And I accepted. The anesthesiologist came in and stepped up the dose, and in a minute I was numb from the waist down. In another minute I was in the operating room. Obstetricians, pediatricians, medical students, and nurses assembled themselves to get a good view of the dark space between my legs. The resident asked me to push. Then he cut, performing an episiotomy, which I had planned to refuse. A hush and a gasp rose from the assembled audience. He pulled out my baby, a purple mass of flesh, and asked David to sever the twisted knot of the umbilical cord.

When the baby was put in my arms minutes later I didn't know whether to love it or hate it. Then I saw the ring on his cheek from the forceps. Then I saw the bruises on his head from his passage down the birth canal. Like me, he had suffered. He had been born at a minute after midnight, the beginning of a new day.

My love did flow. But my demoralization about my labor did not go away. The midwives said I had been a "trooper," that any other woman in my position would have ended up having a cesarean. In an age of medical control over childbirth, I was supposed to be happy that I had not had a cesarean. Yet I felt as though my body had failed me. When relatives called, they assumed my labor had been natural because I had chosen to be cared for by midwives. "All natural, right Ruty?" they said. Silence was my reply; tears welled up in my eyes. I had not had the kind of natural labor I wanted. I had had all the medical interventions I had planned to resist and refuse, and I had come extremely close to having a cesarean.

Emily Martin would object to the way in these lines I have separated myself from the act of laboring, my body from me, the woman.

Avoid the passive voice, guidelines for proper journal writing often tell us.

Labor is like a hand you are dealt, the midwives told me when I came in to the hospital after my waters broke.

Is there a passive voice that is not the voice of defeat but the voice of coming to terms with the hand you are dealt? Is there an active voice that keeps a memory of that passive voice?

\*      \*      \*

March 20, 1990. The incision is giving my mother problems. A corner of it has begun to bleed since her return home and has developed pus. When she calls the doctor to tell him about the bleeding, he thinks she is referring to the "spotting" that is supposed to occur, and at first doesn't understand nor seem interested. He's having trouble with my mother's English. My mother feels she's bothering. I tell her, from Ann Arbor, to please go in for a check, and not to worry about bothering the doctor. She is paying him, after all, I remind her. It turns out that she's had a "wound breakdown," not an infection, the doctor tells her; but she needs to return to his office once a week afterwards for treatment.

March 29, 1990. *Si vieras como me ayuda mi pie izquierdo*, "If you could see how my left foot helps me," my mother says to me on the phone, her voice energetic and playful. I've told her about the film, *My Left Foot*. My mother is left-handed, though her parents forced her into right-handedness as a child. She is doing so much with her left foot: picking up fallen pencils, papers, magazines, books.

April 11, 1990. *Eso de la bikini es un cuento. Si sigo así, me tendré que hacer cirugía plastica*, "All that about the bikini is a sham. If I stay like this, I'll have to go in for plastic surgery." My mother says she now has a bulge coming down now over the incision; the doctor tells her it's the layers of skin healing, my grandmother tells her it's the space left from the organs that used to be there. Give it time, she's told.

Things are not going past my mother. She doesn't need my knowledge or my guilt. Look how she found her left foot. Look how she's questioning the bikini cut. I believe she will find — is already finding — her own sources of power and knowledge.

*     *     *

After her mastectomy for cancer, the African-American lesbian writer, Audre Lorde, made a decision not to wear a prosthesis in the space where her right breast had been. She would wear the mark of her honorable wound like a warrior, the way Moshe Dayan, the Prime Minister of Israel, wore his eyepatch over his empty eyesocket. But when she went to her doctor's office, she was told, "You're not wearing a prosthesis . . . . You will feel so much better with it on. And besides, we really like you to wear something, at least when you come in. Otherwise it's bad for the morale of the office." And when she read the material on breast reconstruction she found that the key concern was to "enable many women who have had mastectomies to wear a *normal bra or bikini*." As Audre Lorde comments, "when a woman has faced the dread of breast cancer and triumphed, for whatever space of time, her primary concern should still be whether or not she can wear a normal bra or bikini . . . not learning to come to terms with her living and dying."

After her mastectomy, Audre Lorde made a conscious decision "to be loving my life rather than to be mourning my breast." But this self-affirmation, she reminds us, is very different from "the superficial farce of 'looking on the bright side of things.'" She would have no obscuring of realities, no false happiness and false breasts. In the second week after her surgery she wrote in her journal of using this chance "to live and speak those things I really do believe, that power comes from moving in whatever I fear most that cannot be avoided. But will I ever be strong enough again to open my mouth and not have a cry of raw pain leap out?" Audre Lorde did find that strength and she has passed it on to other women in her life and her writing. As she says in the last lines of *The Cancer Journals*, "I would never have chosen this path, but I am very glad to be who I am, here."[26]

I wish for my mother, for Marlene, and for women whose stories have yet to be told, that they may find these words in themselves; and that they may move on to discover other ways of telling what their bodies, in paths they would never have chosen, have put them through, and how they have triumphed; and that, having triumphed, they will pass on the knowledge that there's more to their stories than bras and bikinis.

## ACKNOWLEDGMENTS

For their support of my work, which made it possible for me to take time off to write this essay, special thanks to the Harry Frank Guggenheim Foundation and the MacArthur Foundation. My gratitude to my mother, Rebeca Behar, and my friends, Marlene Cromwell and Joanne Leonard, for generously sharing their stories and lives with me.

## NOTES

[1]Anthropological studies in the United States now range from work on the new American fundamentalism, to work on Black American life stories, to work on homelessness in New York City. For examples, see Susan F. Harding, "Convicted by the Holy Spirit: The Rhetoric of Fundamental Baptist Conversion," *American Ethnologist* 14:1 (February 1987), 167–181; John Langston Gwaltney, *Drylongso: A Self-Portrait of Black America* (New York: Random House, 1981); Kim Hopper, "More Than Passing Strange: Homelessness and Mental Illness in New York City," *American Ethnologist* 15:1 (February 1988), 155–167. For a general overview of cultural critique within anthropology, see George E. Marcus and Michael M. J. Fischer, *Anthropology as Cultural Critique: An Experimental Moment in the Human Sciences* (Chicago: University of Chicago Press, 1986).

[2]Emily Martin, *The Woman in the Body: A Cultural Analysis of Reproduction* (Boston: Beacon Press, 1987), p. 13.

[3]Faye D. Ginsburg, *Contested Lives: The Abortion Debate in an American Community* (Berkeley: University of California Press, 1989), p. 5.

[4]On witchcraft surrounding the use of menstrual blood and other products associated with the female body, see Ruth Behar, "Sex and Sin, Witchcraft and the Devil in Late-Colonial Mexico," *American Ethnologist* 14:1 (February 1987), 34–54, and "Sexual Witchcraft, Colonialism, and Women's Powers: Views from the Mexican Inquisition," *Sexuality and Marriage in Colonial Latin America*, ed. Asunción Lavrin (Lincoln: University of Nebraska Press), 178–206.

[5]Susan S. Lanser, "Feminist Criticism, 'The Yellow Wallpaper,' and the Politics of Color in America," *Feminist Studies* 15:3 (Fall 1989), pp. 428–429.

[6]Martin, pp. 115, 153.

[7]Maxine Hong Kingston, *The Woman Warrior: Memoirs of a Girlhood among Ghosts* (New York: Random House, 1977), p. 41.

[8]Margaret Atwood, *The Handmaid's Tale* (Boston: Houghton Mifflin Company, 1986), pp. 73, 135.

[9]Martin, p. 49, 137.

[10]David Margolick, "A Name, A Face and a Rape: Iowa Victim Tells Her Story," *New York Times*, March 25, 1990.

[11]Martin, pp. 128–129, 164.

[12]Onnie Lee Logan as told to Katherine Clark, *Motherwit: An Alabama Midwife's Story* (New York: E. P. Dutton, 1989), p. 140.

[13]Logan, pp. 168–169. Also see Gertrude Fraser, *Afro-American Midwives, Biomedicine and the State: An Ethnohistorical Account of Birth and its Transformation in Rural Virginia* (Ph.D. dissertation, Johns Hopkins University, 1988).

[14]Patricia J. Williams, "On Being the Object of Property," *Signs* 14:1 (Autumn 1989), p. 7.

[15]Diane Cook, "Worker Files Civil Rights Suit Against 'U,' " *The Michigan Daily*, March 22, 1990.

[16]Ellen Goodman, "In 'Fetal Protection,' Woman is the Enemy," *Ann Arbor News*, April 1, 1990. For a detailed analysis, see Katha Pollitt, " 'Fetal Rights'—A New Assault on Feminism," *The Nation*, March 26, 1990, pp. 409–418.

[17]Llaila O. Afrika, *African Holistic Health* (Silver Spring, Maryland: Adesegun, Johnson and Koram, 1989).

[18]Perhaps if American medical researchers raised the "iron curtain" that hangs over their knowledge of the causes of malfunction in the uterus they might find that we have our own late-industrial version of the "haunting veil" that is beginning to be exposed in Eastern Europe. Medical research in an industrial region of southern Poland, for example, found concentrations of lead mercury, cadmium and other toxic metals in the placenta of every woman. See Marlise Simons, "Rising Iron Curtain Exposes Haunting Veil of Polluted Air," *New York Times*, April 8, 1990. In the United States, when such research is done, it seems to focus on the fetus and birth defects rather than on the affected women. For example, see Keith Schneider, "Birth Defects and Pollution: Issue Raised in Texas Town," *New York Times*, April 15, 1990.

[19]Adrienne Rich, "Notes toward a Politics of Location," *Blood, Bread, and Poetry: Selected Prose 1979–1985* (New York: Norton, 1986), pp. 213, 215.

[20]Vicki Hufnagel, with Susan K. Golant, *No More Hysterectomies* (New York: New American Library, 1989).

[21]Hufnagel, p. 62. Hufnagel provides the following comparison with other surgeries performed in the same year: lens extractions for cataracts (506,000), gallbladder removals (485,000), repairs of abdominal hernias (469,000), prostatectomies (361,000), and coronary bypass procedures (202,000).

[22]Susanne Morgan, *Coping with a Hysterectomy* (New York: New American Library, 1985), p. 50–51, 53.

[23]Susan Sontag, *Illness as Metaphor* (New York: Random House, 1978).

[24]Morgan, p. 75.

[25]Later I heard her lecture about "Women and Medicine," and we had a chance to speak personally in more detail. As her lecture made clear, women physicians only make up 15 percent of the total number of doctors in this country, and they are barely represented on medical faculties. Their practices focus primarily on pediatrics, obstetrics and gynecology, and primary care, where they make up a strong 68 percent. On the other hand, the percentage of women surgeons in the United States in 1987 was 2.5 percent. Women do tend to be concerned with the humane side of medicine, particularly during their early years in medical school, but studies indicate that these concerns diminish by the fourth year of residency. As the medical system stands now, it is unclear yet whether women are making a real change in medicine, or whether medicine, as a highly conformist social system, is shaping women into doctors whose first loyalty is to the profession.

[26]Audre Lorde, *The Cancer Journals* (San Francisco: Spinsters/Aunt Lute, 1980), pp. 59–60, 69–70, 74, 77.

MARGARET HOLLEY


# TRASH


"To my knowledge," Ted Hughes reported
of Sylvia Plath, "she never scrapped any
of her poetic efforts." In the end

it was herself she threw, bright torment
that she was, while we move rather more
reluctantly toward an unknown finale,

each one dripping and dropping off debris,
involuntarily donating the body piecemeal
to the failing cause of its own renewal:

wet kleenex, sanitary napkins, towels
diapering blood, feces, the milky phlegms;
spit hitting the earth like a slap;

eyelashes, nail slivers, razor peppers,
and 40 hairs a day, more or less, flying
off from each of us (where is it all?),

the invisible snow of old skin cells
landing on mirrors, lamps, and bookshelves;
in the twilight under the bed, a pollen

blooming into those angelic balls
adrift amid crumbs and crumpled letters
and the spiders' lace in the broom closet

and back hall, haloing the wastebasket
and waiting garbage bags, the cartons
of discarded books, broken furniture,

and bottle shards, even my love for
you, John Wallace, I still come home to
that wreckage, unable to throw it out

yet. The universal law of entropy
promises that everything will break down
into new forms of matter and conversely

matter to energy, flesh and bone, say,
into labors of love, hands moving across
clean sheets, even as the wind vacuums

wavering smoke from the crematoriums,
and gentle rain continues impartially
sorting and redistributing the dust.

For now I celebrate the slowest forms
of ruin: make me mulch for an unannounced
season, raw material for an untold story;

use me now, use me wholly up, before
tossing me back into the radiant furnace
of the sun's daily dancing artistry,

where everything and nothing is finally
transfigured, as each of us shall be
in that famous twinkling of an eye,

at that last trumpet I seem to habitually
sleep through, its gold and silver song
shimmering in the light of every dawn.

# CONTRIBUTORS

Nin Andrews is the fiction editor of *Whiskey Island*. Her work has appeared in *Exquisite Corpse*.

Margaret Atwood is the author of more than twenty books, including poetry, fiction, and nonfiction. Her most recent novels are *The Handmaid's Tale* and *Cat's Eye*.

Ruth Behar, Associate Professor of Anthropology at the University of Michigan, is the author of *Santa Maria del Monte: The Presence of the Past in a Spanish Village* (Princeton, 1986). She is currently completing a book on the life of a Mexican peddling woman.

Susan Bordo teaches philosophy at LeMoyne College; she is the author of *The Flight to Objectivity: Essays on Cartesianism and Culture* (State University of New York Press, 1987) and the coeditor of *Gender/Body/ Knowledge: Feminist Reconstructions of Being and Knowing* (Rutgers, 1989).

Julie Brown is Assistant Professor of Writing and Literature at Youngstown State University. She has published nine children's books as well as fiction and poetry in literary journals.

Debra Bruce's second volume of poems, *Sudden Hunger*, appeared from University of Arkansas Press in 1987. She teaches at Northeastern Illinois University in Chicago.

Carl Cohen is Professor of Philosophy in the Residential College and the Medical School at the University of Michigan. His books include *Civil Disobedience, Conscience, Tactics, and the Law* (Columbia University Press, 1971) and *Communism, Fascism, and Democracy: The Theoretical Foundations* (Random House, 1962).

Robert Creeley, Samuel P. Capen Professor of Poetry and Humanities at the University of Buffalo/SUNY, is the author most recently of a collection of poems, *Windows* (New Directions) and a *Selected Poems* (University of California Press).

Andrea Dworkin is the author of *Intercourse* (Free Press, 1987) as well as *Pornography: Men Possessing Women* (Dutton, 1989), and a novel, *Ice and Fire*. She and Catharine A. MacKinnon wrote a law for the city of Minneapolis that recognizes pornography as a violation of the civil rights of women.

Kim Edwards won the 1990 Nelson Algren Award for short fiction. She has published fiction in *North American Review, Iowa Woman, Ploughshares*, and elsewhere.

Judith Fryer directs the American Studies Program at the University of Massachusetts at Amherst. Her essay is part of her book-in-progress, "Suzanna and the Elders: The Female Body as Cultural Work, 1890–1920." She is the author, most recently, of *Felicitious Space: The Imaginative Structures of Edith Wharton and Willa Cather* (University of North Carolina Press, 1986).

Carol Gilligan, author of *In a Different Voice: Psychological Theory and Women's Development* (Harvard University Press, 1982), is Professor of Education at Harvard University and directs the Harvard Project on the Psychology of Women and the Development of Girls.

Beckian Fritz Goldberg has published work in *Black Warrior Review, Gettysburg Review*, and *American Poetry Review*.

Laurence Goldstein, editor of *Michigan Quarterly Review* and Professor of English at the University of Michigan, has edited *Seasonal Performances: A* Michigan Quarterly Review *Reader* (University of Michigan Press, 1991).

Darcy Grimaldo Grigsby is a doctoral student in the History of Art and Women's Studies departments at the University of Michigan.

Anne Herrmann is Associate Professor of English and Women's Studies at the University of Michigan. She is the author of *The Dialogic and Difference* (Columbia University Press, 1989) and is currently working on "Impersonation: Nature and Illusion in Gender Ideology."

Brenda Hillman is the author of *White Dress* and *Fortress*, both from Wesleyan University Press. She lives in the Bay Area and teaches at St. Mary's College in Moraga, California.

Margaret Holley is the author of *The Poetry of Marianne Moore: A Study in Voice and Value* (Cambridge University Press, 1987). She is assistant to the president of Bryn Mawr College.

Jefferson Humphries is the author of *Metamorphoses of the Raven* (Louisiana State University Press), *Losing the Text* (University of Georgia Press), *The Puritan and the Cynic* (Oxford University Press), and most recently is the editor of *Southern Literature and Literary Theory* (Georgia). He teaches at Louisiana State University.

Stephanie Kiceluk is Rudin Scholar in the Humanities at the Center for the Study of Society and Medicine, College of Physicians and Surgeons, Columbia University. She teaches "Medicine and Western Civilization" at Columbia College and is coediting the course materials for publication by Princeton University Press.

Joanne Leonard is Professor of Art at the School of Art, University of Michigan, where she has been teaching since 1978 after living and working in California for thirty-five years. Her work is exhibited and reproduced widely, most notably in Lucy Lippard's *From the Center* (1976), Janson's *History of Art* (1986), and Gardner's *Art through the Ages* (1991).

Elizabeth McCracken is currently a fellow at the Fine Arts Work Center in Provincetown. Her first book of stories will be published by Random House in 1992.

Sarah Messer won the major Hopwood Award for Poetry at the University of Michigan, where she received her MFA in 1991.

Gregory Orr is director of the MFA program at the University of Virginia. His most recent book is *New and Selected Poems* from Wesleyan University Press.

Joan K. Peters is the author of the novel *Manny and Rose* (St. Martin's Press, 1985). Her travel and political articles have appeared in the *New York Times* and the *Nation*.

Sally Peters currently teaches in the Graduate Liberal Studies Program at Wesleyan. She is completing an interpretive study of George Bernard Shaw's life and art.

Marge Piercy's most recent collection of poetry is *Ark of Consequence*, and her most recent book of fiction, *He, She and It*, both from Alfred A. Knopf.

Elizabeth Socolow received the 1987 Barnard Women Poets Series prize for her book, *Laughing at Gravity: Conversations with Isaac Newton* (Beacon Press, 1988). She teaches at St. Andrews School in Delaware.

Susan Rubin Suleiman teaches French and Comparative Literature at Harvard University. She edited *The Female Body in Western Culture* (1986) and is the author of *Subversive Intent: Gender, Politics, and the Avant-Garde* (1990).

Zona Teti's poems have appeared in *Iowa Review, Literary Review,* and *Atavist.*

John Updike is the author of numerous books of fiction and nonfiction, including the tetralogy of novels culminating in *Rabbit at Rest* (1991).

Lois-Ann Yamanaka writes using the pidgin of the contract workers from various ethnic backgrounds employed by the sugar plantations in Hawaii during the 1800s. This pidgin has been passed down to their third and fourth generation descendants.